ADOBE®
PHOTOSHOP®
FOR VFX ARTISTS

LOPSIE SCHWARTZ

THOMSON

COURSE TECHNOLOGY

Professional ■ Trade ■ Reference

ISBN: 1-59200-487-3

Library of Congress Catalog Card Number: 2004108012

Printed in the United States of America

04 05 06 07 08 BU 10 9 8 7 6 5 4 3 2 1

THOMSON

COURSE TECHNOLOGY

Professional ■ Trade ■ Reference

Course PTR, a division of Course Technology
25 Thomson Place
Boston, MA 02210
http://www.courseptr.com

SVP, Course Professional, Trade, Reference Group:
Andy Shafran

Publisher:
Stacy L. Hiquet

Senior Marketing Manager:
Sarah O'Donnell

Marketing Manager:
Heather Hurley

Manager of Editorial Services:
Heather Talbot

Senior Acquisitions Editor:
Kevin Harreld

Associate Marketing Manager:
Kristin Eisenzopf

Project Editor:
Tonya Cupp

Technical Reviewers:
Lisa Bucki and Mark Abdelnour

Retail Market Coordinator:
Elizabeth Furbish

Interior Layout Tech:
Shawn Morningstar

Cover Designer:
Nancy Goulet

Indexer:
Kelly Talbot

Proofreader:
Kezia Endsley

*This book is dedicated to my absolutely wonderful husband Andrew
and to the night crew of the 24-hour Starbucks,
who saw me through the many long nights of writing.*

FOREWORD

For most of my career I've been happy to watch others experiment with new materials and technologies, taking sidelong glances at the possibilities being opened up, while persisting in my use of the oldest artists' materials, to go with my love of ancient epics and fairytales. While watercolour, charcoal and graphite have always been the methods that are most sympathetic for the kind of books that I was illustrating, it was very often film and TV that provided the excitement, ideas and inspiration for what I was doing, and there has always been a parallel interest in various optical enchantments, from flick books using the margins of old paperbacks, to the amazing stop-motion animation of Ray Harryhausen, as well as all the miniatures and matte paintings that extended the scope of what was filmed in a studio or backlot. So I was more than ready to pack my bags, lock up my studio and head off to New Zealand when I was offered the opportunity to explore, and bring together, all of these interests.

As my involvement with the design work on Peter Jackson's film trilogy of *Lord of the Rings* grew from an initial estimated period of a few months of conceptual design work to six years, and the work shifted from a fairly speculative offering of options on the look of the architecture and costumes of middle-earth, through detailed design work on the sets and miniatures to visual effects design I realized that I would have to come to grips with the mysteries of computers, and in particular, Photoshop.

It wasn't that drawing became redundant —it still underpins everything that I do— it is just that as the raw materials we were working with became increasingly photographic, in the form of bluescreen and other effect shots, tile sets, scenic elements and a large number of miniature shots, it became obvious that I should be using that material directly to design shots. Fortunately, I was working alongside Gus Hunter, a very gifted Photoshop artist, who was able to come to my rescue whenever I ran into difficulties, which was embarrassingly often in the initial stages. I also shared the workload with Jeremy Bennett and Paul Lassaine, whose inspiring production paintings and effects designs guided both the cinematography and the final digital grading of the films.

Jeremy, incidentally, held on to his favourite medium, acrylics, for the entire time he was working on LOTR, despite our promptings to him to "come over to the dark side," and changed to Photoshop only when he switched to working on *King Kong*. He mastered his new medium almost immediately and has been producing copious amounts of brilliant and distinctive work ever since.

Another factor which helped in my own conversion was a proximity to the large numbers of very gifted compositors, modellers, texture painters, matte painters and other digital masters at Weta, Peter's SFX facility. That they were more than happy to share their skills, while happily tolerating my very shaky learning curve, contributed hugely to the ease with which I was able to adapt to coping with an increasingly heavy workload.

The job, in the post-production phase, consisted of helping to design new shots and scenes that would require effects, miniatures or set extensions, and also producing artwork for scenes already shot, that would be used to guide the digital artists at Weta and the other effects houses that did work on the films.

In some of the busier scenes, there may be upwards of twenty bluescreen shots, where the drama in the foreground needs to be located in some kind of digitally created environment. We would show artwork for all these to Peter, which, once approved, would be distributed to the camera department, whose job it is to track the camera moves into a simple 3D environment, to Alex Funky's miniatures unit, the matte painting department and the compositors who would be putting all this material together in the final shots. Many scenes would involve animation, which would also require the skills of the creatures department, who have to construct a working anatomy, as well as skin and body masses that behave in a believable way. Texture painters also play a vital role in this process, as do those who add light and shade to these moving virtual characters and creatures so that they will match the live action. A busy production like *Lord of the Rings* may involve 200 or so digital artists, animators and technicians, and we were fortunate in having very skillful, and level-headed supervisors like Joe Letteri, Jim Rygiel, and VFX producer Dean Wright, as well as Peter Jackson, to oversee the project.

The artwork would have to be available as a first point of reference for all these different disciplines, though it would quickly be superseded as the shots were refined, and it was vital that it could be distributed as quickly as possible after the scenes were edited and handed over to Weta.

Photoshop became an essential part of this process because, in many ways, it closely parallels the methods used in compositing. Bluescreens can be eliminated with a touch of a magic wand, tiled photographic backgrounds, much larger than the canvas being worked on, can be rotated into place, the effects of different lenses can be reproduced by enlarging, reducing and defocusing. There are even tools for creating the equivalent of motion blur.

The real revelation for me though, and the reason that I shall continue to rely heavily on Photoshop in my work on books, as well as films, is the speed with which it is possible to work, and the number of variations that it is possible to produce in a small amount of time. I also love the fact that I can take an image from the loosest sketch to the most highly finished end result in one uninterrupted continuum, and, if I wish, keep a version of it at every stage along the way.

So, I'll leave you now in the capable hands of one of those skilled and supremely patient digital artists. You probably already know a lot more about the wonders of Photoshop than I do anyway. Lopsie certainly does.

Alan Lee, Conceptual Designer,
Lord of the Rings

Devon, England
October 2004

Acknowledgments

This book would not have been possible if it weren't for the patient and hardworking team at Thomson Course Technology. I would like to thank Kevin Harreld for giving me the opportunity to author this book and for his continued patience with all the occurrences and delays. I would also like to extend my gratitude to the hard-working Tonya Cupp, who not only edited diligently all hours through nights and weekends, but did so while pregnant too. My thanks to LB and MGA, the technical editors of this book, who I know only as initials on my red-markered pages, and to the rest of the publishing team who work behind the scenes to bring this book to life.

I would like to extend special thanks to Tom Capizzi, who gave me my first writing experience, and without whom I would not have had this opportunity.

I am eternally grateful to Alan Lee, who took the time out of his busy schedule, which spanned continents and hemispheres, to write the foreword for this book.

I would also like to take this opportunity to mention and thank two people who were early influences in my career: Duane Stinnett, who first introduced me to the world of 3D with 3D Studio 2.0, and Alfredo Cartagena, who gave me my first glimpse into video and compositing.

Of course, no acknowledgement would be complete without a heartfelt thanks to my loving husband for his always-present care and support. What other husband would bring a warm throw at 4am to the 24-hour Starbucks where his wife is typing furiously away?

And last but not least, I would like to thank all my friends and family who have lent their support directly or indirectly. Accolades to Adobe for an unbeatable product, and my sincere gratitude to Rhythm and Hues Studios and Art Department Manager Stacy Burstin for providing a warm, creative environment where artists can thrive.

ABOUT THE AUTHOR

Lopsie Schwartz has worked in TV, web, multimedia, and graphic design before finding her passion in the film VFX world. On her very first film, she catapulted from an apprentice to a lead texture painting position, and has been going strong ever since.

Lopsie freelanced for years, working for different companies in different capacities and traveling to various wonderful locations. She has worked as a lighting technical director, a matte painter, an environment technical director, and a texture painter and supervisor. The list of movies she has worked on is too long to list here, but a quick search on IMDB.com would reveal such high-profile films as *Hollow Man*, *Harry Potter and the Sorcerer's Stone*, and *Lord of the Rings: The Two Towers*.

Lopsie Schwartz now lives in the South Bay area of southern California with her husband and dog. She has hung up her wandering robe and is happily in a staff position for Rhythm and Hues Studios, CA, as the lead texture artist in the art department. As of this writing, she is working on several movie projects—*The Interpreter*, *Serenity*, and *The Chronicles of Narnia: The Lion, the Witch and the Wardrobe*—but is eagerly awaiting the release of her greatest work yet: her baby boy, who is due out February 28th, 2005.

Contents

PART II:
TEXTURES   93

Chapter 6
Starting with Color Maps 95

Chapter 7
Bump Maps and Grayscale 113

Chapter 8
Custom Brushes 127

Chapter 9
Tiling and Transformations 139

Chapter 10
Variations 163

Chapter 11
Automating Tasks 181

Part III:
Matte Paintings   195

Chapter 12
Matte Paintings from Pictures 197

Chapter 13
Quick Fixes for Common Problems 219

Introduction

When I was contacted to write this book, I responded as most people in my situation would: Why would you want yet another Photoshop book out there? How about if I come up with a better idea for a different book?

Their response was not "How about you just do what we say?" Rather, they patiently explained that there weren't any Photoshop books out there addressed specifically to VFX artists. Despite owning about 100 pounds worth of books—that's by weight, not by British currency—I didn't believe them. Surely I must have just missed the section on Photoshop for VFX artists, been at the wrong bookstore, or missed the last copy that was just sold. So I didn't answer my e-mail and went to the bookstore. A few bookstores later, my fingers bleeding from paging through the shelves upon shelves of Photoshop books, I returned to my computer and I answered my e-mail: "You're right." (Okay, so maybe I was exaggerating about my fingers bleeding, but isn't poetic license part of the benefits of being an author?)

There are plenty of Photoshop tomes, a plethora of digital photography Photoshop books, and an abundance of web-focused Photoshop books. There are a few books on texturing 3D models that obliquely refer to Photoshop. As a wilder whose degree is not in VFX (not that there were any 3D degrees at the time anyway, but I'm dating myself), I started off self taught, learned everything the hard way, and am acutely aware of how hard it can be to teach yourself a tool, let alone the jargon of an industry. As a supervisor, I am surprised at how many times I have had to explain the same principles to people who were already working in the industry or who were freshly out of school and not yet exposed to these insider tips. As an artist, I am always looking to learn more and increase the depth of my knowledge. Knowledge is the real tool in bringing fantastic paintings to fruition.

What I wanted to create was a book that would be informative to those who are already in the industry yet clear enough for those who are just coming into the VFX industry. I wanted full color (because a black and white Photoshop book just doesn't make any sense), cool images (photorealistic should look photo-real!), and something that would make a great reference book long after you have gone through its covers.

What I didn't want was inane descriptions ("this button is a button…"), boring litanies, or an entire section devoted to all the cool things that Photoshop can do for web designers. Not that I have anything against web designers—I just don't want my book weighed down by information I don't use and therefore don't really care about.

What You'll Find in This Book

Throughout the book you find some elements that give you additional information—Photoshop tapas, if you will.

- **Cautions:** Things that need the extra highlight, because the world can crumble if you skim the instructions and miss this part. Generally, missing this point can cause quite a bit of pain.

- **Notes:** Information you might find helpful to know and alternate ways of doing things. Something that others might say (and which is correct), but not my way. Sometimes the information is an aside and not necessary for the basic functioning of the program—sort of trivia.
- **Tips:** Wisdom gleaned from experience and often a useful shortcut.

Who This Book Is For

You need to have Photoshop, but hopefully you figured that part out. Ideally, you should have the latest version, but if you have an older version, you can still participate in most of the book. If you are working on Photoshop 3 or earlier, this book is pretty useless. Then again, why would you be buying a book now for a program version that is more than 10 years old?

It's easy to say that this book is for intermediate to advanced users, since it is aimed at the visual effects industry. In actuality, I think I explain the steps clearly enough for a novice to follow, but keep it interesting enough to keep the attention of the advanced users. Plus, I don't believe that just because someone is already in the industry that that person is an advanced user.

However, if you just purchased the software and you're not sure how to install it, or if you don't know what it means to click or double-click with your left mouse button, you can stop right here and put this book down. There are other books out there that you should probably start with. Once you have become a little more familiar with computers in general, then you can pick this book up for the techniques.

How This Book Is Organized

Part I, "Starting," is the reference section of the book. It starts with an overview, explains the nitty-gritty details of a few important areas, and finishes with an essential guide to VFX.

Part II, "Textures," is the texture-emphasis area, and Part III, "Matte Paintings," is where I focus on matte painting. Both parts have techniques that can be applied to either, but Part II's techniques are most often used for painting for 3D, and Part III's techniques are most applicable to 2D painting. Of course, since a texture for a 3D model is still a 2D painting, it makes sense that there is crossover. The techniques used in Part II, such as the customizing of brushes, can be very applicable to matte painting.

You can do the straight cover-to-cover thing, but if you are not a linear type of person, you can pretty much jump in for whatever piece you want. In other words, this is not a ramping book where each chapter builds upon the last. My usual method is to just scan the table of contents and see what interests me, or look something up in the index and find the chapters that deal with that topic.

Companion Web Site

What about the photos I use in the examples? You can go to this book's companion Web site at www.courseptr.com to download the specified pictures. Although most people like to apply the technique to their own pictures right off the bat, I think it's good to use the example pictures so you have a control image to compare your results. What else is on the companion Web site? Besides the images specified in this book, you can download a few of my custom libraries—free of charge!

PART ONE

STARTING

CHAPTER 1

PREFERENCES AND SETTINGS

This chapter ensures a common understanding of terminology. That way when I say to "go to the options bar" or "undock your Layer Comps palette," then you know what I am referring to. So even if you are an experienced user, you might want to at least browse through this chapter. Personally, I like lots of pictures. I think they allow experienced people to faster find what they need and novices to understand that much quicker. It follows that I would include heaps of pictures as well!

Do This First

Start by resetting the default preferences and ensuring that the examples here match what you see on your screen. You need to make sure there are no customized preferences to follow the examples laid out in this book. Customization may thwart your progress by giving unexpected results.

Caution

If you're using a friend's version or are at work, make sure the presets and such are saved before resetting Photoshop. Otherwise, any customization is irrevocably lost during the reset.

1. Launch Adobe Photoshop.

   If you have an alias on your desktop (or in your Dock if you have a Mac), you can launch by double-clicking the icon. Otherwise, go to your Applications menu (Start, Programs or All Programs in Windows) and click Adobe Photoshop CS.

2. Immediately hold down Option+ Command+Shift (Windows: Alt+Ctrl+Shift) while Photoshop is still launching to reset the default settings.

   If the dialog box in Figure 1.1 doesn't pop up, then you probably didn't hold down the keys long enough or soon enough. Close Photoshop and try launching again with the reset keys.

3. When the window pops up, click Yes to confirm that you want to delete the Adobe Photoshop Settings File.

Note

You may receive a warning message recommending that you change the primary scratch disk to a different drive. If so, click OK to continue past the warning message. The Color Setting dialog box pops up after that. Later, when you have completed resetting your Photoshop settings to default, you can go to Chapter 4, "Customizing Your Workspace," for custom settings.

4. Another window asks if you would like to adjust your color setting.

   Since you can do that later, select No for now. See Figure 1.2.

5. The last pop-up window is Adobe Photoshop CS's Welcome Screen. Click Close in this window.

Figure 1.1 You should see this dialog box after Step 2.

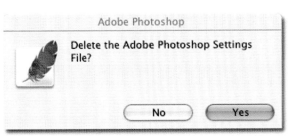

Figure 1.2 Say no to this. You can adjust your color setting by going to your preferences at any time.

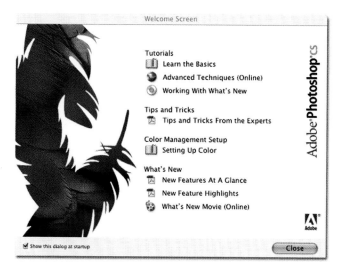

Figure 1.3 You can access this great resource at any time by going to **Help > Welcome Screen**.

If you're reading this chapter, then you will probably find helpful the tutorials, tips, tricks, and other information contained within the Welcome Screen. You can also access tutorials, links, and informational movies from this screen. Some of the information is in PDF format, which requires Adobe Acrobat Reader. (A free download is available from www.adobe.com.) You can return to the Welcome Screen anytime by going to **Help > Welcome Screen**.

N o t e

Some people prefer to just delete Photoshop's preferences directly by deleting the actual folder within the system. On startup, Photoshop builds a new folder with the default preferences and starts Photoshop using those default preferences. The problem with this is that you have to know where your preference folder is and make sure you don't delete the wrong thing. If you feel so inclined, you can do a search for Adobe Photoshop CS Settings and delete the file named AdobePhotoshopCSPrefs.psp. Restart Photoshop and follow the same steps as given previously.

Work Area

Now your default Photoshop screen area should look like Figure 1.4.

Notice how the Windows and Mac versions look virtually identical. The main differences are in the menu bar and the background. The Mac has the program (Photoshop) menu and the ever-present Apple menu. Windows generally likes to hide the desktop when a program is maximized, whereas Mac shows the desktop unless you have a document maximized. Although this book uses screen captures from a Mac, I bring up any big differences that might cause you to stumble.

Since I refer to Photoshop's basic layout in just about every chapter, you should know some basic terminology that defines this area. Table 1.1 lays it out for you and Figure 1.5 shows you. Each of these elements is covered in more detail following this overview.

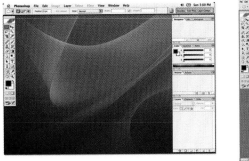 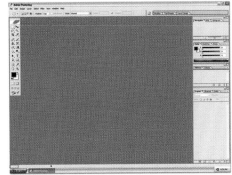

Figures 1.4 Photoshop is an ideal cross-platform application because it has so few user interface differences between the Mac and Windows versions.

Table 1.1 Basic Layout Elements

Element	Definition/Function
Menu bar	This bar, across the top of your screen, holds all your general options in the form of menus.
Toolbox	A Photoshop-specific designation for the specific palette that holds its common tools. It provides access to Photoshop's image-manipulation tools.
Options bar	Tools that have modifiable attributes list your options here.
Palette	This window holds specific options or information, usually with a fixed layout. Palettes left open while working and that can be moved around the screen to any location are referred to as *floating palettes*. Palettes that are put into the palette well are called *docked palettes* (hidden when not specifically clicked open, but are not completely closed).
Palette well	Part of the options bar, the palette well is a management tool used to store, or dock, palettes while still making them easily available. Each tab in the palette well represents an available palette.
Status bar	Displays useful information such as resolution, efficiency, or file size in megabytes. This is on each canvas window for the Mac or on the bottom of the program window for PCs.
Canvas window	The image window is often referred to as the *canvas*—an obvious reference to traditional painting.

Menu Bar

The menu bar at the top of the screen contains all the major commands that enable you to navigate and manipulate files. The commands are accessed like most other computer programs; just click the menu option so the drop-down menu appears. Then click an option from the drop-down menu. See Figure 1.6.

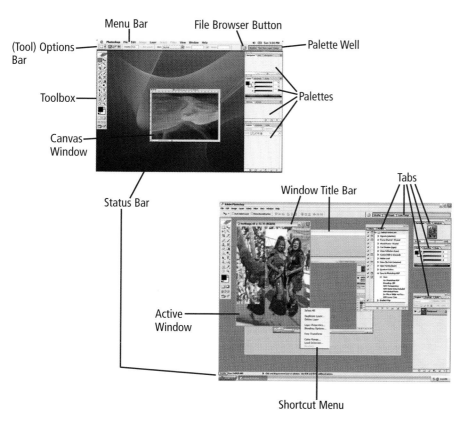

Menu Bar

File Browser Button

(Tool) Options Bar

Palette Well

Toolbox

Palettes

Canvas Window

Tabs

Window Title Bar

Status Bar

Active Window

Shortcut Menu

If I went on a litany of each and every menu option of the menu bar, would you remember all of it? Probably not. The best way to find out what an option does is to use it in context. It does help to have a general overview of what each menu title holds, so you can basically deduce where to find what you are looking for. You can find that in Table 1.2.

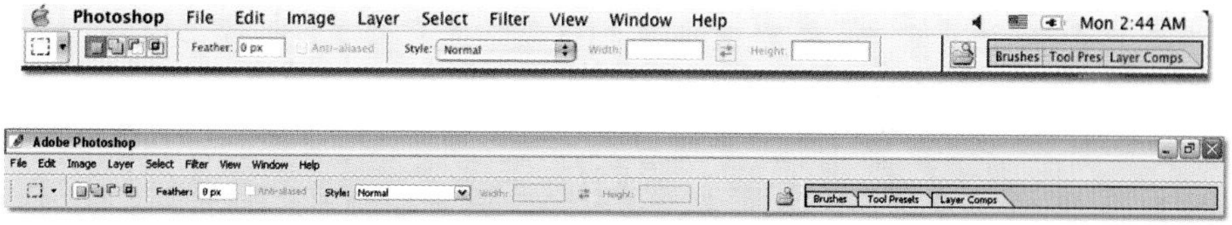

Figure 1.5 Terms in blue are Photoshop-specific components; those in black are general terms.

Figure 1.6 The menu bars for Window's version of Photoshop CS (bottom) and MacOS's version of Photoshop CS (top).

Table 1.2 Menu Title Contents

Menu	What You Find Here
Photoshop	Mac only. Some of the file and edit functions are located here for the Mac. See Figure 1.7 for the differences and comparison between Mac and PC menu items.
File	Addresses opening, closing, and saving files, including the automation of these functions.
Edit	Specifies some of the fundamental image functions used to change an open image on a standard global, or general, level. The generic cut, paste, and undo options are located in this menu.
Image	Contains the fundamental image functions such as the image mode, color adjustments, canvas, and image sizes.
Layer	One of Photoshop's most essential and powerful features is the capability to work on different layers. The Layer menu covers all the layer-specific options, and you find most of these same controls on the Layers palette menu.
Select	Controls selection options, such as feathering the borders and other adjustments and variations of a selection, within the program.
Filter	Contains the image processing effects called *filters*. In addition to the Photoshop native filters, you can install third-party plug-in filters such as Alien Skin's Eye Candy or Andromeda to give yourself even more options! Notice that the last filter you apply is at the top of the menu for easy reapplication and the Fade Last Filter command allows you to reapply the last filter in varying strengths ranging from zero (none) to full (exactly like last).
View	Basically deals with the look of imagery within the Photoshop interface and some drafting tools to help guide you.
Window	So many palettes are available that it makes sense to have a menu item to organize it all. The Window menu arranges and brings up palettes and open documents.
Help	The place to go for assistance. To get the maximum benefit, you must have Internet access; many of the help pages are accessed from an online database.

Figure 1.7 shows all of the menu bar's drop-down menus. Photocopy this page and keep it next to your computer as a quick reference. (It beats having to click each menu header and looking through to find where that particular command is located.) Notice that the Mac has an additional drop-down menu under the Photoshop heading. All the options listed there are located throughout the other menus in the Windows version.

Note

Personally I like dissection views, because I would otherwise sometimes forget where to find things. I find myself wondering if Crop is under Image or Edit, for instance. (That change actually happened between versions.) Where is the Define Brush option? If even a seasoned Photoshop user finds herself in such a situation, you may even more often find yourself searching if you're unfamiliar with Photoshop. Make a copy of these exploded views and keep them handy when working on your own. In all my tutorials I have tried to take it step by step, but trying to remember everything a few days after the tutorial can be a bit more difficult. You can always dog-ear this page, but keeping a copy nearby is a little more compact, don't you think?

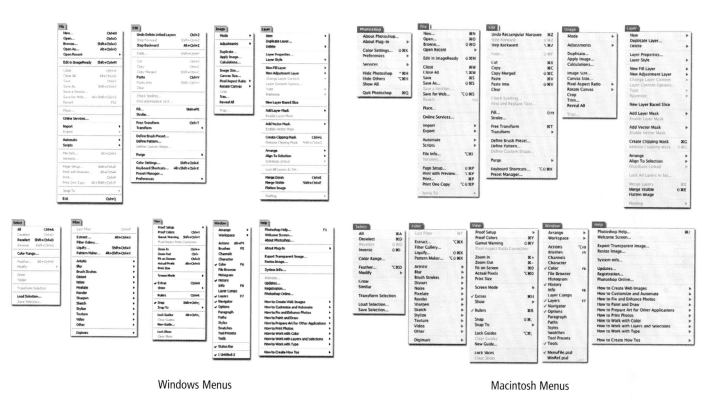

Windows Menus   Macintosh Menus

Figure 1.7 Here are all of the menu bar's drop-down menus for both the PC and the Mac.

Toolbox

I'm not going to provide an exhaustive detail of each and every tool. (Boring!) Rather, I want to familiarize you with the names and shortcuts and help you conjecture how to use each tool. You end up using most of the tools in the tutorials through this book (and Chapter 2 covers the details of the Brush palette). If you want to look further into a particular tool, Adobe has plenty of help in the form of its user manual and online help, but this book should cover everything you need to the capacity that you need it for VFX work.

To select a tool, click it. If the tool button contains a small triangle in the lower-right corner, additional hidden tools or alternate versions of the current tool exist in a flyout menu. To access this menu, click and hold the tool; you don't have to click the tiny triangle, but you can try if you're into that kind of thing. If you have a two-button mouse, you can just right-click to get the flyout menu. Drag through the flyout menu to select one of the additional tools. Positioning your pointer over a tool displays the tooltip with the tool's name and keyboard shortcut. The flyout menu also contains this information. See Figure 1.8 for an example.

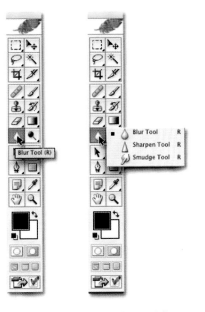

Figure 1.8 Both the tooltip and flyout menu contain the tool's name and keyboard shortcut.

Tip

If you have a Mac and still just have the Mac mouse, get a three-button mouse. Most Wacom tablets nowadays come with a three-button mouse or a scroll mouse (two buttons with a middle 'wheel' that can also be used as a button), but many Mac users never get around to fully utilizing the three-button mouse, instead using the standard Mac one-button mouse with their tablet. Trust me—once you start using the right-click function, you begin wondering why anyone still uses a one-button mouse!

The toolbox is arranged into loose categories: tools, swatches, and modes. You can select a tool by clicking it or access the tool via its shortcut (by pressing the letter indicated in the flyout menu). For example, pressing R selects the Blur tool. Holding Shift and pressing the shortcut key cycles through the hidden tools. Repeatedly pressing Shift+R cycles between the Blur, Sharpen, and Smudge tools.

Beneath the tools are the color, masking, screen mode, and ImageReady choices, respectively. Some tools, such as Paintbrush, use the foreground color. Some tools, such as Gradient, use both the foreground and background colors. To switch between the back ground and foreground color swatches, click the curved arrow icon to the upper right of the swatches. Click the Default Colors icon on the lower left to reset the colors to the default of pure black and pure white. When you click the bottommost icon, you launch Photoshop's sister program, ImageReady.

Table 1.3 provides more information about the toolbox and Figure 1.9 offers an exploded view.

Table 1.3 Toolbox Arrangement

Tool	Function	Tool Type
Marquees	Selects polygonal areas of an image.	Selection
Move	Moves a selection or layer.	Selection
Lasso	Selects areas of an image.	Selection
Magic Wand	Selects pixels based on color.	Selection
Crop	Trims off unwanted surroundings from the edge of an image.	Image editing
Slice	Slices an image into smaller, faster download pieces or for creating image-editing hot spots within an image for the web.	
Healing Brush, Patch, and Color Replacement	Advanced cloning and color tools for repair work.	Image editing
Paintbrush and Pencil	Applies color to the current layer. Brush has variable-edge strokes and Pencil has only hard edge strokes.	Image editing
Clone and Pattern stamp	Paints with pixels drawn from another part of the image, a separate image, or a pattern.	Image editing
History brush and Art History brush	The History brush paints to restore from a previous History state, and the Art History brush paints with artistic strokes that create a watercolor-like effect.	Image editing
Eraser, Background Eraser, and Magic Eraser	Erases pixels from a layer to transparency or to the background color.	Image editing
Gradient tool or Paint bucket	Fills an area with color or pattern.	Image editing
Blur Sharpen, Smudge	Increases or decreases sharpness.	Image editing
Dodge, Burn, Sponge	Increases or decreases exposure locally.	Image editing
Path Selection and Direct Selection	Moves paths or anchor points.	Vector
Type	Adds text to your pictures.	Vector
Pen	Creates vector paths.	Vector
Shape	Creates vector-based polygonal shapes such as rectangles, rounded rectangles, ellipses, lines, and custom polygons.	Vector
Notes and Audio Annotation	Adds text messages or sound messages to a picture.	Vector
Eyedropper, Color Sampler, and Measure	Samples color from an image, sets a marker for a color sample, or measures between two user set points in the image.	Vector
Hand	Pans the image relative to the viewable window area. Hold down the spacebar to temporarily switch to the Hand tool.	Viewing and utility
Zoom	Magnifies or reduces your view of an area on the current active image onscreen.	Viewing and utility

Table 1.3 Toolbox Arrangement *(continued)*

Swatch	Swatch Type
Foreground Color	Represents the current foreground color.
Background Color	Represents the current background color.
Default Colors	The small black and white swatches represent the default colors of a pure black foreground and a pure white background.

Mode	Mode Type
Mask modes	Standard or Quick Mask.
Screen modes	Standard, Full with menu bar, or Full.
Program mode	Photoshop or ImageReady (toggle).

Tip

Another shortcut that isn't obvious: Double-clicking the Hand tool fits your current window to the available workspace area. Double-clicking the Zoom tool puts your current window to 100 percent.

More about Mask and Screen Modes

The Mask mode buttons are for editing in standard or quick-mask modes. The left button is the Edit in Standard Mode button, and the right button is the Edit in Quick Mask Mode button. Quick Mask offers a way to view, make, and edit a selection using a painting technique. This is hard to explain without an example, so leave the mode set to Standard right now. You can find out more about the Quick Mask mode in Chapter 14, "Masks and Mattes."

From left to right, here are your screen modes, which affect the way you see the work area:

- **Standard Screen mode.** This default setting shows your entire Photoshop desktop, with menu bars, scrollbars, and other screen elements.
- **Full Screen mode with menu bar.** This mode hides your desktop background and other open images, enlarges your view of the image, and keeps the menu bar in view.
- **Full Screen mode.** Use this mode to hide your desktop background, any open images, and the menu bar. In addition, the Photoshop window turns to black. (You can now move an image even when it is in Full Screen mode.)

Note

You can move the toolbox by pointing to the title bar and dragging it where you want it. However, you cannot group the toolbox (nor the tool options bar) with other palettes, resize the toolbox or tool options bar, or dock the toolbox in the palette well.

Tool Options Bar

A design introduced in Photoshop 6, the tool options bar (see Figure 1.10) shows a tool's modifiable attributes, if available. Some settings in the tool options bar are common to several tools and some are specific to one. It simply says there are no options if nothing's modifiable. If your tool options bar has mysteriously disappeared, you can bring it back by pressing Return (Win: Enter) or choosing **Window > Options**. (Note that Return [Win: Enter] is *not* a toggle for the tool options bar, it merely retrieves it.)

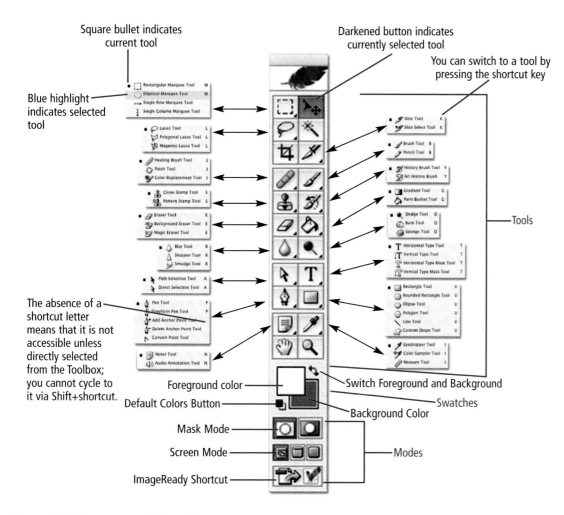

Figure 1.9 Keep a copy of this handy.

Palette Well

The tool options bar also holds the palette well. The well is great for organizing and managing palettes because you can dock most of them there. To dock your palette, drag its tab into the palette well so the palette well is highlighted. Then you can use the palette just by clicking its tab in the palette well. The palette remains open until you click outside it. See Figure 1.11.

If your screen resolution is less than 800×600, you do not see the palette well and many of your dialog boxes may get cut off. The user's guide recommends at least 1024×768.

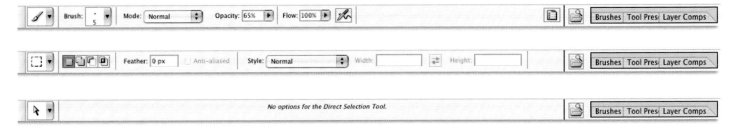

Figure 1.10 The tool options bar as it appears with three different tools.

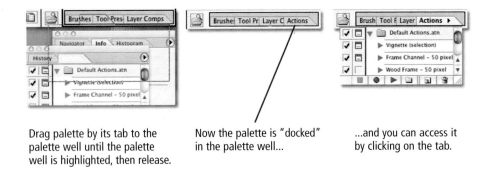
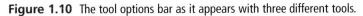

Drag palette by its tab to the palette well until the palette well is highlighted, then release.

Now the palette is "docked" in the palette well...

...and you can access it by clicking on the tab.

Figure 1.11 If you don't see your palette well in the options bar, check your resolution.

Palette Navigation

Some palettes are grouped by default. You can modify the way palettes are presented with these actions:

- If the palette you want is not at the forefront of the group window, left-click its tab. The triangle in the upper-right corner of the palette signifies a palette menu with options related to the functionality of the associated palette. For example, if you click the triangle on the Layer Comps palette, you get a submenu with options such as New Layer Comp, Delete Layer Comp, and Update Layer Comp.

- Check Show Tool Tips in the General Preferences dialog box (found through the main menu bar under **Photoshop** > **Preferences** > **General** if you have a Mac or **Edit** > **Preferences** > **General** if you have a PC) and hover over a button at the bottom of a palette's shortcut buttons. You see the button name.

- Double-click a palette tab or the palette title bar to collapse a group. This way only the title bar and its tabs are visible. Double-click again to restore the expanded view.

- Click the palette tab and drag it out of its group window to separate any palette from its group. When you release, the palette is in its own window.

Tip

Inevitably you will have messed with the palettes so much and wish you had just left it at the default layout. No fear! Just go to **Window** > **Workspace** > **Reset Palette Location**. The palettes are restored to their original visibility status and location. For more on creating custom workspaces with custom palette locations, go to Chapter 4.

Visual Palettes Overview

I have grouped the following palettes according to how they're organized by default in Photoshop CS. You do not have all the palettes if you're using an older version, and some are grouped differently. (For example, in Photoshop 6, the Color, Swatches, and Brush palettes were grouped.) These dissection views should get you acquainted with each of their functions.

Navigator/Info/Histogram

These palettes all give image information. Navigator previews the image you are working on, along with zoom informa-tion. Info displays pixel color information under the mouse pointer (no matter what tool is selected) and relates positional data. Histogram is a graphical representation of your image's tonal range. Figure 1.12 shows all three.

Color/Swatches/Style

These palettes all deal with your tool's paint, whether that be the Brush, Paint Bucket, or any other painting tool. Color displays the color information for the currently selected foreground and background colors. Swatches holds a selection of predefined color samples. Style enables you to apply a predefined style to your layer. A style is a combined effect of different filters that holds true for the entire layer. Since the swatches and styles are presets, you can also access the preset manager from each palette's submenu. Figure 1.13 reveals these palettes.

History/Actions

Both of these palettes deal with recording steps you take while using Photoshop. The History palette displays every task you perform in Photoshop, which allows you to selectively edit your steps. Actions holds semiautomated routines, which are Photoshop's version of macros or scripts. These palettes are shown in Figure 1.14.

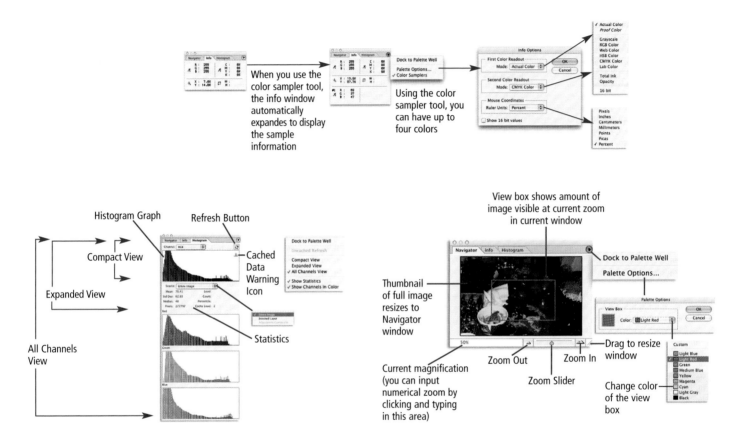

When you use the color sampler tool, the info window automatically expandes to display the sample information

Using the color sampler tool, you can have up to four colors

Histogram Graph

Refresh Button

Compact View

Expanded View

All Channels View

Cached Data Warning Icon

Statistics

View box shows amount of image visible at current zoom in current window

Thumbnail of full image resizes to Navigator window

Current magnification (you can input numerical zoom by clicking and typing in this area)

Zoom Out

Zoom Slider

Zoom In

Drag to resize window

Change color of the view box

Figure 1.12 The Navigator, Info, and Histogram palettes with all their submenus.

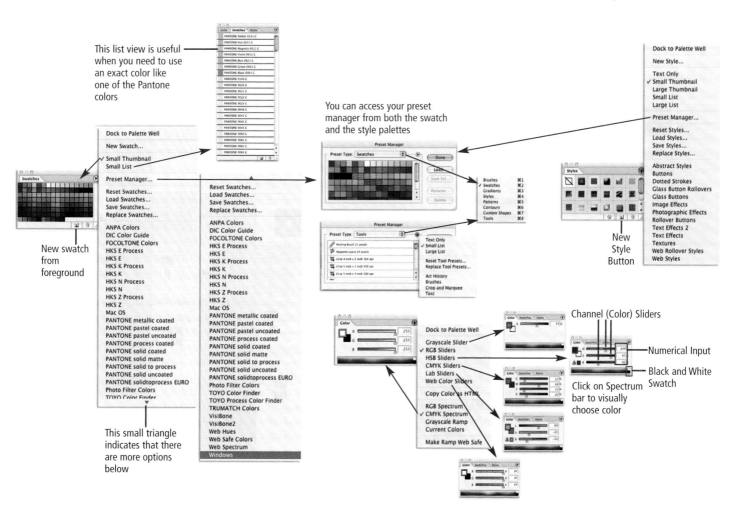

This list view is useful when you need to use an exact color like one of the Pantone colors

You can access your preset manager from both the swatch and the style palettes

New swatch from foreground

This small triangle indicates that there are more options below

New Style Button

Channel (Color) Sliders

Numerical Input

Black and White Swatch

Click on Spectrum bar to visually choose color

Figure 1.13 The Color, Swatches, and Style palettes with its submenus. Notice that the preset manager is accessible via the submenu.

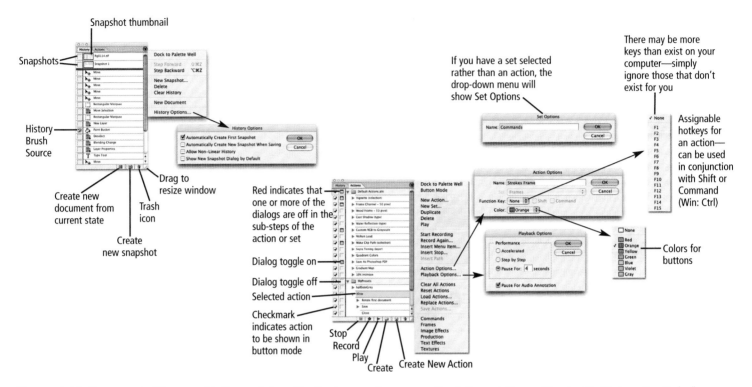

Snapshot thumbnail

Snapshots

History Brush Source

Create new document from current state

Create new snapshot

Trash icon

Drag to resize window

If you have a set selected rather than an action, the drop-down menu will show Set Options

There may be more keys than exist on your computer—simply ignore those that don't exist for you

Assignable hotkeys for an action—can be used in conjunction with Shift or Command (Win: Ctrl)

Red indicates that one or more of the dialogs are off in the sub-steps of the action or set

Dialog toggle on

Dialog toggle off

Selected action

Checkmark indicates action to be shown in button mode

Stop
Record
Play
Create
Create New Action

Colors for buttons

Figure 1.14 These are the History and Actions palettes with all submenus; for more on the Action palette, see Chapter 11, "Automating Tasks."

Layers/Channels/Paths

Layers, Channels, and Paths are types of content that are layered within the image, contributing to the overall image. The Layers palette displays the current image layers, with the foreground on top and the background bottommost. Each file in Photoshop is comprised of channels that store information (typically color information) in the image. Depending on the mode, Channels reflects this information and lets you manage and edit the separate channels. Paths holds the different vector lines created using the Pen tool. Figure 1.15 shows these palettes.

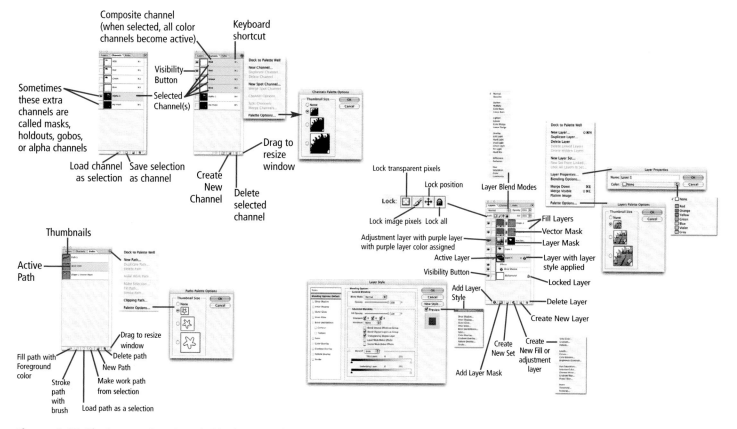

Figure 1.15 The Layers palette is probably the most often used in Photoshop.

Character/Paragraph

As you can guess, both of these palettes deal
with text. Character provides formatting
options, such as font and size for individual
characters. Some of these options are available in the tool options bar when you select
the Text tool. Paragraph gives you paragraph-
formatting options, such as justification and
line spacing. By default, these palettes are
not out; you have to go to **Window** >
Character or **Window** > **Paragraph** to
bring up the palettes, which you see in
Figure 1.16.

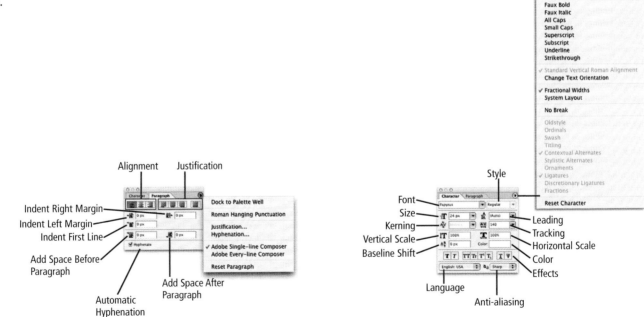

Figure 1.16 Seldom do I need to use Character or Paragraph palette for VFX work, but it's here just in case you need to create a sign on a building or something.

Brushes

By default, this palette is located in the palette well, but you can access it by going to **Window** > **Brushes** (though why would you do so when it is actually faster to just click on the tab in the palette well). Every Brush palette option, shown in Figure 1.17, is covered in Chapter 2.

Tool Presets

By default, the Tool Presets palette is located in the palette well, but is also available via the tool options bar. You can see its two locations in Figure 1.18. For any tool that can set presets, this palette can be seen in a flyout palette by clicking the inverted triangle next to the tool icon in the options bar. Tool Presets allows you to save and easily reuse a particular tool's specific settings.

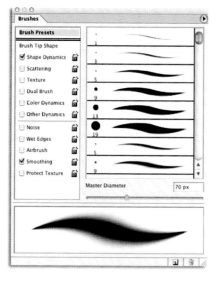

Figure 1.17 Just so you know what the Brush palette looks like: The brushes and all related functions are covered in depth in Chapter 2.

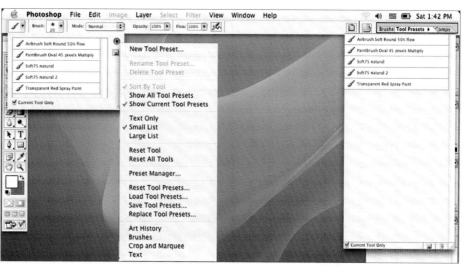

Figure 1.18 Notice that you can access Tool Presets from two different locations.

Layer Comps

Layer Comps is also located in the palette well, and is of course available via **Window > Layer Comps**. Layer comps are especially handy when dealing with variations, as you see in Chapter 10, "Variations." This palette acts a bit like a History palette for layer composite snapshots. It's shown in Figure 1.19.

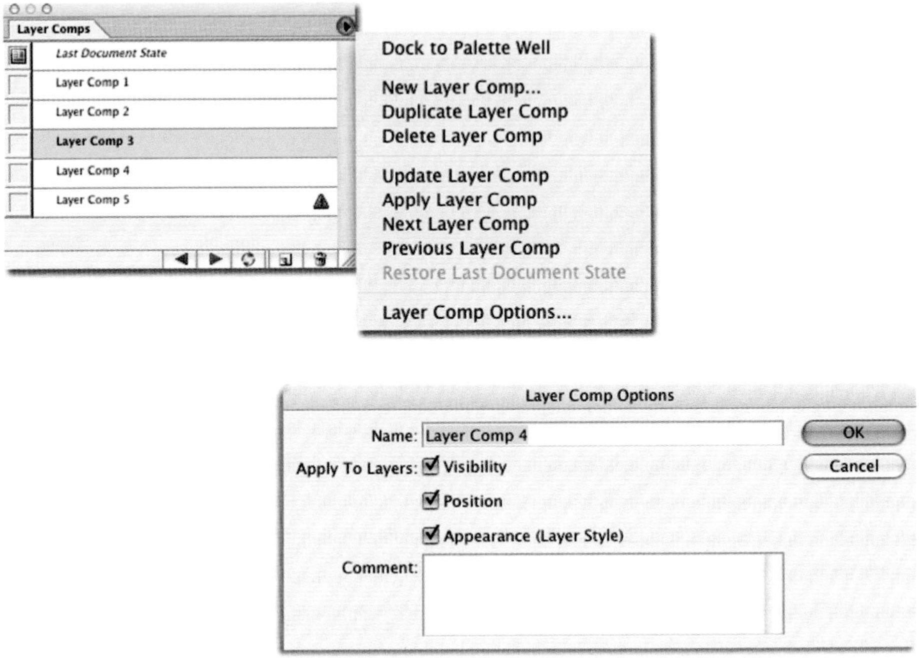

Figure 1.19 Layer Comps, introduced in Photoshop CS, is covered in Chapter 10.

CHAPTER 2

BRUSHES

This book isn't a complete dissertation of Photoshop. Plenty of books weigh in at 10 pounds, covering just about every nitty gritty detail. Although I know an overview is a necessary evil, my eyes glaze over just thinking about a litany of menu functions.

Of course, every rule has an exception.

As a painter, how can you not get excited about brushes? Especially the new and improved brush capabilities introduced in Photoshop 7?

Nonetheless, if the idea of spending an entire chapter going through each brush's options sends you into a coma, skip over to Chapter 8, "Custom Brushes," to create a custom dirt brush and see some of the functionality in action. Then watch yourself skip back here to read through the other options. You can't say I didn't tell you so.

Finding Brush Controls

As is common in Photoshop, you have several ways to access brush controls. On the options bar at the top of the screen, when you have the Brush tool selected, you see the brush shape and size assigned to your brush. Clicking the Brushes submenu brings down the Brush Presets menu (see Figure 2.1), which has some brush tip control sliders.

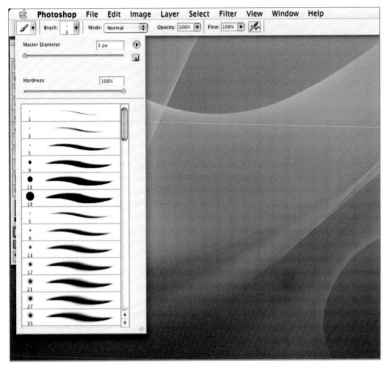

Figure 2.1 This simplified palette, the Brush Preset picker, works for the basic controls.

In contrast, you can open the Brushes palette by either choosing **Window** > **Brushes** or clicking the Brushes tab in your palette well. Figure 2.2 shows the Brushes palette.

Speed Tip

The keyboard shortcut for the Brushes palette is F5 for both Windows and Mac. If you are on a Mac laptop or other integrated system that has a function assigned to this key (such as volume), hold down the fn key on the lower-left corner of your keyboard as you press F5.

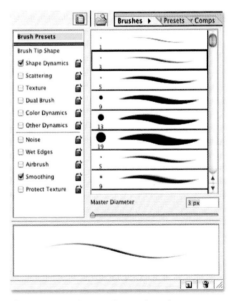

Figure 2.2 The Brushes palette has many wonders to behold!

The Brushes Palette

Open your Brushes palette from the palette well and drag it to your workspace so it stays open. You can see your available brush presets, heaps of brush-editing options, and a handy-dandy brush preview window. The preview window instantly reflects the attributes you assign to the brush, so you can ensure that the brush behaves the way you intend. The preview is only black and white. As you can see in Figure 2.3, no color information is reflected.

Brush Presets

The first setting on the Brushes palette's left frame is the Brush Presets choices. Clicking Brush Presets at the top of the left list reveals the available brushes in the scrolling list at the right side of the palette. This is the same list that is accessible in the Brushes submenu in the options bar. By default, Photoshop shows them as stroke thumbnails, which is the best way to familiarize yourself with what each brush looks like.

Choose the Scattered Maple Leaves brush. Click the brush preset and deselect all of its default settings. Figure 2.4 points out the checkboxes in the list on the left of the palette. Now you can see how the preview instantly reflects the brush changes.

Brush Tip Shape

All the brush options appear below the Brush Presets choices on the left side of the Brushes palette. The first option is the brush tip shape. Do you want to be able to paint a flurry of leaves? Duplicate the look of a traditional airbrush? The shape of your brush is a major contributing factor.

Brush Editing Options

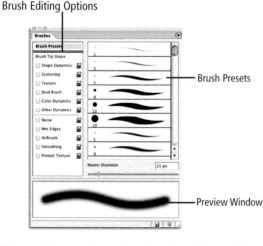

Brush Presets

Preview Window

Figure 2.3 Drag the palette from the palette well to the desktop so that it stays open during this overview.

Holding your cursor over a preset will show you its name

The blue highlight indicates that we have this selected

We have deselected all of the brush dynamics

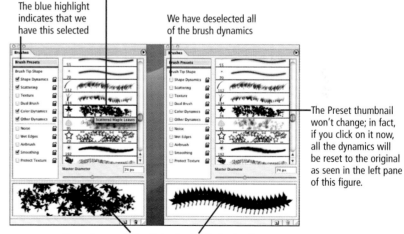

The Preset thumbnail won't change; in fact, if you click on it now, all the dynamics will be reset to the original as seen in the left pane of this figure.

The preview reveals the effects of each of the brush options

Figure 2.4 You chose Scattered Maple Leaves and deselected all its options to show the influence on the brush.

Click Brush Tip Shape. You see the options for changing the fundamentals of the brush in the right frame: the diameter, angle, roundness, hardness, and spacing. The first option is the diameter. Your brush tip can have a pixel width of 1–2,500 pixels. The Use Sample Size button appears if you modify a custom brush, allowing you to revert to your originally created size.

Speed Tip

Want to nudge your brush size up or down? Use the left bracket ([) to decrease and the right bracket (]) to increase the size of your brush.

You can adjust angle and roundness interactively or numerically. Note that if you have a symmetrical brush, you don't see the angle change. The allowable angles are –180 to 180 degrees, comprising an entire 360 degrees. The hardness slider controls what falls off the edge of the brush tip. *Falloff* is the rate at which the ink decreases from the center of the brush; 100 percent makes the edges very sharp and 0 percent gives the softest edge. This option is not available on custom brushes.

Spacing controls the amount of overlap that falls between the brush shapes as it is stroked across the canvas and can be anywhere between 1–1,000 percent. A spacing of 100 percent lines up the shapes edge to edge, a spacing of 200 percent leaves the brush shapes exactly one shape width apart, and a spacing of 50 percent puts each shape overlap halfway through the last one. Of course, instead of thinking numerically, you can just play around with the slider until you get the look you want.

Take a look at the settings in Figure 2.5.

With just these settings, you can create a variety of brushes. Changes in one setting may give the illusion of a different adjustment. Table 2.1 shows a comparative example of different settings. Changes in diameter (measured in pixels [px]), horizontal mirroring (Flip X), vertical mirroring (flip Y), angle, roundness, hardness, and spacing can give quite a variety of looks. The Comment column allows you to quickly see the relationship of one brush stroke to another; brush stroke 2 is the same as brush stroke 1 but with a spacing difference, for example. Take a look at the brush strokes in Figure 2.6 and compare the settings depicted in Table 2.1.

The Use Sample Size button only appears on custom brushes that have been changed from their original size

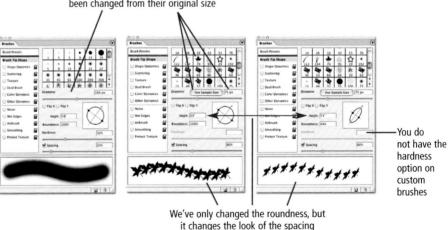

You do not have the hardness option on custom brushes

We've only changed the roundness, but it changes the look of the spacing

Figure 2.5 Photoshop 7 introduces the ability to change the ratio aspect and rotation of any brush, including custom brushes. You didn't change the spacing, but the change in the roundness gives the effect of more space between each leaf.

Table 2.1 Brush Stroke Settings

Stroke	Diameter	FlipX	FlipY	Angle	Roundness	Hardness	Spacing	Comment
1	19 px	N	N	0°	100%	100%	25%	Hard round 19
2	19 px	N	N	0°	100%	100%	100%	#1 w/ space diff
3	19 px	N	N	0°	100%	0%	100%	#2 w/ hard diff
4	19 px	N	N	0°	50%	0%	100%	#3 w/ round diff
5	19 px	N	N	90°	50%	0%	100%	#4 w/ angle diff
6	19 px	N	N	0°	100%	100%	200%	#1 w/ space diff
7	19 px	N	N	0°	100%	100%	75%	#1 w/ space diff
8	74 px	N	N	0°	100%	N/A	25%	Scattered Maple Leaves
9	74 px	N	N	0°	100%	N/A	100%	#8 w/ space diff
10	74 px	Y	N	0°	100%	N/A	100%	#9 w/ X flip
11	74 px	N	Y	0°	100%	N/A	100%	#9 w/ Y flip
12	74 px	Y	Y	0°	100%	N/A	100%	#9 w/ X and Y flip
13	74 px	N	N	0°	100%	N/A	50%	#8 w/ space diff
14	74 px	N	N	0°	100%	N/A	200%	#8 w/ space diff

Shape Dynamics

The Shape Dynamics setting enables you to specify randomness and variation in a stroke. Some of its options are only available if you are using a pressure-sensitive digital tablet. What?! You say you don't have a tablet? Using Photoshop without a tablet is sort of like going snorkeling without a mask. As long as you have the snorkel, you technically are snorkeling, and yeah, you can see…sort of…mostly…but you really miss out on a lot. So get a tablet!

Note

A *tablet* is another form of input interface with your computer, as your mouse and keyboard are. A tablet acts like a map of your screen and you use a digital pen to interact—like painting on paper with a pen. Many options are available for purchase, with Wacom Tablets being the most popular and predominant brand in the industry.

Click to highlight the Shape Dynamics option on the left frame of the Brushes palette. You can see your options for the shape dynamics on the right.

Angle Jitter lets you control or randomize the brush tip angle, which is great in a couple instances:

- You're creating a texture that has to follow some logical change in angle. An example is arrows pointing along a path (0 percent jitter, but using direction).

- You want to give a more natural look to a shape (leaves blowing in the wind, 100 percent jitter).

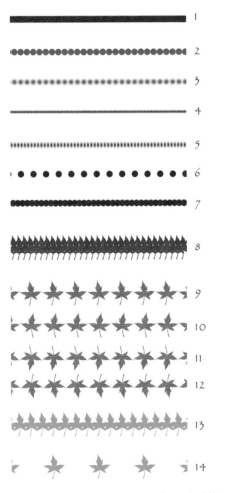

Roundness Jitter controls the roundness that you have set for brush tip shape. Minimum roundness sets a limit to how flat the brush can go.

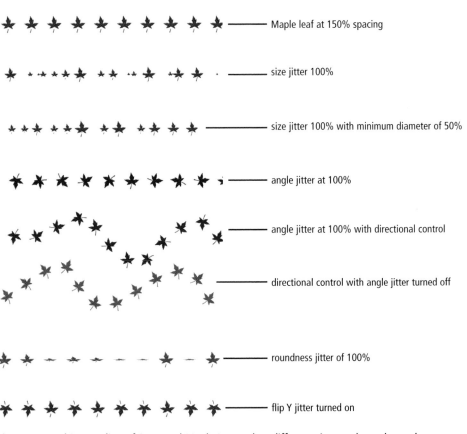

Figure 2.6 Brush strokes 2 and 3 only differ in their hardness, but it looks like the spacing has increased in 3. It's because the edge of the brush is fading to transparent.

Maple leaf at 150% spacing

size jitter 100%

size jitter 100% with minimum diameter of 50%

angle jitter at 100%

angle jitter at 100% with directional control

directional control with angle jitter turned off

roundness jitter of 100%

flip Y jitter turned on

Figure 2.7 This sampling of Scattered Maple Leaves has different size, angle, and roundness jitters applied.

Scattering

Click Scattering on the left frame of the Brushes palette to see the options available on the right side. Scattering distributes the amount and position of brush marks on a stroke. The higher the scatter percentage, the farther the brush mark may be from the line of the stroke. Selecting Both Axis scatters the marks radially, while deselecting the option scatters only on the perpendicular of the stroke.

Count specifies the number of brush marks at each spacing point, and Jitter randomly varies that number along the stroke by the percentage you set. Setting the count and variation to 0 percent uses your brush tip shape settings. Setting jitter to 100 percent gives the maximum randomness. See Figure 2.8.

Texture

Texture control applies either a preset or user-defined texture pattern to a brush stroke. It makes the stroke look like it was done on a textured canvas. To see the texture options, click the texture option on the left frame of the Brushes palette; see Figure 2.9. The texture controls are listed on the right frame of the Brushes palette.

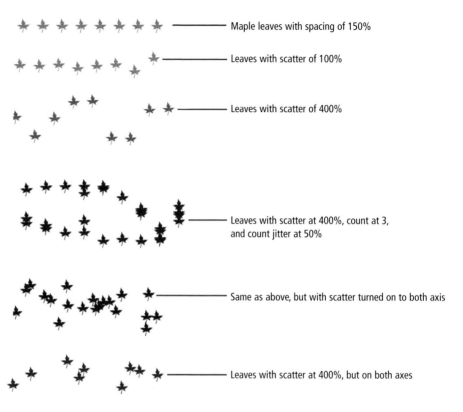

Figure 2.8 Scattering controls the number and placement of brush marks on a stroke.

- Invert reverses the light and dark pixels in the pattern.
- Scale sizes the pattern in each stroke.

- Texture Each Tip activates the Minimum Depth and the Depth Jitter controls. This option adds the randomization to the texture application over the stroke as it's applied to the canvas. Texture Each Tip renders each tip as it is stroked, giving a more saturated effect.

- Depth controls the amount of the pattern integrated with the stroke, specifying how deep the paint penetrates the texture. The lower the number, the more covered the pattern; at 0 percent, the pattern is completely obscured. Specifying a setting for Minimum Depth limits how low this percentage can dip to when you are using Depth Jitter.

- Depth Jitter randomizes the depth. At 0 percent there is no change over the course of the stroke. The higher the percentage, the more randomized the depth.

- Mode lets you choose one of Photoshop's blending modes, which determine how the texture and paint interact. These modes are the same as the brush-blending modes covered later in the chapter.

Dual Brush

Dual Brush uses a second brush tip, blended in, in a single stroke. This is great once you're familiar with all the brushes. You can even specify and control the mode with which the second brush is applied to the first brush.

To display these settings, click the Dual Brush option on the left side of the palette. You can see the option in Figure 2.10. The settings appear on the right side of the palette. (You do see the trend here, don't you?)

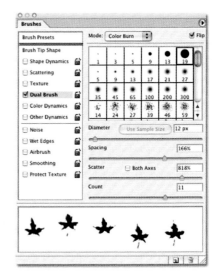

Figure 2.10 The second brush gives your Scattered Maple Leaves brush a stamped quality. It breaks up the clean edges and gives it a more organic feel.

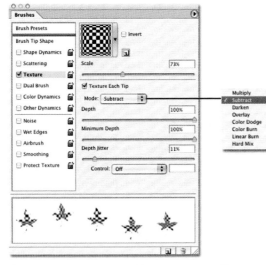

Figure 2.9 Texture can add an interesting effect.

Color Dynamics and Other Dynamics

The last set of options are the Color Dynamics and Other Dynamics. By now you will have figured out that you need to click the left side to see the options on the right side.

Color Dynamics allows color variation in a stroke, which gives a natural, organic feel. Foreground/Background Jitter determines how paint varies between the two colors. To the left (0 percent) is all foreground color, but to the right (100 percent) is not all background color: It is a full mix. Think of it as a 0-percent mix and a 100-percent mix. See Figure 2.11 for examples.

Note

Unfortunately, you can't see the Color Dynamics settings you're creating in the preview window. Kind of defeats the purpose of a preview window, doesn't it? One day, I know it will happen—color thumbnails. Until then, I continue to pine away. Nonetheless, this is one of my favorite options.

The Hue, Saturation, and Brightness Jitter choices introduce variation to their respective aspects. The higher the percentage, the more the variations deviate from a numerical setting. The best way to understand this is to think of painting in HSB (hue, saturation, and brightness).

Looking at an HSB slider, you can see how the variance affects you. Painter had this option long ago, and I'm glad to see Photoshop has finally included it.

Purity is simply the saturation level. At 100 percent it is fully saturated and at −100 percent it is fully desaturated (grayscale).

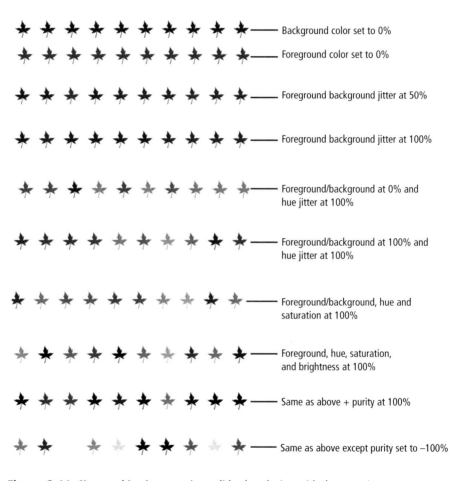

Figure 2.11 Since nothing in nature is a solid color, playing with these settings at a more subtle level gives some very organic results.

Other Dynamics, shown in Figure 2.12, introduces jitter to the opacity and the flow aspects. The settings do not override the main brush opacity setting, but give variation from the point at which they were set. For instance, an opacity jitter of 50 percent does not jitter around 50 percent, but jitters 50 percent of the opacity set. In other words, if you have a brush set at 50 percent opacity, a 50 percent jitter randomizes between 25–75 percent opacity, a 100 percent jitter randomizes between 0–100 percent opacity, and a 10 percent jitter gives you an opacity between 45–55 percent. The Flow Jitter option works on the same concept.

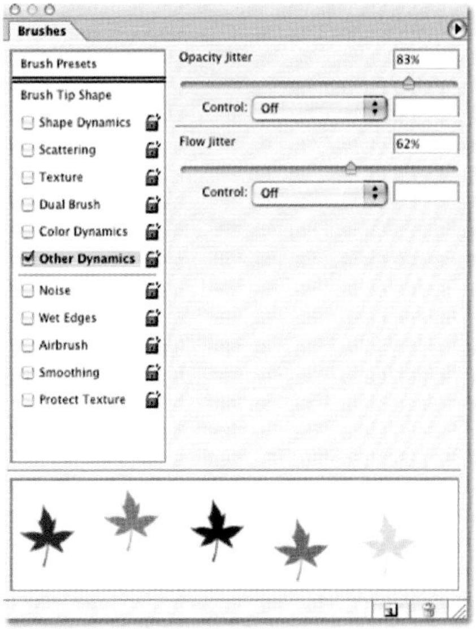

Other Brush Tip Characteristics

These brush tip characteristics are toggles; they are on or off. Clicking these options on the palette's left frame does not bring anything up on the right frame; notice the line that separates these characteristics from the earlier options.

- Noise applies additional randomness to the brush tips, but does not fade the noise to match the edges of a soft brush. Brush tips that contain gray values (fading areas) see the effect more prominently.

Figure 2.12 Randomness in the opacity and flow gives a feeling of more depth.

- Wet Edges lightens the central portion of the stroke, giving a watercolor brush look due to paint buildup at the outer edges.

- Airbrush is represented on the options bar as well as the Brushes palette. It emulates a traditional airbrush, producing a soft buildup that increases the paint saturation. This gives the wider buildup airbrush effect if you hold your brush down in one spot.

- Smoothing works on freehand strokes to eliminate any hard edges.

- Protect Texture overrides any brush texture preset so that if you're painting with several brushes, the texture remains consistent over the entire image.

Putting the Brushes Palette to Use

You put most of the Brushes palette options into effect throughout the book, but here's an example of how the brush controls have made life so much easier. The graphic of leaves in Figure 2.13 swooping in on the wind was made with little more than one sweep of a brush. All the settings are shown in Figures 2.14 through 2.20, so you can emulate them—in case you don't believe me!

Figure 2.13 This figure was created with a few dabs of a paint brush. All the options and colors are depicted in Figures 2.14 through 2.20.

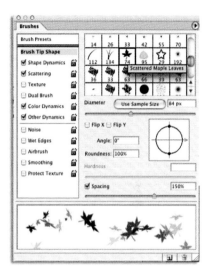

Figure 2.14 Brush Tip Shape settings.

Figure 2.15 Shape dynamics.

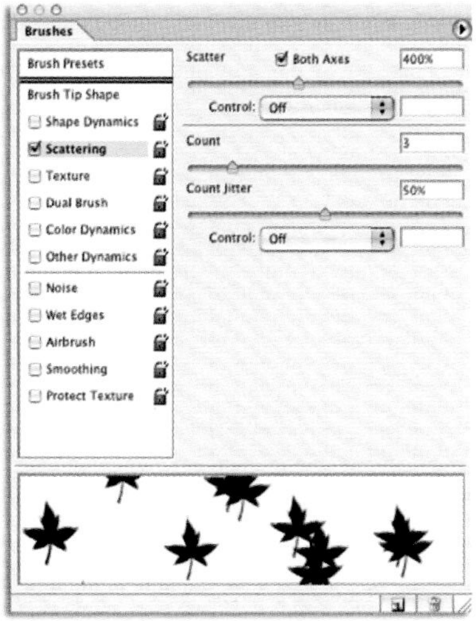

Figure 2.16 Scattering.

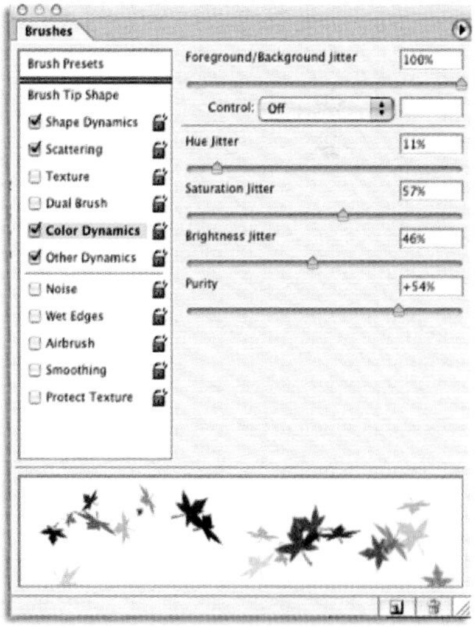

Figure 2.17 Color dynamics.

Figure 2.18 Other dynamics.

Almost overwhelming isn't it? Well, hold on to that almost because all of the brushes can be applied with different blending modes, which are much like layer modes.

Note

Save your new Scattered Maple Leaves brush settings as a new brush preset if you want to keep the brush. Otherwise, you lose all your settings with the next brush you use. To save a new brush preset, simply go to the Brush Presets in the options bar and click the New Presets button.

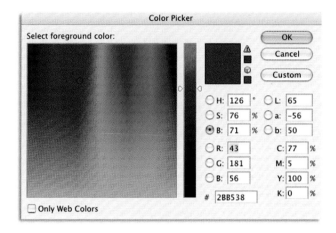

Figure 2.19 Foreground color.

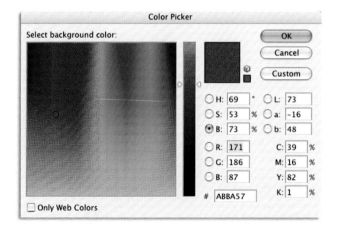

Figure 2.20 Background color.

Brush Blending Modes

You've seen how you can adjust the brush's behavior in the sense of its shape and color, but how does the paint interact with the canvas? If this were real paint, I would have to say it depends on the paint type and how dry the base layer is. You'd also probably have quite a mess all around the canvas. Or maybe that's just me. Then again, I can't eat without getting food on my clothes…but I digress. Figure 2.21 shows you the original photo on which I'm going to test blend modes.

Photoshop has 25 blend modes that you can select for a brush, and these blend modes determine how the colors interact with the base image. You can find these modes in the options bar when you've selected a painting tool. See Figure 2.22 for the brush stroke examples and Figure 2.23 for where you can access them.

Figure 2.21 My dog, Auggie, is here to test the blend modes.

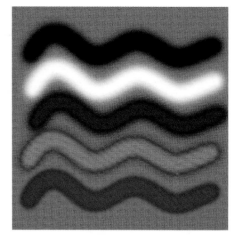

Figure 2.22 Here are the brush strokes at 100 percent normal on a 50-percent gray background.

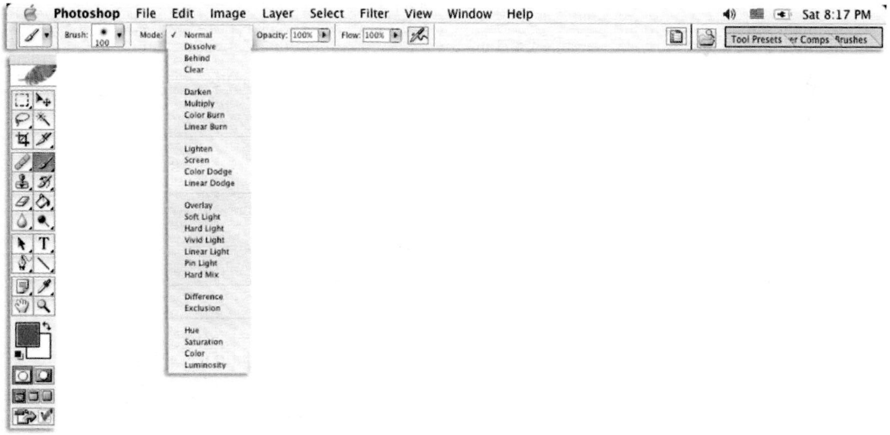

Figure 2.23 This is where you can find the blend modes.

For the most part, the blend modes for the brush and for the layer react identically. A couple of brush blend modes don't exist as a layer blend mode, and a few brush blend modes react a bit differently than its layer counterpart. The following subsections cover each and every possible blend mode. To illustrate this, each of the modes are followed by three figures.

- The first image shows the brush stroke at 100 percent.

- The second image shows the same brush at 50 percent opacity.

- The third image is the brush stroke at 100 percent normal, but on a separate layer with the layer blend mode set to the corresponding mode.

Dissolve

Dissolve only comes into effect when the opacity is less than 100 percent. It allows randomized pixels to show through.

Normal

Normal is the default mode, which appears as Threshold in a bitmap or an indexed color-image mode. At 100 percent opacity, your application colors are unaffected by the base layer. In other words, whatever color you choose appears the same—there's no blending or influence from the base layer.

Figure 2.24 This is pretty much what you're used to seeing: the standard in digital paint.

Figure 2.25 The 50 percent opacity strokes show the dissolve blend mode better than the others, but you can still see a bit of the dissolve on the edges where the brush strokes feather.

Behind

Behind affects only transparent parts of a layer, giving the illusion that the strokes are behind the layer. You can liken it to painting on the back of a sheet of acetate. Obviously, there is no "behind" layer blend mode. You would just put the layer, well, behind another.

Caution

The Behind and Clear modes are not an available option on any locked layer. By default, you can't use these modes on the background layer.

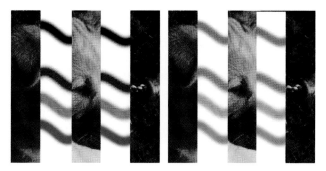

Figure 2.26 To show how the brush blend mode works, I cut out slices of the image so the brush had a transparent section on which to paint.

Clear

With this mode pixels are made transparent, like the eraser.

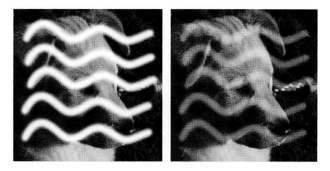

Figure 2.27 There is no such effect for the layers; you can't have a layer on top negate a layer on bottom to transparency, though it is an interesting concept.

Darken

Darken compares each color at the channel level and selects either the base or selected foreground (aka blend) color—whichever is darker—as the result color. Ergo, colors in the base are changed if they are lighter than the applied color, but colors that are darker than the applied color are not changed.

Figure 2.28 Despite its name, the Darken blend mode does not just darken, but colors the result by the application color.

Multiply

Darkening all colors until they reach black is what the Multiply mode does. It looks at the color information in each channel and multiplies the base color by the foreground color. Using a light color allows more control over the effect, and painting repeatedly over the same area produces progressively darker colors, much like coloring with a marker.

Figure 2.29 The marker analogy is fairly accurate: not much different from Darken.

Color Burn

A darker color darkens and saturates the base layer when you use Color Burn mode. It darkens by increasing contrast.

Figure 2.30 Blending with white on either the base or application produces no effect.

Linear Burn

If you want to darken your work, use Linear Burn. It does its thing by decreasing the brightness of the base layer, which tints and affects white.

Figure 2.31 Even light colors subtract from the base layer.

Lighten

The opposite of Darken, the base colors that are darker than the applied color are lightened. However, colors that are lighter than the applied color stay the same when you use Lighten mode.

Figure 2.32 Lighter colors stay the same.

Screen

The opposite of Multiply, the end result is always lighter with Screen mode. It looks at each channel's color information and multiplies the inverse of the application and base colors.

Figure 2.33 Painting with black gives no effect, but even an almost-black color lightens the base.

Color Dodge

Another lightening effect, Color Dodge infuses the base with the applied colors and brightens the base. The opposite effect of Color Burn, this lightens by decreasing contrast.

Figure 2.34 Here is the first example of how the brush reacts differently than the layer blend mode. Notice how the brush eats away much more than the layer.

Linear Dodge

Similar to Screen mode, Linear Dodge brightens the base to reflect the application color. It's a bit harsher than Screen, and it tends to go to white faster.

Figure 2.35 There is a subtle difference between the brush and the layer blend mode; the edges of the brush burn in just a bit with the brush blend mode, whereas the layer blend mode just fades at the edges.

Overlay

Overlay *multiplies* (darkens) dark areas and *screens* (lightens) light areas.

Figure 2.36 The base color is tinged with the application color.

Soft Light

Similar to Overlay, but softer, Soft Light applies a color lighter than 50 percent gray lightens, and an application of a color darker than 50 percent gray darkens.

Figure 2.37 Luminosity values in the base are preserved.

Hard Light

This works similarly to Soft Light but tends to emphasize contrast and exaggerate highlights.

Figure 2.38 This effect is harsher than Soft Light.

Vivid Light

Vivid Light is like the Soft Light and Hard Light modes, but instead of multiplying and screening, it uses a combination of Color Burn and Color Dodge. If the *blend color* (light source) is lighter than 50 percent gray, the image is lightened by decreasing the contrast. If the blend color is darker than 50 percent gray, the image is darkened by increasing the contrast.

Figure 2.39 You can see a dramatic difference between the brush and the layer blend modes.

Linear Light

Linear Light uses Linear Burn and Linear Dodge. If the blend color (light source) is lighter than 50 percent gray, the image is lightened by increasing the brightness. If the blend color is darker than 50 percent gray, the image is darkened by decreasing the brightness.

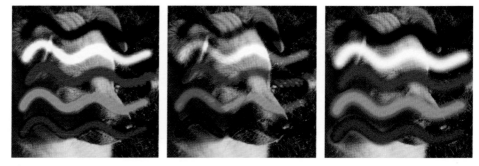

Figure 2.40 It's the same concept as Vivid Light, but uses Linear Burn and Linear Dodge.

Pin Light

Like Overlay, Pin Light divides and affects those pixels that have a brightness greater than 50 percent one way, and pixels that have a brightness of less than 50 percent another way. If the color applied has a brightness greater than 50 percent, then it replaces any affected pixels that are darker than 50 percent brightness. If the color applied has a brightness lower than 50 percent, then pixels lighter than it in the underlying image replace the color applied.

Figure 2.41 Pin Light works similarly to Overlay.

Hard Mix

Hard Mix creates a posterized, graphic effect by reducing all colors to eight colors: black, white, red, green, blue, cyan, magenta, and yellow.

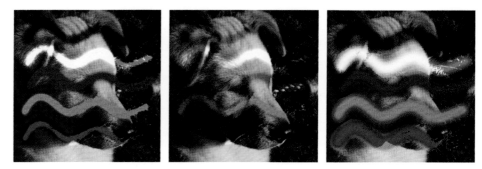

Figure 2.42 Graphics effects abound with Hard Mix mode.

Difference

Difference creates a negative, or inverted, effect by subtracting the applied color from the base color or the base color from the applied color, depending on which has the larger brightness value.

Figure 2.43 A white application inverts the base colors.

Exclusion

A lower contrast version of Difference, Exclusion also has less saturation. A dark application color tends to convert the base colors to shades of gray.

Figure 2.44 It's interesting how the 50 percent white reacts in the middle frame.

Hue

The *color*, or hue, of the applied color is applied to the *luminance* (brightness) and *saturation* (intensity) values of the base color.

Figure 2.45 Notice how both the black and the white affect the image the same way. Both of them have no hue, per se, and result in a grayscale.

Saturation

Use the applied color's saturation to blend with the hue and luminance of the base color.

Figure 2.46 Since the red, blue, and green have equal saturations, they give the same effect when used in the saturation mode. The same theory applies for the black and white.

Color

Color uses both the saturation and hue of the applied color to colorize the base's luminance.

Figure 2.47 The luminance on this base is colorized.

Luminosity

Luminosity uses the applied color's luminance to blend with the saturation and hue of the base color.

Figure 2.48 Luminosity is the opposite of Color.

Note

The Brush tool shares its space with the Pencil tool. Some have asked why you'd even use the Pencil at all. Isn't it the same as setting the brush to a hard edge? Actually, they exhibit a few differences not only in their hardness, but in their function. With the Pencil, you Shift+click and create straight lines. An auto-erase option automatically switches your pencil to the background color when you try to draw on a color that matches your foreground color. The Brush does not have such an option.

In addition to these functional differences, take a look at Figure 2.49. A hard brush tool is still anti-aliased, so on close inspection it's quite different from the hard stroke of a pencil tool. The main difference between a brush with a hard edge and a pencil is the anti-aliasing, which is less visible if you use a large brush.

Figure 2.49 The top scribble was done with a Pencil tool, the middle with a hard Brush (hardness of 100 percent), and the bottom with a soft Brush (hardness of 0 percent).

CHAPTER 3

FILE BROWSER

Whether you are a texture painter, a matte painter, or part of any other digital painting field, you inevitably come across a slew of reference images that you need to access and work with. Photoshop's file browser has so much to offer in this regard. The *file browser* is a visual file-management system that was introduced in Photoshop and has been further developed in Photoshop CS. With a customizable layout and fast thumbnail views, the file browser is much preferable to the standard **File** > **Open** command. But wait—there's more! If you act now, you also receive all the features of a cataloguing program. (Actually, you get the cataloguing features whether you act now or not, but this makes it even more exciting, doesn't it?)

Basic Navigation

You navigate the file browser much like you do Windows Explorer (not to be confused with Internet Explorer, the web browser). To bring up the file browser, click the file browser button in the tool options bar. It is the button directly to the left of the palette well that looks like a folder with a magnifying glass.

When the file browser first comes up, you see these things in the left frame: a file tree on the top, a preview thumbnail in the middle, and the metadata and keywords in separate tabs on the bottom. File thumbnails are on the right. You know that I love exploded and dissection views, so here you go: Figure 3.1 shows this very thing.

To open an image from the file browser, simply double-click the thumbnail on the right. You can open multiple images by pressing Shift or Command (Win: Ctrl) and highlighting multiple files before double-clicking (any one of them).

There you go! Pretty basic. Now come the more interesting parts.

Finding Your Keys

Keywords are descriptive labels that help organize your files. You can attach one or more to any image and use them later to organize your view in the file browser. Do you want to see all the images of your dog? If you had assigned the keyword *dog* to each of your dog image files, you could easily find and display them! Click the Keywords tab in the file browser's bottom-left frame. Adobe provides a few default categories. You can either leave, hide, or delete these. For now, leave them.

Want to create a new keyword? Follow along:

1. Go to the level at which you want the new keyword.

   For example, I have pictures from Australia that I want located under one of the default categories/keywords, Place.

2. Click Place to select it.

   If I want the new keyword on the same level as Place, then I don't highlight anything.

3. Click the New Keyword icon (the new layer icon's twin brother) at the bottom of the Keywords palette. See Figure 3.2.

4. In the label that opens up, type your own new keyword, and press Return (Enter)

   I entered Australia as a keyword, as you can see in the text box of Figure 3.3.

You say you want to get even slicker with your keywords? Table 3.1 can help.

You can see what keywords are assigned to an image by looking for the checkmarks next to the keywords in the Keywords palette when you have the image thumbnail selected, as shown in Figure 3.4. You can toggle the checkmarks to assign or unassign keywords to the image. If you already have a keyword assigned to an image, don't worry: Assigning a keyword simply adds the keyword to any existing keyword(s).

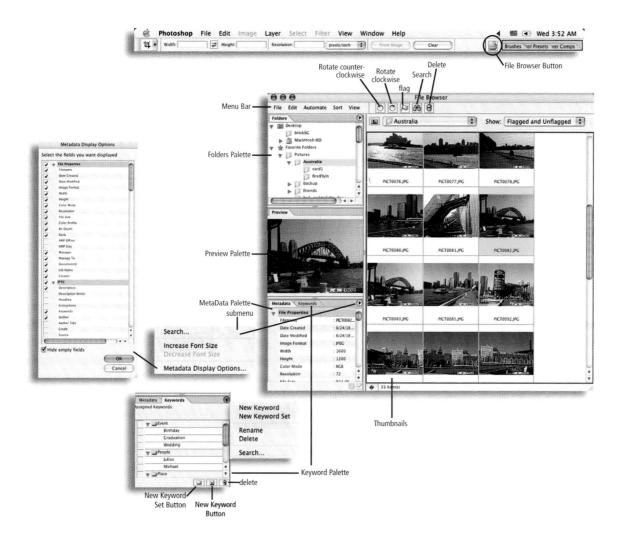

Figure 3.1 You can click the file browser button in the tool options bar or go through **Window** > **File Browser** in the menu bar to bring up the file browser.

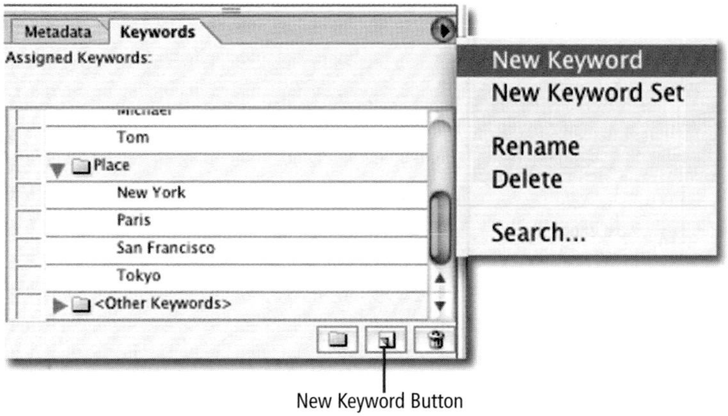

New Keyword Button

Figure 3.2 You could press the new keyword button or go through the Keyword palette's submenu to create a new keyword.

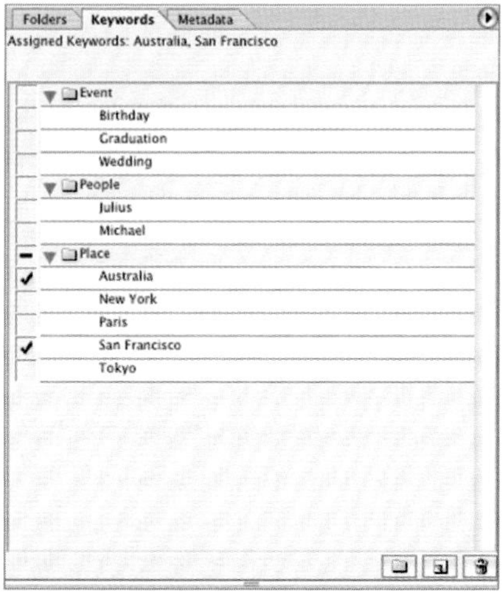

Figure 3.3 Create your own keywords to catalog your images.

Table 3.1 Keyword Tricks

You Want to Do What?	Here's How
Assign the keyword (Australia, in this case) to the image you have highlighted.	Click the picture thumbnail, and then double-click the keyword in the Keywords palette.
Give all the images in this file the same keyword.	Go to the file browser's bar menu at the top of the dialog box and click **Edit > Select All** (or press Command+A [Win: Ctrl+A]), then double-click the keyword.
Put a keyword in a folder.	Photoshop refers to the grouping of keywords into a common folder as a *keyword set*. First create a folder, or new keyword set, by clicking the new keyword set button at the bottom of the Keyword palette. If you already have keywords you'd like gathered under a new keyword set, drag your keywords to the newly created folder. To add a keyword to the new keyword set, highlight the folder before creating the keyword.
Remove a keyword from one or more images.	Just choose the image thumbnails and click the checkmark next to the keyword to deselect the image's assignment to that keyword.

Figure 3.4 When you click an image, all its keywords are visible in the Keywords palette.

Using Your Keys

That little button that looks like binoculars is not the bird-watching or voyeur button, but a search button. (Now, now, don't be so disappointed.) Clicking it brings up a dialog box that allows you to search by a variety of criteria, including keywords; check out Figure 3.5. Unfortunately, no pop-up lets you select from existing keywords. Instead, you have to know the word and enter it.

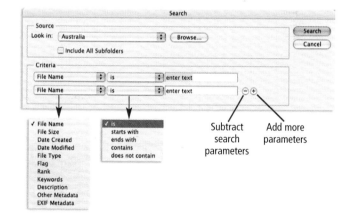

Figure 3.5 You can do a search on all of your images by keyword, name, date, rank, and many other options.

Keywords are one way to go about shuffling through pictures, but you may have noticed quite a few options in the search criteria. One of them is rank. You can assign an alphanumeric rank to any of your pictures. Whatever you type in the Rank box is ordered; numbers have a higher value than letters and values are evaluated from left to right. So 1 comes before 2, but 10 also comes before 2. A is equal to a (no distinguishing between uppercase and lowercase), but A comes before b, and A1 comes before A2. To get a better idea, assign a rank to a few pictures.

1. Either go to **Edit** > **Rank** or right-click and choose Rank.

2. Type in the rank in the dialog box that pops up, and click OK.

   You could do something with a theme or something witty, but being the under pressure to finish this book, I have entered a simple single letter and number combination for Figure 3.6.

Rank Files

Rank: A3   OK

                             Cancel

Figure 3.6 You could enter something a little more creative, like Dinner. Which would come after Appetizer and before Full.

Follow these steps to view the images by rank:

1. Go to the file browser menu bar and choose **Sort** > **Rank**.

2. Refresh by either going to the Folders palette submenu and clicking Refresh, choosing **View** > **Refresh** in the menu bar, or by pressing F5.

Note

Remember to refresh after sorting. This is worth repeating because it's a detail that people forget. Photoshop doesn't seem to do so reliably, so pressing the Refresh button ensures that you are looking at the proper results of your change. For example, after choosing **Sort** > **Rank** and changing the rank of one of the images, you notice that you need to refresh for that changed image to pop into its rank. To be on the safe side, refresh!

If you want to see the rank of each of your images, either go to **View** > **Details** to display your thumbnails in detail form (which displays data next to the thumbnail) or go to **View** > **Rank** to see just the rank displayed underneath the thumbnail. You need to have larger thumbnails for this to be an option, so if the Rank option is grayed out, increase the size of your thumbnails. If you really messed up, you can get rid of all the rankings and start over: Select all the images, go to the file browser's bar menu, and select **Edit** > **Clear Ranking**.

Say you don't need such a complex ranking. All you want to do is flag the images you like out of the virtual pile that was thrown at you. You can do this by selecting the image thumbnail and (surprise!) clicking the flag button at the top of the file browser. Then you have the option of showing only the flagged or unflagged images using the Show drop-down list; in Figure 3.7. This is great if you have to sort through a plethora of images and just need to make a yeah or nay pile.

If you accidentally flag an image that you didn't want to flag, or change your mind and decide to reverse a particular image's flag, all you have to do is select the image again and click the flag button. The flag toggles off.

Figure 3.7 Clicking the flag button allows you to quickly divide any group into two and view them separately.

Batch Renaming Your Files

I don't know about you, but I hate the camera's generic image names: DSCF0459 or img2356. It would help on so many different levels if I could just rename all of them to Hawaii0001 through Hawaii1234. Luckily, Photoshop makes this a lot easier with its Batch Rename function.

1. Copy the images into a folder.

   Do this as a general rule of thumb, especially if you are not sure that renaming is Pok2Do (Perfectly okay to Do). One example of when this step is not necessary is when you are renaming images from a CD. (Photoshop can't overwrite files already burned to CD.) I'm of the paranoid but lazy type (read: worried enough to really want to back up everything, but generally procrastinating so long it never gets done). I like to copy the images to a folder and save myself the ulcer, in case something goes wrong.

2. Go to your newly created folder in Photoshop's file browser.

3. Choose **Edit** > **Select All**, as shown in Figure 3.8, or press Command+A (Win: Ctrl+A).

   This selects all the image thumbnails in the folder. (This is the same keyboard shortcut for **Select** > **All** that you take when selecting all the content on a layer an image.)

4. Go back to the file browser's bar menu and choose **Automate** > **Batch Rename**, shown in Figure 3.9.

   The Batch Rename dialog box, which you see in Figure 3.10, appears.

5. You can choose the Rename in Same Folder option since you already have your images in a separate folder.

Caution

Move to New Folder does *not* copy the renamed files to the new folder. Instead, this option moves the image files to the new folder after renaming them.

Figure 3.8 You don't have to select all of the files. You could do a noncontiguous selection by holding the Command key (Win: Ctrl) and selecting images.

Figure 3.9 This renames all of the selected images.

6. Under the File Naming area, either type in a name or choose an option.

Since these are my photos from Australia, I give it the name Australia in the first field. To distinguish each one from the other, I give them a four-digit number, followed by the file extension. Finally, I want the numbers to start from 67 (to match the previous numbers), so I enter 67 at the Starting Serial # text box at the bottom.

At the top of the File Naming area, a sample of what the name looks like reflects your selections. It always uses GIF as the sample extension, so don't worry that your 16-bit TIF will be converted to a GIF—it won't be.

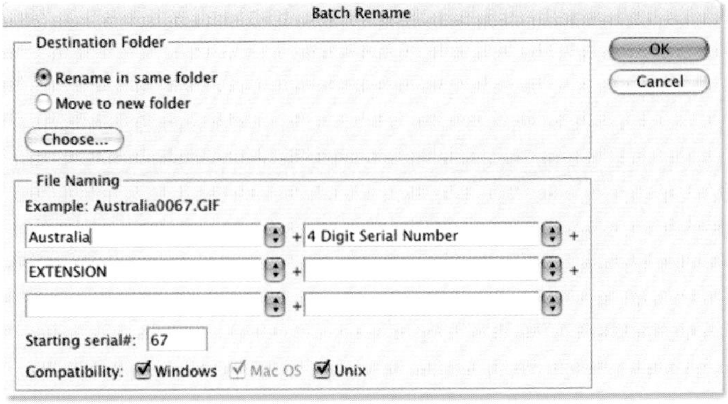

Figure 3.10 The Batch Rename dialog box.

7. Click OK and you see all of your selected images have been renamed! Figure 3.11 shows my renumbered images.

If you navigate through a system window, you see that the actual files have been renamed. Of course, the file browser reflects this also.

Creating a Custom Layout

You don't need to create your own layout, but most likely you have a particular ritual that sets up your file browser just so. Rather than repeating that ritual each time you start Photoshop, you can create a custom layout!

1. Open the file browser by clicking the button beside the palette well.

Take a look at the default layout. It should look like Figure 3.12.

Figure 3.11 The images are renamed.

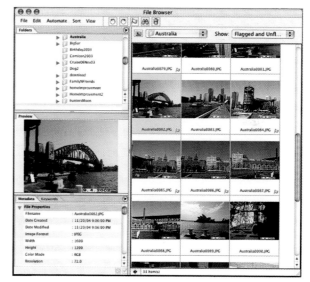

Figure 3.12 The default layout.

2. Save this setting before making any changes: **Window** > **Workspace** > **Save Workspace**.

A dialog box asks for a name; see Figure 3.13.

3. Enter **PSdefault** into that space for Photoshop Default and click Save.

4. Click the Keywords tab at the file browser's lower-left frame.

5. Drag the palette by its tab to the topmost part of the frame, where the Folders tab is.

You see a dotted outline of the tabbed section, like that in Figure 3.14, move as you drag.

6. Do the same thing for the Metadata tab.

Now you have a blank, gray area underneath your preview where the two tabs were before you moved them.

7. Simply drag the bottom bar of the pane that holds the Preview palette all the way down to get rid of the gray space and increase the Preview palette space.

8. Now drag the vertical bar to the right until you have a nice, medium-sized preview like that in Figure 3.15.

In this case, I have also dragged down the top of the preview bar to give myself more room for the tabbed information at the top.

9. Set the thumbnails to Medium.

Since the oversized preview window helps you see details, you don't need the large thumbnails.

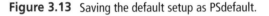

Name: PSdefault

Figure 3.13 Saving the default setup as PSdefault.

10. Go to the file browser's menu bar and select **View** > **Medium Thumbnail**.

This layout, shown in Figure 3.16, is what I generally like to work with. It allows me a better view of the images and easy access to its info while looking at the image. All the while I can navigate easily.

Figure 3.14 Drag the lower palettes to the topmost palette.

Figure 3.15 Drag the frame bars out to create a new view mode.

Figure 3.16 A whole new file browser.

11. Save this setup using the same command as you did for the default: Go to **Window** > **Workspace** > **Save Workspace**.

12. Type a name in the Save Workspace dialog box that appears, and click Save.

    Of course, you don't need to call it GenView, which is what I named it. You can call it anything you want. I like the name Andy, but thought GenView was more descriptive.

    Another popular file browser layout is to increase the thumbnails to a custom size and have the text info on the left as you need it. Make your thumbnails huge.

13. Go to your preferences by selecting **Photoshop** > **Preferences** (Win: **Edit** > **Preferences**) or by going to the file browser's menu and choosing **Edit** > **Preferences**, as in Figure 3.17.

Figure 3.17 One of many ways to access Photoshop's preferences.

14. In the Preferences dialog box, shown in Figure 3.18, enter the width you would like for your custom thumbnail in the Custom Thumbnail Size text box, and then click OK.

   The default of 256 pixels is fine for my laptop, but at work, with my dual monitor setup and much larger screens, I like to use 420 pixels for thumbnail width. It may take some back and forth work to figure out which size works best for you.

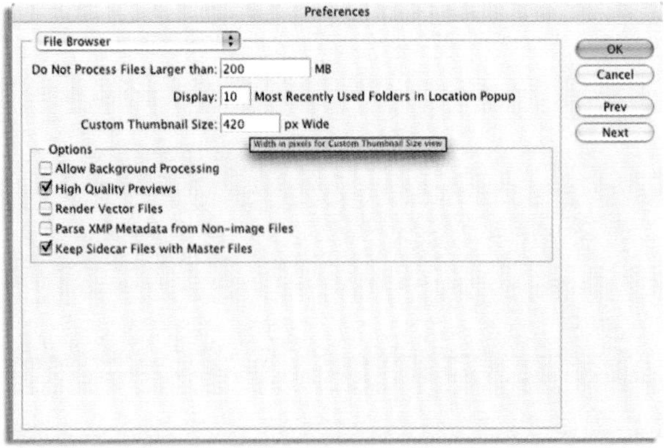

Figure 3.18 Enter the custom thumbnail size.

15. To view the custom size, go to **View > Custom Thumbnail Size** in the file browser's menu bar. See Figure 3.19.

    A small button that gets rid of the left frame appears on the bottom of the file browser, shown in Figure 3.20. Clicking this button hides and redisplays the file browser's left pane. With a large custom thumbnail size, you may want to use this button, bringing back the left frame only as you need it to navigate or to check out the image information.

16. Save this the workspace using custom layout with whatever name you want.

    I call it BigBrow. You can call it Bob or Mom or anything else. I recommend some psychotherapy if you decided to name it Mom, though.

    Now you have three different layouts accessible by going to **Window > Workspace** and then choosing from the names at the bottom of the pull-down menu.

Note

Saving a workspace is just that: A complete workspace, including the location of all of your other palettes. Keep this in mind when you go to save your workspace; double-check the entire screen for the location and visibility of the other palettes.

Figure 3.19 Show your custom thumbnails.

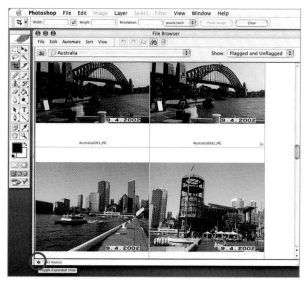

Figure 3.20 Your third layout option. Hide and show the other palettes by clicking the expand view button on the lower left of the file browser window.

Exporting Your File Browser Changes

You have rotated, renamed, annotated, and a few other spiffy changes, all in the file browser. Now you want to make sure that anyone else on the network can see the image modifications the way you do. Or you want to burn it all to a CD. How do you ensure that others have all that information? If you're like me, you just burned it to a CD and found out the hard way that none of this information was passed on.

It is pretty easy to remedy the situation: Go to your file browser's bar menu and choose **File > Export Cache**. A dialog box lets you know the cache has been exported. See Figure 3.21.

Three files are in the same folder area where the images appear. As long as the files are there in the same folder as the images, anyone using the file browser to view the folder contents can see the rotation changes you made and the picture thumbnails load more quickly. If you burn the folder of images to a CD, all is well if you include the three cache files in the folder with the images.

Figure 3.21 Can't find the Export Cache option? You're probably looking in Photoshop's main menu bar rather than the file browser's menu bar.

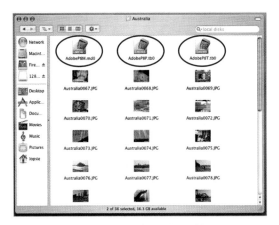

Figure 3.22 Make sure these three files accompany your images

CHAPTER 4

CUSTOMIZING
YOUR WORKSPACE

P hotoshop is a flexible program; you can accomplish the same thing so many ways. The more you learn, the more you start developing your own workflow preferences. This, in turn, affects how you want to interface with Photoshop. This chapter gives you a solid place to start and the means to change your workspace to fit your needs.

Preferences

I remember looking through books, trying to find what settings I should set Photoshop to. Each time I went to the chapter about setting your preferences, it has some inane description—"Checking 'Beep when done' enables Photoshop to beep when it has finished a function"—and absolutely no suggestions—"There is no real reason to have Photoshop beep at you unless you simply like annoying sounds; keep this unchecked."

At that time I swore upon my dead hamster's grave that I would give specific suggestions. I figure the best place to start is to have you set your computer up like mine. Of course, there are no absolute right ways to configure your setup. You may not agree with my suggestions, but you have to admit it at least gets you started finding the right settings for you.

General Preferences

To get to the preferences, go to **Photoshop > Preferences > General** (Win: **Edit > Preferences > General**). A window like the one in Figure 4.1 opens, revealing the General Preferences options. The other preference categories can be reached in the drop-down menu located at the top. Since the General Preferences are the most applicable in your day-to-day use of Photoshop, it is important to understand and set these preferences first.

Color Picker

Leave the default setting of the Adobe color picker as is. The chance that you need to use any system specific color picker is highly unlikely, and it is better to stay with Adobe's own.

Image Interpolation

When resizing an image, Photoshop has to determine how to create or combine pixels for the new image. For our purposes, stick with Bicubic (Better) interpolation; it has the best quality for resampling photographs. Bicubic Smoother or Bicubic Sharper applies varying amounts of softening that you probably won't need on a regular basis.

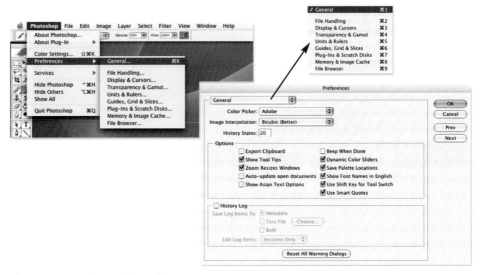

Figure 4.1 Getting to the preferences.

History States

This is one setting that I change every so often. This determines how many of your actions on a document Photoshop remembers, and therefore affects the number of undos you can do. I generally leave this setting at the default 20, but find that if I am working on a very large file, reducing it to 3 helps Photoshop run a bit smoother. On the other hand, when I am doing a lot of cloning or lots of tiny, brisk touch ups, I increase the number to 50 so I can go back further.

Export Clipboard

Keep this option deselected. If not, you get long pauses between switching programs with a Converting Clipboard to Pict Format dialog box or an Export Failed, Image Too Large warning. Even if you need to cut and paste a small image to another program, the quality is better when you save out and import a file. There really isn't a real good reason for keeping this option on.

Show Tooltips

Some people prefer to have this off, claiming that it is only good for novices. I however, prefer to have it on. I know the functions of most buttons in Photoshop, but may not know their official names. If I get a call from someone asking me how to do something, I can give clear directions, rather than telling him to press "that button with the circle thingy on it."

Zoom Resizes Windows

I prefer to have this on. I would rather have the windows resize to the image as I use Command++ (Win: Ctrl++) or Command+- (Win: Ctrl+-) to zoom in or out. If I want to zoom without resizing, I can simply use one of these shortcuts:

- Command+spacebar+click (Win: Ctrl+spacebar+click)
- Option+spacebar+click (Win: Alt+spacebar+click)

Autoupdate Open Documents

I keep this off because I often go between Deep Paint 3D and Photoshop and don't want the document to change in Photoshop just because I made a change in Deep Paint 3D. I manually update by using the Revert option in the File menu in Photoshop. This also allows me to undo whatever I did in another program by simply saving over the existing file.

Show Asian Text Options

Uh…no. There is a reason this is off by default. If you need this, you know who you are. All the rest can keep this off.

Beep When Done

This is what I used as the introductory example to this section. This option made sense when computers were slower and while computing a filter we wanted to go off and make better use of our time. Now, however, it is more annoying than useful and I suggest you keep it off or suffer your officemate's wrath.

Dynamic Color Sliders

This option allows the sliders in the Color palette to match your settings in real time. Generally you want this on, but if you have a very slow computer, you might benefit by turning off this feature.

Save Palette Locations

This feature has Photoshop remember where you had all the palettes the last time you shut down; it restores them to the same location the next time you start up. This is completely a personal preference and does not really affect general performance either way, since the save only happens at shutdown. Most people keep this on.

Show Font Names in English

This is to show Chinese, Japanese, and Korean (CJK) fonts in English. As I would not like to see anything in my interface not in English, I keep this selected.

Use Shift Key for Tool Switch

Keep this option on. Turning it off means that the Shift key is not required to cycle through the tool variations when using the shortcut key. For example, if you want to use the oval marquee, you could press Shift+M when this option is on. With the option off, pressing M twice takes you to the oval marquee. More often than not, this causes more accidental, problematic, and annoying tool selections.

Use Smart Quotes

Another one of those options that just doesn't really matter to a VFX artist. Smart quotes are the curly kind and straight (not smart) quotes are the straight kind. The only time anyone has ever mentioned a reasonable preference is when my editor pointed out the primes and double primes (mathematical annotations) would look like quotation marks if you chose curly over straight. Otherwise, this is purely an aesthetic choice. You choose.

History Log

Check this only if you really need a record of all the steps of getting to your finished image. That means leave it deselected unless you are being audited or are writing an article or book and need to have a record of each tiny little step. Hmm. Maybe I should have used that for some of the chapters of this book.

Figure 4.2 shows a sample of the resultant text from activating the History Log option.

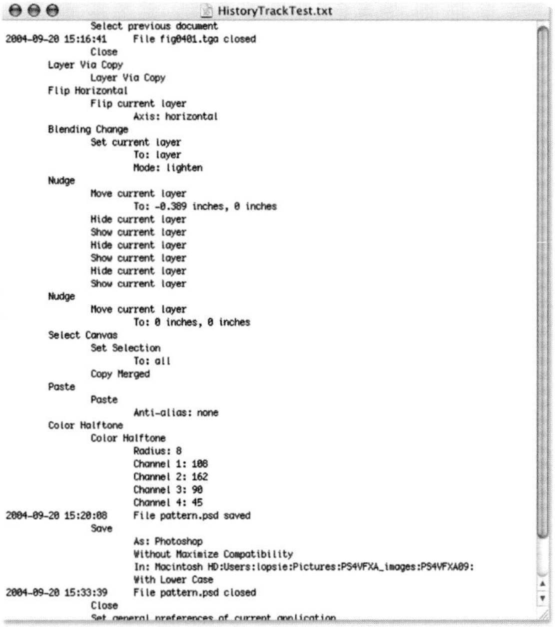

```
HistoryTrackTest.txt
                Select previous document
2004-09-20 15:16:41     File fig0401.tga closed
                Close
        Layer Via Copy
                Layer Via Copy
        Flip Horizontal
                Flip current layer
                        Axis: horizontal
        Blending Change
                Set current layer
                        To: layer
                        Mode: lighten
        Nudge
                Move current layer
                        To: -0.389 inches, 0 inches
                Hide current layer
                Show current layer
                Hide current layer
                Show current layer
                Hide current layer
                Show current layer
        Nudge
                Move current layer
                        To: 0 inches, 0 inches
        Select Canvas
                Set Selection
                        To: all
                Copy Merged
        Paste
                Paste
                        Anti-alias: none
        Color Halftone
                Color Halftone
                        Radius: 8
                        Channel 1: 108
                        Channel 2: 162
                        Channel 3: 90
                        Channel 4: 45
2004-09-20 15:20:08     File pattern.psd saved
                Save
                        As: Photoshop
                        Without Maximize Compatibility
                        In: Macintosh HD:Users:lopsie:Pictures:PS4VFXA_images:PS4VFXA09:
                        With Lower Case
2004-09-20 15:33:39     File pattern.psd closed
                Close
                Set general preferences of current application
```

Figure 4.2 A sample text history log.

File Handling Preferences

The file handling preferences determine how Photoshop handles files as they are opened and closed. While still in the General Preferences window, press Command+2 (Win: Ctrl+2) to get to the File Handling Preferences dialog box shown in Figure 4.3.

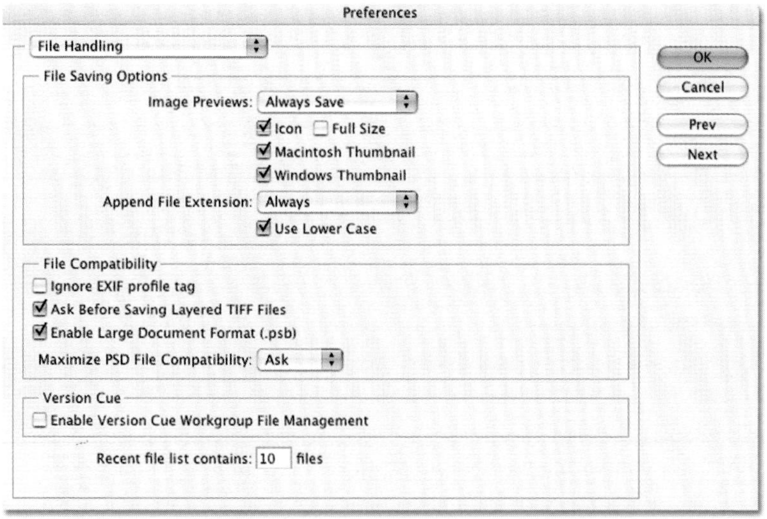

Figure 4.3 These preferences affect your day-to-day use of Photoshop.

Tip

Need to get the General Preferences dialog box back up onscreen? Press Command+K (Win: Ctrl+K)!

Image Preview

Do you want Photoshop to save an image *preview*—a thumbnail for visual identification—when it saves a file? It can create a significant increase in file size and slow down the saving of files, but the convenience of having a visual cue may be worth it to you.

In Windows OS, you only have these options:

- **Never Save** saves files without previews.
- **Always Save** saves files with specified previews.
- **Ask When Saving** assigns previews on a file-by-file basis.

If you are using Mac OS, you have the same Windows options but the addition of selecting one or more of the following preview types:

- **Icon** uses the preview as a file icon on the desktop.
- **Full Size** saves a 72ppi version of the file for use in applications that can open only low-resolution Photoshop images. For non-EPS files, this is a PICT preview.
- **Macintosh Thumbnail** displays the preview in the Open dialog box.
- **Windows Thumbnail** saves a preview that can display on Windows systems.

Append File Extension

Generally, it is a good idea to have this set to always save with lowercase extensions. This maximizes compatibility with different operating systems.

Ignore EXIF Profile Tag

Do you care about camera data? You should, but ultimately it is up to you. If you have absolutely no use for the image's camera settings, then you can select this and Photoshop ignores the data. If you either take your own images or receive images from others, it's a good idea to keep this deselected; that way you can see the camera's settings. This can help in obscure ways (such as in lining up a model to an image) as you can get the lens information and match it in your 3D program without distortion.

Ask Before Saving Layered TIFF Files

It is a good idea to have this on, as it is easy to accidentally save a layered TIFF that is too large and unusable to most other graphics packages. Programs that support layered TIFFs are far and few in between. Come to think of it, right now I only know of Adobe products that support it. In addition, my technical editor pointed out that TIFF images can be large to begin with, so keeping the layers creates an even huger file! If you are going to save layers, I would recommend saving them in PSD format.

Enable Large Document Format

This option enables limitless file sizes (save Photoshop's 300,000 × 300,000 pixel size limit and whatever your computer hardware can handle). You must explicitly save to the PSB format, but if you have images above the 2G limit of most formats, then you might want to consider enabling the large document format.

Maximize PSD File Compatibility

Although this seems like something you would want on, this is such an outdated compatibility point it's better turned off. This option saves a composite version along with the layered file, and it may lose some features that are incompatible with older versions. In addition, each time you save, a dialog box alerts you that the file is being maximized. Furthermore, you pay in disk space and time.

Unless you are working with an older program to open a PSD or with a program like Illustrator that requires a composite with the file, you might as well turn this option off by choosing Never from the drop-down menu. Of course, you could choose the Ask option to have Photoshop annoy you with yet another dialog box each time you save, but maybe you like telemarketers and Internet pop-up ads, too.

Version Cue

Unless you are being told you can work in a Version Cue workspace, leave this deselected. It is for Creative Suite users and their chosen ones only.

Recent File Lists

Another one of those personal choice things. This controls the number of files listed under **File** > **Open Recent** submenu. The default is 4, but I like to have 6. My dog likes 10. The max is 30. Do you really want to know and list the last 30 files you opened?

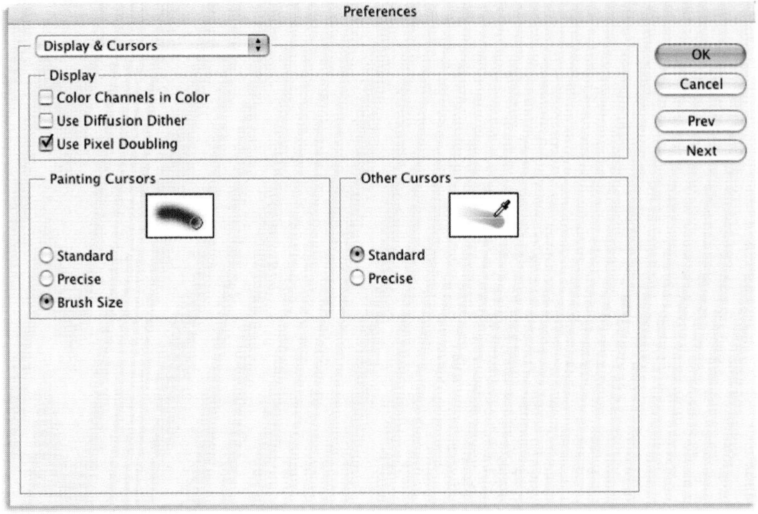

Display & Cursors

To change the shape of painting and other tool cursors, go to the Display and Cursor Preferences. Press Command+3 (Win: Ctrl+3) to switch the Preferences dialog box to the Display & Cursor Preferences dialog box shown in Figure 4.4.

Color Channels in Color

Although this may seem like a nice little visual option, it is better to have this off. The color overlay makes it difficult to see the details of the channel images, thereby affecting your channel manipulation.

Figure 4.4 The most common settings for this preference set are shown.

Use Diffusion Dither

Another holdover from the old days, this option allows displays limited to 256 colors to blend colors to emulate full 8-bit color (24-bit images, 8 bits per channel, with 3 channels, RGB). However, the system requirements to run the current version of Photoshop guarantee it can show full-color images.

Use Pixel Doubling

Anything that speeds me up is a good thing, so I turn this on. This option doubles the size of the pixels in dialog box previews; it reduces the resolution of the preview, but speeds the display. This does not affect the display of your actual image in Photoshop, nor does it affect the actual file.

Painting Cursors and Other Cursors

For the tool settings, keep the Painting cursor at the default (Brush Size) and the other cursors at Standard. The precise cursor can be a bit tough to see at times. Plus, if you need to use the precise cursor, you just need to press Caps Lock. Your cursor toggles to the precise cursor.

Transparency & Gamut

Transparency & Gamut preferences are accessed by pressing Command+4 [Win: Ctrl+4] while in the Preferences window. The dialog box in Figure 4.5 allows you to change the transparency grid and out-of-gamut colors. (*Gamut* is the continuous range of colors that a device can reproduce.) Of course, you can choose any grid colors you wish—it is totally a personal preference. However, I recommend changing the gamut warning color to an extremely bright and generally unused color.

Note

The term *out of gamut* means that colors from one device (such as a monitor) are not supported in another device (such as the film printer). The bright color you assign marks colors out of the range of reproducible colors for an assigned profile.

To turn on the out-of-gamut option, you must go to **View** > **Proof Setup** and choose the proof profile you want to use. The VFX artist who uses this option generally has a profile provided by the company or client representing the film stock that is used. You may, however, use the Adobe-provided NTSC or PAL (the two formats used worldwide in television) profile if you are doing work for television and need to make sure none of your colors are illegal.

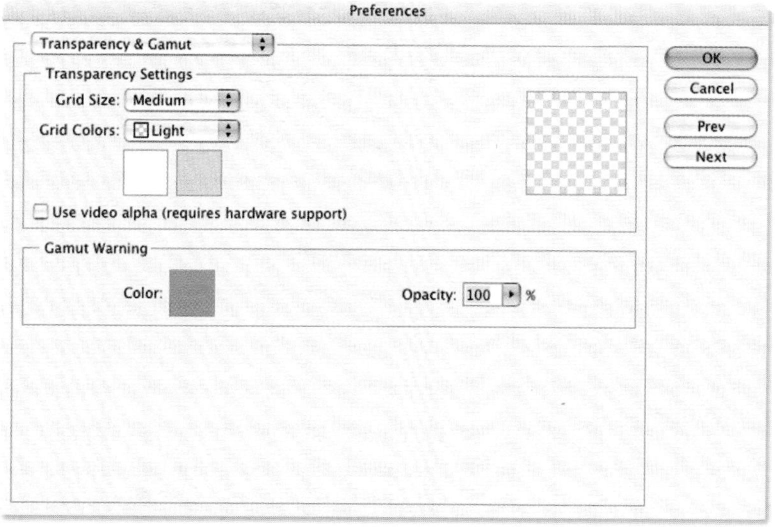

Figure 4.5 The Transparency & Gamut dialog box.

See Figure 4.6 for the Adobe options. Once you have chosen your warning color and gamut profile, you must go to **View** > **Gamut Warning** to highlight pixels outside the gamut range.

Units & Rulers

These preferences control not only the rulers on the top and side of a Photoshop canvas, but also how you determine a new document's size and how the measuring tool displays. Intimidating? Not really.

Units

Under here you see the subcategories: Rulers and Type. Rulers is pretty self explanatory. Your choice determines the units used for the rulers on the canvas and for the measuring tool. Type is not the type of units, but rather the units of choice for alphanumeric type (text you add into the image). I have left Type set to its default (points), but I prefer to set the Rulers to use either percent or pixels.

Column Size

This is more useful for those doing page layouts, which you rarely have to do for film or television, so I have left it at the default values. This information is used for the New, Image Size, and Canvas Size commands that let you specify image width in terms of columns.

New Document Preset Resolutions

The default Print Resolution and Screen Resolution entries here are pretty standard. Leave this at its default settings until you have a real compelling reason to change it (for example, your company has a different standard; your Mom tells you she'll disown you unless you change it).

Point/Pica Size

Again, another thing that rarely comes into play for VFX artists. I have left this dialog box intact in its entirety.

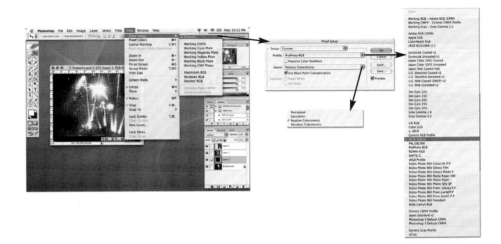

Figure 4.6 Adobe profile options.

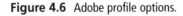

Figure 4.7 The Units & Rulers guide.

Guides, Grid & Slices

You probably won't deal with slices unless you work on the web, so you probably wouldn't care what color Photoshop uses to indicate them. However, if you happen to be working on a cyan image, this is the place to go when you need the guides to be a different color. Or maybe you want the grid to be some color other than gray. It's usually more of an aesthetic choice than anything else. Figure 4.8 shows my Guides, Grid & Slices settings.

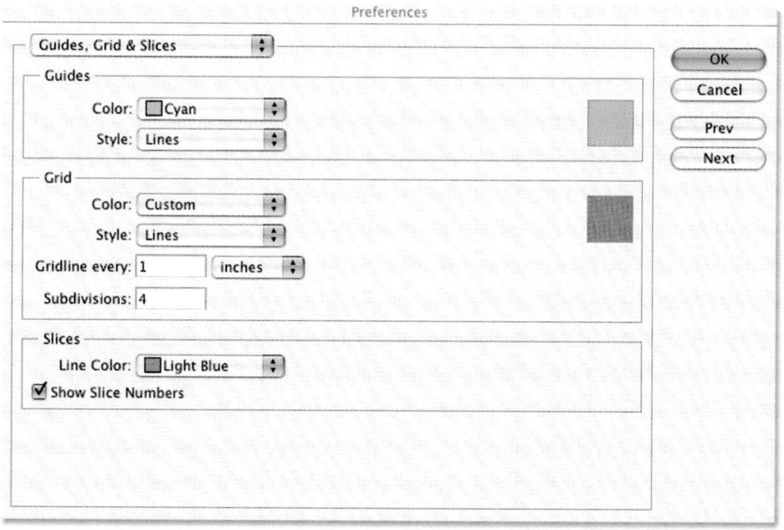

Plug-Ins & Scratch Disk

Most of the preferences for Photoshop are fine for the average user right out of the box. The one exception is the scratch disk preferences. When you work on an image, Photoshop first uses RAM to store the working data and then it uses parts of your hard drives to store the overflow. (Until you save the image to the hard disk, that is.) The hard-drive space used as a temporary RAM supplement is referred to as the *scratch disk*.

The scratch disk is Photoshop's virtual memory technology and can be any drive or partition with free space. The act of going between RAM and the scratch disks is called *swapping*. Ideally, you avoid any swapping to get the fastest performance. Realistically, this is not going to happen for most of your work.

The Plug-Ins & Scratch Disk preferences dialog box is where you assign the scratch disks. Obviously, the more memory Photoshop can access and the faster it's accessed, the better your performance. This won't overcome the standard factors of hardware and technology, but it definitely tends to enable Photoshop to work more smoothly and reduce much of its hang time in performing memory-intensive actions.

Press Command+K (Win: Ctrl+K) to access the general preferences if you do not still have them open. Press Command+7 (Win: Ctrl+7) to get to the Plug-Ins & Scratch Disk dialog box. The first area of the dialog box enables you to access plug-ins that are, for some reason, not in the default plug-ins folder. Once you select the checkbox to activate the Additional Plug-ins folder, you can click the Choose button and navigate as you would any program that asks for a path.

Figure 4.8 This is my setting, but the default setting generally works just fine as it is.

Below the Plug-In area is the scratch disk allocation area. The first one is, by default, the hard disk on which the operation system is installed. You can change this first scratch disk and you can assign up to three more scratch disks. If you have others, use your largest, fastest drives for the second drive. Regularly defragmenting the scratch disks helps performance. See Figure 4.9.

If you are still unsure how you should assign scratch disks, Adobe posts some guidelines in its help section:

- If possible, assign the scratch disk drive as a drive other than where your large files are located.

- Choose a different drive than what your computer operating system uses for its virtual memory.

- Don't use network drives as scratch disks.

- Don't use removable media such as thumb drives (USB drives) as scratch disks.

- Raid disks/disk arrays are ideal scratch disks.

- Defragment scratch disk drives regularly.

Of course, finding your best setup may take some trial and error.

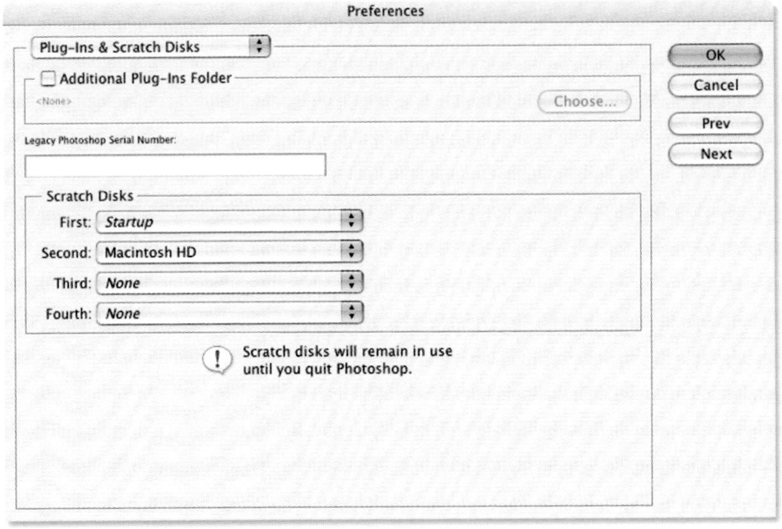

Figure 4.9 Your choices are limited if you have a laptop, as you won't have four drives to access.

Memory & Image Cache

Mac's pre-OS X operating systems dealt with memory quite differently, and pre-Photoshop CS requires specific and varying instructions. For CS, you just give a percentage of your total RAM to Photoshop. If you don't have a lot of memory, you should actually be allocating less: Leave the Memory Usage's Maximum Used by Photoshop allocation at the default 50 percent. If you have a lot of memory, you can allocate more to Photoshop (say, 80 percent).

Initially you may think that the opposite is true, but because you don't want to interfere with the functioning of your computer, the lower your RAM, the greater the ratio of RAM necessary for basic functions. If you take a look at Figure 4.10, you can see my settings for my laptop, which has a low amount of RAM. I hope this is encouraging, as my laptop is very functional, even with the minimum RAM. Of course, my desktop with 2G of RAM performs quite a bit better!

As for the Cache Levels setting, the larger the number (8 is the max), the more RAM and disk space are eaten when you open a file. Photoshop can hold up to eight levels of lower-resolution versions that are used for faster onscreen redrawing. A larger image cache gives you a faster update on larger files, since Photoshop makes file copies in different sizes and uses the smaller versions for updating when working with layers, navigating, and so on. Of course, having so much cached can cause its own slowdown, so experiment to find the level that works for you.

Also note that you have to restart Photoshop for these changes to go into effect.

Tip

Have you allocated enough memory? Photoshop has a nifty way of letting you know. An efficiency percentage display option appears on the status bar. Click the triangle on the status bar, and then click the Efficiency option in the menu that opens. If the status bar area to the left reads 100 percent, then it is using 100 percent of RAM and not swapping. If it is 50 percent, it is swapping then half the time. Ideally, you are between 100 percent and 70 percent.

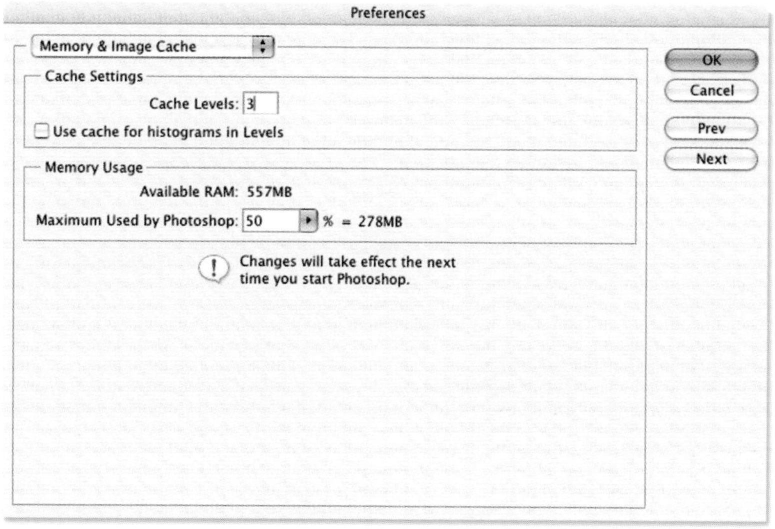

Figure 4.10 Alas, my poor little laptop has so little RAM…but these settings let me work quite well.

File Browser

If you want to know what size you should make the custom thumbnail, you probably skipped Chapter 3, "File Browser." It's okay, I'm not upset…where *did* I put that axe….

All right, I'm over it now. Take a look at my settings, shown in Figure 4.11, for the file browser preferences.

Do Not Process Files Larger Than

A safeguard, since large files can slow down the file browser.

Display (X) Most Recently Used Folders

I don't need more than 6 and sometimes wonder if I should reduce the number to 4. The maximum is 30.

Custom Thumbnail Size

Specify the pixel width of the thumbnails for custom views. See Chapter 3 for details on deducting a good size. (You knew I was going to say that.)

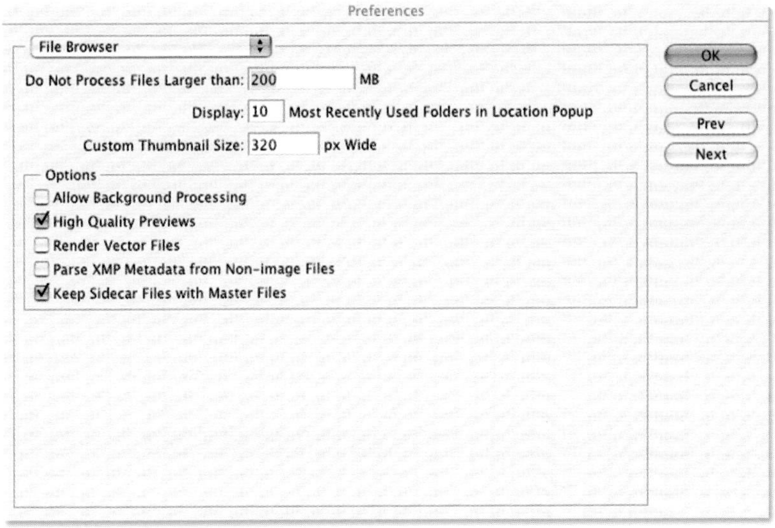

Figure 4.11 My settings for the file browser.

Allow Background Processing

When checked, this option enables Photoshop to use extra processing power to pregenerate cache information such as previews and metadata. Since I prefer to keep what processing power I have, I have deselected this.

High-Quality Previews

Since I love the file browser and love the ability to have high-quality previews, I prefer to select this. If you don't have the disk space, you can deselect it.

Render Vector Files

If you use Illustrator, then you should probably have this selected to see thumbnails of vector files.

Parse XMP Metadata from Non-image Files

Do you really want to be able to see the metadata on NON-IMAGE files in PHOTOSHOP?

Exactly.

That's why I don't have it selected.

Keep Sidecar Files with Master Files

Sidecar files are the XMP and THM files that help other applications process the metadata associated with a file. Generally a good idea to select.

Color Settings

You open a file and you get a warning: "Embedded Profile Mismatch. The document's embedded color profile does not match the current RGB working space…." What does that mean and what should you do?

Your Photoshop settings are part of the reason behind some of these warnings. These settings are not in the Preferences dialog box, but in their own Color Settings dialog box: **Photoshop > Color Settings** (Win: **Edit > Color Settings**).

Now this is one of those catch-22 situations. If you are not doing high-end production, you may not need to worry about the color setting options. If you are in high-end production, you probably have dedicated people taking care of this and won't need to worry about the color setting options. So why am I still writing? Because knowledge is power and you need to at least know whether you should really turn off those annoying warnings.

Entire books are dedicated to color management and theory, if you are interested. What I do here is simply what you need to know for now.

That said, if unopened, open the Color Settings dialog box by going to the main menu bar and choosing **Photoshop** > **Color Settings** (Win: **Edit** > **Color Settings**). See Figure 4.12.

Figure 4.12 Open up the Color Settings options.

Settings

The drop-down menu gives you a selection of settings. Normally, most people set this to ColorSync if they are on a Mac and to North American General Purpose defaults if they are on a PC; see Figure 4.13. However, being an VFX artist is different monster altogether: You have to customize your settings.

Most people put their color settings at one of three popular predefined settings: Color Management Off, ColorSync Workflow (Mac only), or North American General Purpose Defaults. None of those options is optimal for VFX work. Take a look at Figure 4.13.

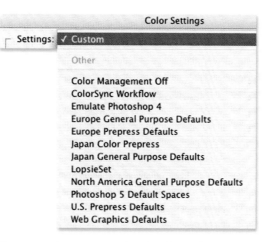

Figure 4.13 PC users notice that their pull-down menu does not have the ColorSync option.

Color Management Off

Why not just set the entire thing off, if the setting causes different interpretations of color? Because there really is no such thing as turning off a color-management system. Whatever file you open has to be seen, which means that some type of interpretation took place for the image to display. All this option really means is that the image is displayed according to the current monitor profile, but when the image is saved, the untagged images change, and may be identified as being in a particular color space (*tagged*). The tagged images remain tagged with the same *tag* (color space) that they had coming in, but that you did correction without being in that particular tagged space.

Here's how Adobe describes this option in its help documents (emphasis added): "…this option tells the color management system to use *passive* color management techniques *to emulate* the behavior of *applications that do not support color management*."

Now does that sound appealing to you? No. I didn't think so. So don't turn off color management.

ColorSync Workflow (Mac OS Only)

Only available to Mac users, many Macs are set to this just because it is Mac-exclusive. The ColorSync Workflow is a generally good choice for Mac users because it is considered a robust profile format, but the configuration is not recognized by Windows systems or by versions of ColorSync earlier than 3.0. I still do not recommend this for those who work in film, as the gamut is not quite as large as the Adobe RGB space.

North American General Purpose Defaults

This is the default that Photoshop gives to North American customers. Generally this doesn't do anything for anyone other than just having a name for a random PC setting.

Custom

If you make any changes to the working spaces, the setting automatically switches to Custom. For example, I set my settings to ColorSync, but then go and change the RGB workspace to Adobe RGB. This causes the setting to switch to Custom. See Figure 4.14.

For film and VFX work, you want the largest color space with which you can work. For your RGB space, use Adobe RGB (1998) or ProPhoto RGB. (See the "Color Management and Color Space" sidebar.) Although our monitors may not be able to display all the colors, the machines printing to film can display the wider gamut of colors.

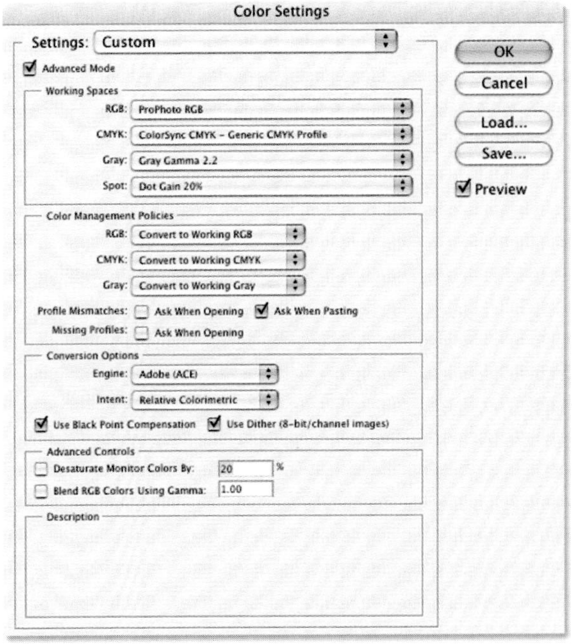

Figure 4.14 Here are the color settings for my iBook.

Color Management and Color Space

Every device (monitor, digital camera, scanner, and the like) has its own internal method of assigning a value to a given color. In other words, each device has its own unique *color space*, or *color gamut*. If you were to take a picture with a digital camera, open it up with Photoshop on your computer monitor, and compare both to a film strip, the image looks different. Color management's aim is to reduce the amount that colors differ across devices and software.

When it comes to choosing a working color space, the greatest consideration is size in relation to your possible workflow. The working space must be large enough to contain all the colors that all your devices can capture and reproduce. The main working spaces follow:

- **SRGB** was designed to simulate the average uncalibrated CRT monitor, and therefore has become the premier choice for web graphics. Its aim was to be a useful lowest common denominator output color space for the web (most web browsers assume sRGB in all untagged web graphics), which makes sRGB a less than optimal working space for VFX artists.

- **Adobe RGB (1998)** is a much larger and excellent choice for any color managed 8-bit graphic workflow. Until recently, I would have suggested Adobe RGB (1998) for VFX artists and anyone else who wanted to maintain the fullest integrity of their images.

- **Adobe Wide Gamut RGB** is an update to Adobe RGB (1998) and has a slightly wider range than its predecessor. For some reason, it seems to have not garnered much attention.

- **ProPhoto RGB** is the widest color space and even encompasses colors outside of the visual spectrum! (RGB is the common shorthand for the additive Red-Green-Blue color space.) Of course, you can't use the colors that are outside of the visual spectrum, but such boundaries were necessary to obtain more of the visible spectrum within the color space profile. As you can guess, this color space is recommended for professionals such as photographers and movie professionals or anyone using a high bit-depth image. Of course, since Photoshop CS now is fully functional in true 16 bit, a lot more people can benefit from the ProPhoto working space.

Color-Management Policies

The second section of the Color Settings dialog box controls the Color Management Policies. The settings for this section tell Photoshop what to do when you open, create, save, or paste images. Each of the three working spaces—RGB, CMYK, and Gray—has three options.

Off

Remember the neurosis I mentioned about this option in the previous section? It still applies. It is better to choose and have to change, than to turn it off and have no idea what is going on or why you have to change.

Preserve Embedded Profiles

This is generally the simplest way to proceed if people are maintaining the company's color space or if multiple clients demand a specific color space. This option preserves the original color space of the document, allowing each image to be in its own color space. This ensures that Photoshop does not make unwanted color space conversions. However, if you have a set protocol for color space, then you should use the next option, Convert to Working (*space name*).

Convert to Working (Space Name)

This option is good for large organizations because it encourages a single, consistent working space, thereby supporting a standardization. On the downside, you may lose information from the original color space, losing detail captured by, say, your digital camera.

Profile Warnings

Within the Color Management Profiles section of the Color Settings dialog box, you have the option to deal with profile warnings. If you are in a large company with color space standardization, turning off all the warnings is generally a good idea. In case of a set protocol, you probably have the preferences set to Convert to Working Space and won't need any of the warnings. However, if you are independent, turning *on* all the warnings is generally a good idea. That way you have the option to customize how Adobe Photoshop deals with each image. The warnings do not just alert you to the color mismatch, but give you the option to override the default behavior of your color-management policy with several choices. The choices follow.

Profile Mismatch

Photoshop checks an image's profile during two instances: when opening and when pasting. You can see the warning dialog boxes in Figure 4.15. When opening, you are given the choice to work in the embedded profile, change to the working profile, or completely discard the profile. When pasting, you can convert to the current space or leave it.

Missing Profile

This warning occurs at opening if the image does not contain an embedded profile. It lets you either leave the images untagged or assign a profile. See Figure 4.16 for a look at the Missing Profile dialog box.

Note

Let me reiterate: Color management is a field in itself. These settings, however, should reduce the number of times you scratch your head trying to figure out why your image doesn't look the same.

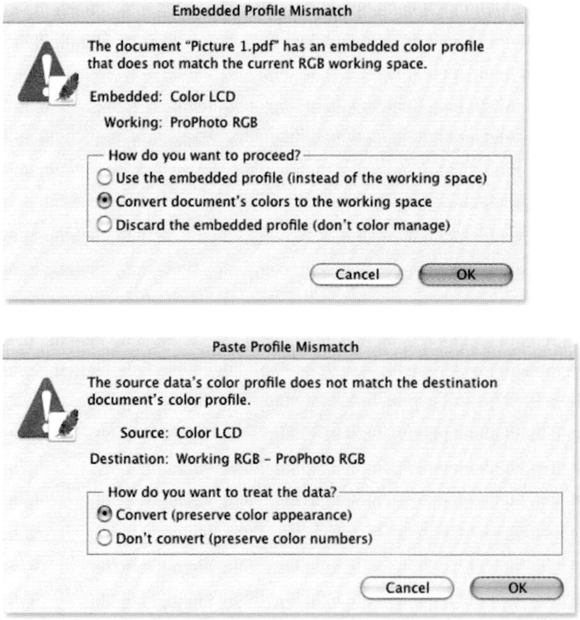

Figure 4.15 Profile Mismatch has two different dialog boxes.

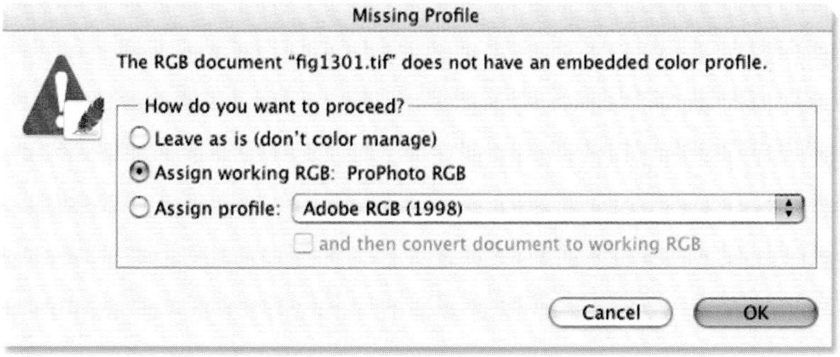

Figure 4.16 The Missing Profile dialog box.

The following sections holds the most exciting development from Adobe Photoshop in the realm of customization.

Keyboard Shortcuts

Yes, it's true Virginia: Photoshop now offers customizable keyboard shortcuts. Yay! You can create shortcuts for just about anything offered via any menu. The many prayers of Photoshop users everywhere have been answered!

Default Shortcuts

Before you change shortcuts, you probably want to know all the preexisting shortcuts. You can print out your own version: Go to **Edit** > **Keyboard Shortcuts** and click the Summarize button. This creates a file for viewing with your Internet browser.

Customizing Shortcuts

Go to **Edit** > **Keyboard Shortcuts**. This, ironically, somehow seems shorter than the keyboard shortcut of Option+Shift+Command+K (Win: Alt+Shift+Ctrl+K). I end up getting Color Settings or Preferences because I didn't apply even pressure to all the buttons!

1. If you haven't created any keyboard shortcuts, create an editable set by clicking the Create a New Set Based on the Current Set of Shortcuts button in Figure 4.17.

2. In the resulting dialog box, shown in Figure 4.18, give your new customized key set a descriptive name.

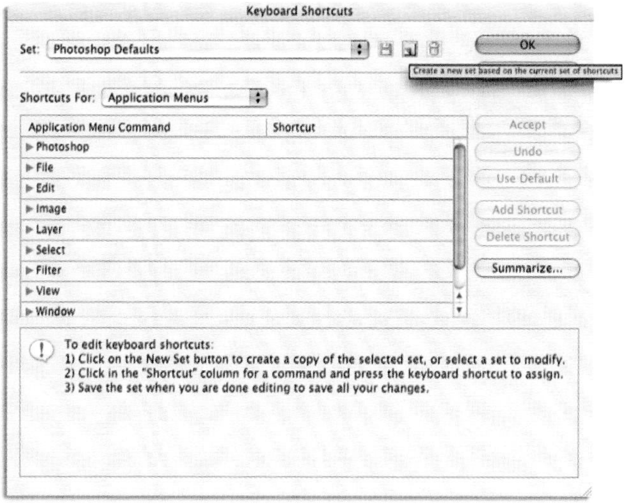

Figure 4.17 Create a new set to customize.

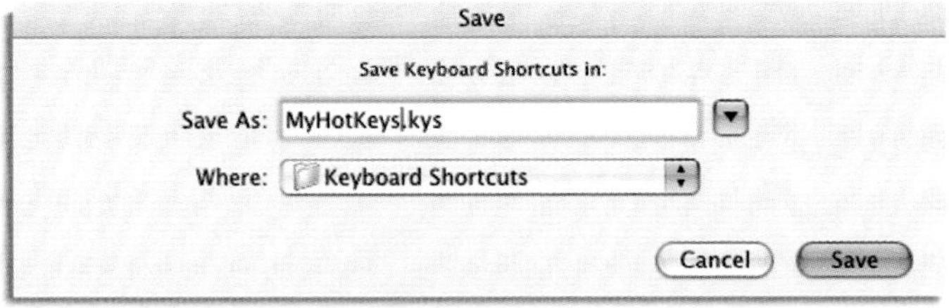

Figure 4.18 This is the name for your new set of shortcuts.

3. Select your category from the Shortcuts For drop-down menu accessed by clicking on the triangles on the far right of the bar and choose your desired command from the list that appears.

4. Type your personal shortcut into the shortcut field to assign it to the command.

   The shortcut must contain Command (Win: Ctrl) and/or an F key (function keys such as F1). If a shortcut exists, you are informed so you can decide whether to overwrite the previous assignment. See Figure 4.19.

5. Choose to Accept or Undo the customization.

6. When you are finished, click the Save All Changes to the Current Set of Shortcuts button beside the Set pop-up menu.

   Since it is easy to forget what you assigned to what, Adobe is so kind as to include a Summarize button that creates an HTM file you can view in your web browser and print for reference. Figure 4.20 shows an example.

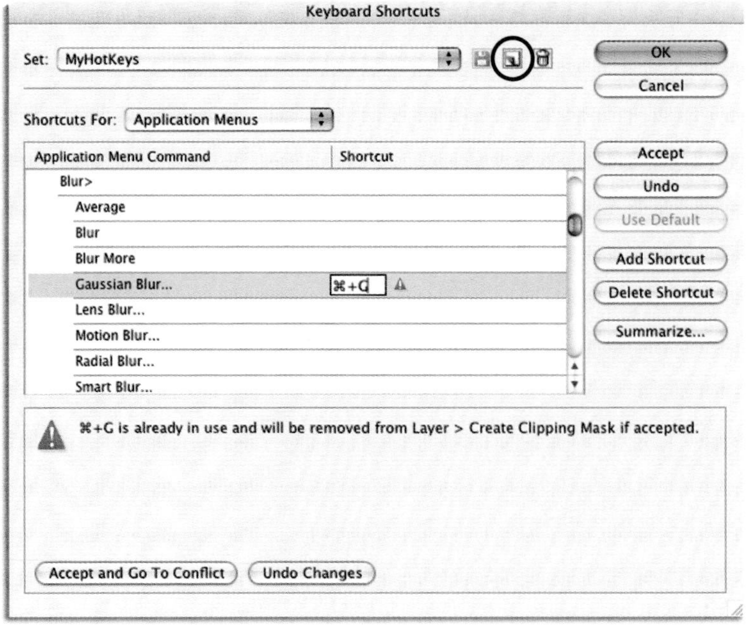

Figure 4.19 If the shortcut you type is already being used, Photoshop gives you a warning.

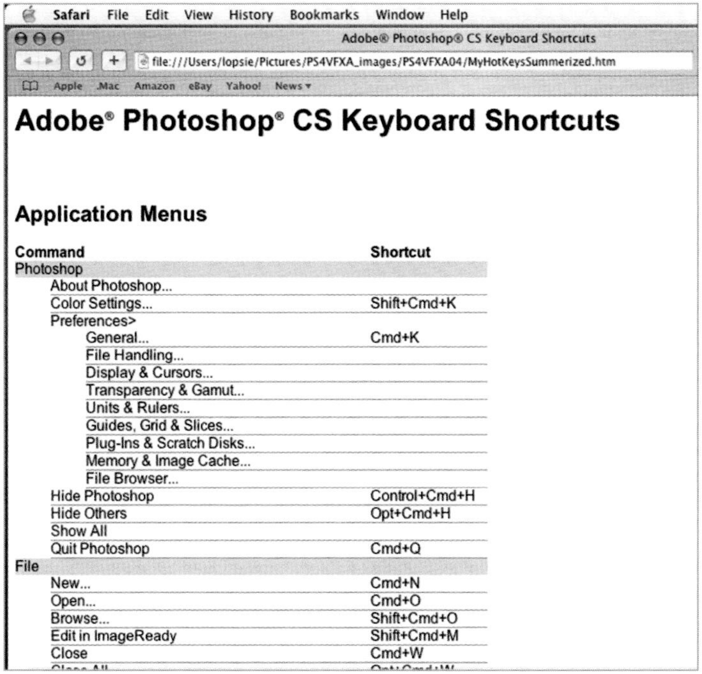

Figure 4.20 You can print a reference sheet of all your keyboard shortcuts from your Internet browser, or just bookmark it for easy reference.

Doesn't this chapter seem a bit short to you? It should, because there is no mention of how to save your palette locations and file browser settings. As you can guess, those points are covered in Chapter 3, "File Browser."

CHAPTER 5

IMAGE ESSENTIALS

"2K textures should be fine."

"We're delivering one-six-six, but work on it full ap."

"Hard mask it at two-three-five."

If you were ever a film student, that might make sense to you. If you haven't been in the business for a while, and you didn't take film classes at any point in your life, that direction sounded like a military launch code.

Life in the VFX world is a lot less confusing with some basic image essentials.

File Formats

Each Photoshop book I ever picked up had a section on file formats. Each time I browse through one, I am disappointed to realize that they never discuss the formats I use every day in the film/entertainment/movie industry. EPS, one of the most used and arguably important formats for print and advertising, is almost never used in VFX work. Usually the less well-known formats used in the industry have a little blurb (if mentioned at all) that reads "extremely high-end formats used in 3D animation."

The following is a description of the formats you commonly use. Some of these formats need special plug-ins to open or save the file formats, so don't be surprised if you don't have a particular option on you version of Photoshop. I follow the common formats with some formats you will probably run into or hear about, but are not used in the special effects industry (along with the reasons why they're not used).

PSD

Of course, the first option on the list of supported file formats is Photoshop's native format, PSD. See Figure 5.1.

You are probably saving your working file as a PSD. This is logical and wise. Obviously, using Photoshop's native format makes the program operate more efficiently, and you are assured that it can support every program option, whether it is a vector mask layer, an adjustment layer, or an annotation. In addition, PSD format is generally more efficient at applying lossless compression to the file than any other format. TIFF can sometimes do better compression, but you give up the ability to save certain Photoshop functions. I go into TIFF in the next section, but first a word on PSD 2.0 format.

Ultimately, you probably have to save a flattened version of your image for the pipeline, but are likely to always use PSD in some capacity while working.

TIFF

Arguably the most popular image format, *TIFF* stands for Tagged Image File Format and can be suffixed as .tiff or .tif. That alone should clue you to the possible problems that can arise. Although well known across the gamut of digital artists, it is misleading to call it a format; TIFFs are an *extensible format*, which means that others can modify the original specifications. This can lead to incompatibilities with programs that only support the baseline TIFF standard.

Figure 5.1 This is the first and most common option for saving files in Photoshop.

PSD 2.0 and Miscellany: All for Naught?

Simply stated, I don't know why the PSD 2.0 format is there. I could understand it when many studios were still using SGI (Silicon Graphics, Inc.) machines. Adobe stopped supporting UNIX Photoshop after Photoshop 3, but most studios kept it on their SGIs. If you were creating an image on a PC or Mac that a UNIX machine was to tweak, then you would save it in some way that the UNIX machine could read. Of course, you could just flatten and save it as a TGA, for example, since Photoshop 2.0 didn't support layers yet. That is a moot question, since just about every place I know is phasing out (if not completely out already) its SGIs and UNIX machines for Linux, PCs, and Macs.

While I am on confusing Photoshop formats, I might as well discuss Photoshop RAW. This is not the same as a camera RAW image. It is a format designed to transfer images to devices that don't support the standard graphic formats. I could go into how it saves its information in an uncompressed binary format, but why? You'll never use it.

Then there are Photoshop DCS 1.0 and Photoshop DCS 2.0, which are not the same as PSDs. DCS stands for Desktop Color Separation and is used primarily by those who deal with print. I have yet to meet anyone in the film industry who has used either of these formats.

Photoshop, for example, supports layered TIFFs; you can save something as a TIFF but maintain the layer information. The problem is that other programs can't see that info. Another example is the 16-bit and 8-bit TIFF. Many programs try to read a 16-bit TIFF as an 8-bit TIFF, which leads to other imaging troubles. Then there is the question of byte order. When in doubt, save using the IBM PC option. Saving in Mac byte order can sometimes cause problems with PCs, but Macs can generally interpret the PC byte order.

Nonetheless, the TIFF format is still popular, due to its prior years of being the safest bet on transferring images between platforms and programs and its continued importance in the publishing world. Although more image formats are supported by graphics programs nowadays, most of which are cross platform, TIFFs can be confidently used as long as you specify your bit depth.

One of TIFF's advantages are its compression options:

- **LZW and ZIP.** Two very common lossless compression formats, where no information is deleted to compress your image.
- **JPEG compression.** A lossy compression that compresses into smaller files at the expense of image degradation.

Another TIFF advantage is that it can be up to 4GB in size—a definite boon in the film matte painting world, where the 2GB limit of some other formats can be prohibitive.

TGA

Although the TGA (Targa) format was designed for systems using the Truevision video board, this stable and commonly supported format is always 8 bit. This means that each channel is no more than 8 bits. It is a bit confusing, because the images are referred to as 16-, 24-, and 32-bit images. This means Targa supports these:

16-bit RGB images: 5 bits × 3 color channels + 1 unused bit

24-bit RGB images: 8 bits × 3 color channels

32-bit RGB images: 8 bits × 3 color channels + 1 8-bit alpha channel

The Targa format also supports indexed-color and grayscale images without alpha channels. This was the file format of choice in many studios I worked at, including Rhythm & Hues Studios and WETA Digital. However, I think, with Photoshop CS now able to paint in true 16-bit color, that other formats will be used more and more.

PSB (Large Document)

Photoshop's solution for huge files, PSB is new to Photoshop CS. You must first select the Enable Large Document Format option in your preferences. Most formats have a 2G limit to their file size, but PSB can handle larger files and keep Photoshop features such as layers and filters intact. Of course, as of this writing, Photoshop is the only program that supports this format.

CIN

Developed by Kodak, Cineon, used interchangeably with DPX (Digital Picture Exchange) is a 10-bit-per-channel logarithmic digital format used mostly by compositors. The 10-bit log file emulates 16- or 12-bit images that capture the dynamic range of film. (A 10-bit linear file lacks the range.) Of course, this means that saving a matte painting for a compositor will often use this format. Despite increased support for other formats, and with 16-bit per-channel capabilities being more prevalent, this format is used often in transferring film to digital and is still prevalent in the VFX world.

IFF

Most commonly associated with Alias/Wavefront (or with Amiga, for you old-school people), IFF (Interchange File Format) is a general-purpose data storage format that has extensions that support still picture, sound, music, video, and textual data. Most of the time, however, IFF is for opening a Maya-rendered image or saving an image for use in a Maya pipeline.

Filmstrip

The Filmstrip format is used for RGB animation or movie files created by Adobe Premiere. I haven't used this format in any of the studios that I have worked at—even the small, boutique shops. Premiere is used by quite a few smaller shops, so I assume quite a few request this format. Photoshop does caution that if you resize, resample, remove alpha channels, or change the color mode or file format of a Filmstrip file in Photoshop, you can't save it back to Filmstrip format. Kinda makes me wonder if this is useful after all.

3D Programs

3D programs include Wavefront RLA, Alias PIX, Electric Image, SoftImage, 3D Studio Max, or proprietary formats. Just about every 3D program has a Photoshop plug-in that allows you to save an image in its native image format, whether that be RLA, PIX, or 3DS. More often than not, wherever you're working has a pipeline that optimizes this, and you work with that format because your supervisor tells you so.

SGI RGB

When I was working on UNIX machines, I almost always saved with SGI's RGB format. It is an 8-bit RGB or grayscale image, and can have the suffix SGI or RGB. The confusion came when someone would say to "Save it out as an SGI," but expect an RGB suffix. Just in case you are working on UNIX machines, I will reiterate: RGB and SGI are used interchangeably.

PhotoCD

Another format developed by Kodak, the PhotoCD (PCD) format allows five resolutions to be contained in a single file. Often, reference CDs are in this format and you simply read it in and save it as a different format for your use.

Pixar

Do you work at Pixar? Then you know this format and know when you are supposed to save this way. Everyone else? You don't work at Pixar and won't be using this format.

RAW

Photoshop supports most camera RAW formats. This format not only saves uncompressed image data, but also the image's metadata. You do not save in this format, but may occasionally use it to import reference or source images. Usually the RAW formats are converted and delivered as TIFFs, but you have to deal with this format if you end up taking the images directly off the camera's drive.

Now here are some of the other available formats that you hear a lot about, but probably will not use in the course of painting for special effects.

JPEG

One of the most popular formats almost never used in film or television, the Joint Photographic Experts Group (JPEG) format is very effective at compression and lets you choose the level at which you wish to compress. This format is most commonly used to display photographs and other continuous-tone images over the Internet. A JPEG compresses information by looking at an 8×8 block of pixels and combining similar-color pixels. It is a lossy compression, resulting in the irrevocable loss of data—especially apparent after multiple saves. Because of this, you do not use this format for film.

JPG2000 is the newest rendition of the standard JPG. JPG2000 now has a lossless compression option, supports 16 bit, and has a new feature called ROI for Region of Interest. This allows you to define a region (via alpha channel) that has a lower compression rate than the rest of the picture. Sounds intriguing, but like anything new, there isn't yet widespread support for this version of JPG.

This format is used, however, to show clients, in-progress work, as its compact format is ideal for teleconferences and rough viewing.

Caution

It should be reiterated that the master file should never be continually saved as a JPEG, as it degrades and permanently loses information.

GIF

One of three most common formats for the web, the Graphics Interchange Format (GIF) is highly compressible, but is 256 colors—much too limiting for film work.

EPS

Encapsulated PostScript is a format commonly used in the publishing world. You never use this format, unless, of course, you are getting a file from an advertising or publishing company. Okay, I take that back. If you like to use Adobe Illustrator, this file format allows you to save clipping paths and link it to your Photoshop file rather than embedding the clipping paths. Still, the majority of VFX artists never see this format.

PDF

Adobe Acrobat's native format, PDF is the acronym for Portable Document Format. Mostly used for documents, it is good for showing someone images because the reader is available for PC, Mac, and UNIX, and is a free download at Adobe's web site. My supervisor, however, prefers to just come by my desk to see the images.

BMP

The bitmap format (BMP) is the standard Windows graphics file format.

PICT

PICT, short for Macintosh Picture, is the native Mac graphics file format.

By now you may be wondering what happened to all the pretty pictures. Didn't I say I was going to put in as many pictures as possible? Well, my young grasshopper, take a look at Figure 5.2 to see some of the differences between the formats.

A Word about HDRI

Generally, all of the preceding "normal" formats are *low dynamic range images (LDRI)*. A scene's *dynamic range* is the contrast ratio between its brightest and darkest parts. A *high dynamic range image (HDRI)* is an image made by combining multiple normal images of the same scene taken with different exposure levels; each end-result pixel in an HDRI stores the amount of light in a floating-point number with no upper limit. Compare this to the RGB image integer values of 0 to 255, and you can imagine the difference. Figure 5.3 shows you.

Image with area of focus

GIF 1.09M

TIF w/LZW 3.55M

File sizes are for entire image, not the cropped area of focus. The area focus is for comparison of image details.

JPG 488K

PSD 4.44M

TIF 4.53M

Figure 5.2 A taste of the difference between some of the formats; take a look at these close ups of the same picture.

The beautiful luminance resulting from the use of HDRI is absolutely stunning. Unfortunately, as of this writing, working with an HDRI in Photoshop is, at best, convoluted. I can't wait until a plug-in is released for Photoshop to deal with HDRI.

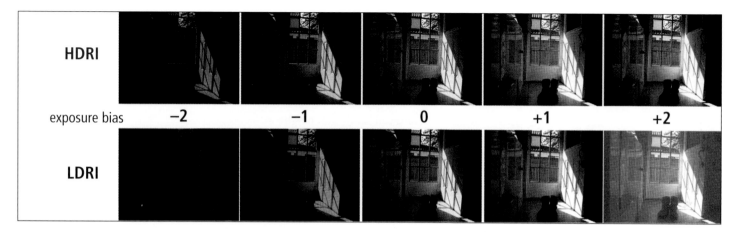

Figure 5.3 An HDRI and LDRI at different exposure settings.

Aspect Ratios

Aspect ratio is a way of expressing an image's proportions, which are always stated as the horizontal size versus the vertical size. Therefore, 1.78:1 means that the width is 1.78 times as long as the height. You may also see this expressed as 16:9. The *normalized* ratio (1.78:1) is often used because it is easier to calculate the dimensions from this ratio. When speaking of the normalized aspect ratios, usually just the first number is recited without the decimal. In that case, 1.78:1 would be recited as "one-seven-eight."

You can see a graphical representation of some common aspect ratios and their relation to each other in Figure 5.4.

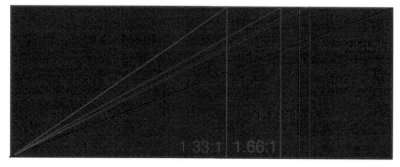

Figure 5.4 Some common aspect ratios expressed with the height normalized.

At one point, television and film shared the same aspect ratio. That is, the ratio of width to height was 1.33:1. This ratio was called the *Academy Ratio* because the Academy of Motion Picture Arts and Sciences had this ratio as its standard for film. When television was developed, the designers kept the same ratio for the screen. Makes sense, right?

As human nature would have it, people started staying home, watching more television, and fewer people saw any reason to go to a movie. The movie industry decided to make movies "grander" than television by making the aspect ratio different, and now we have to deal with the plethora of film formats.

These two aspect ratios are most common for film today:

- 1.85:1 (also known as *Academy Flat*)
- 2.35:1 (also known as *Anamorphic Scope*)

These are less common but still used aspect ratios:

- 1.66:1 (common for overseas/ European releases)
- 2.20:1 (70 mm)

Film Format Nomenclature

Although easier to calculate, normalized ratios are a bit misleading. Generally, movies are shot on 35-mm film stock; the width is common and the height is reduced. In reality, when a widescreen movie is shown in letterbox on television (pixel resolution aside), the movie is not squeezed to fit the screen, but rather the film had been masked in the first place. Take a look at Figure 5.5.

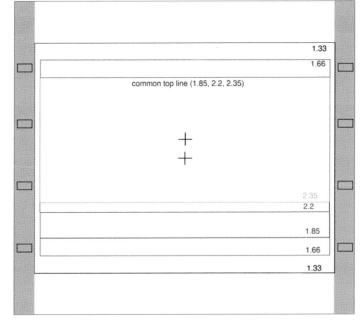

Figure 5.5 This is a better depiction of the ratios. Notice the Common Top Line. This allows the filmmaker greater flexibility in determining the aspect ratio and makes the editing easier by keeping consistent headroom.

As you can see, each of these ratios shares a common width. The height is cut out to create its respective aspect ratio. Also notice there are no lines for the soundtrack depicted in this diagram. This type of film is called *Super 35*. Sometimes directors film with Super 35 to give leeway for shifting in the editing process, though the camera operator frames the picture with all of the action within a 2.35:1 rectangle. Of course, not having space for the soundtrack changes the aspect ratio of Full Aperture. Academy Full Aperture is 1.37:1 due to the sound strip on the film, but Super 35 Full Aperture is 1.33:1.

Table 5.1 associates common names to their aspect ratios. As you can see, often several names are associated with a single aspect ratio. You can't deduce what ratio is associated with a name. You can copy this table and memorize them, but luckily, most people refer to the aperture numbers rather than the film format names (or at least follow up the name with its respective ratio).

File Resolution

Knowing the terms and their implied aspect ratios, how do you determine what size your matte painting or texture should be?

Table 5.1 Film Aspect Ratios

Ratio	Film Type
1.33:1	Full Aperture 35 mm, 16 mm, 8 mm
	NTSC
	Standard Television
	Academy Standard
1.66:1	European Film Standard
1.78:1	Digital HDTV
16:9	Digital HDTV
2.35:1	Anamorphic Scope
	CinemaScope
	Panavision
1.85:1	Academy Flat
	Matted Spherical
	VistaVision
	Modern Standard
	Widescreen

Resolution is actually a misnomer, because in the strict sense, *resolution* refers to the pixels per unit length. Artists also refer to *resolution* as document's pixel dimensions.

Common resolution terms for textures are 1 K, 2 K, and 4 K. Kilo (or 1000) is what *K* stands for, but since you are dealing ultimately with binary digital machines, K is actually equal to 1024 (or 2 to the power of 10).

1-K texture is 2^{10} or 1024×1024 pixels

2-K texture is 2^{11} or 2048×2048 pixels

4-K texture is 2^{12} or 4096×4096 pixels

half-K texture is 2^{9} or 512×512 pixels

You may be asked to make things to half K for small textures or television. Or you may have to make something 256×256, which is usually just called 256 (not *quarter-K*) and 128×128. These are all powers of 2: 2^{9}, 2^{8}, and 2^{7}, respectively.

Occasionally you hear someone refer to a 3-K map, which is a break in the math. You don't get 3 K from a power of 2. This just means that someone wants a 3072×3072 map. It won't be optimized, since it is not a power of 2, but is still a common texture size.

That all seems clear until you hear someone asking for a 1-K render or comp, and you are supposed to know that you are to deliver a 1024×778 image. If you are a genius, you probably looked at that and realized, "Hey, that's a 1.32:1 ratio based on a 2^{10} image width, so it's probably because we're working with Academy Full Aperture!"

Yeah.

The rest of us have to resort to memorizing the most common resolutions. Better yet, make a copy Table 5.2 and keep it near your desk.

Even with these resolutions memorized, determining texture map dimensions takes a bit of calculation. You must know how close to camera your 3D object will get or how much of the frame your rendered object will take up. Take a look at the following two images in Figure 5.6.

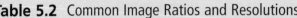

Table 5.2 Common Image Ratios and Resolutions

Format	Aspect Ratio	2 K	1 K
Cinema Scope	1.17	2048×1743	1024×871
Full Ap1	1.32	2048×1556	1024×778
Full Ap2	1.33	2048×1536	1024×768
Euro	1.66	2048×1234	1024×617
HDTV	1.78	2048×1150	1024×575
Standard Hard Masked	1.85	2048×1108	1024×554
Scope	2.35	2048×871	1024×436

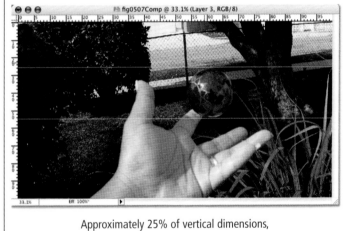

Approximately 25% of vertical dimensions, or 277 pixels of screen space

Approximately 75% of vertical dimensions, or 831 pixels of screen space

Figure 5.6 Where will your textured object be in the frame?

At the 2-K film resolution, the texture for the right ball must be larger than the texture for the left ball. You can make a guesstimate by figuring out the proportion of the texture map seen in the context of the render, then apply the size to get the final texture dimension. This is a bit easier to understand with pictures. Take a look at one of the pictures from Figure 5.6 and approximate the pixel size of what is showing. Then take a look at the portion of the map that is seen in the render and approximate what ratio of the entire map is seen.

Correlating these values, you can safely guess that a 2-K map works fine in this case. Doing the same calculations, you also see that you could have gotten away with a 1-K map in the other setting.

Matting

Even if the film you are working on is going to be 2.35:1, you have to work in a larger aspect ratio if it is *not* going to be hard masked (sometimes called *soft matted* or *soft masked*). *Hard masked* means there is permanent black padding added to the image to fill in the rest of the Full Aperture frame. Therefore, you need not worry that something that isn't meant to be seen will somehow enter the cut in the final edit.

Figure 5.7 What portion of the texture map is seen?

Approximate Visible Area

It is very common to give a little bit of leeway, so you may hear "We're supposed
to deliver 2.35:1, but we're protecting to
1.85:1." This means you should make sure
everything within the 1.85 mask is clean,
but that the final film is shown at a 2.35:1
ratio. The 1.85:1 matte still saves you from
having to work at the 1.37:1 ratio of Full
Aperture. See Figure 5.8.

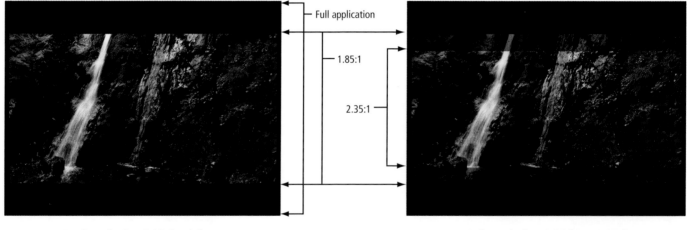

Full application

1.85:1

2.35:1

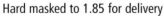

Hard masked to 1.85 for delivery

Soft masked to 2.35 from 1.85 for
internal visualization

Figure 5.8 The grayed-out area denotes a soft mask, and you can see what the audience sees versus what you deliver.

PART TWO

TEXTURES

CHAPTER 6

STARTING WITH COLOR MAPS

Texture painters and modelers have to work together to share the duties of creating the textured object's look. Should we create displacement maps or do we model it in? How shall we assign the UVs? A great book to check out for this kind of information is Tom Capizzi's *Inspired 3D Modeling & Texture Mapping*. He gives an in-depth view of all things that should be considered and how to go about attacking them.

Note

As a texture painter, you need to be able to separate the characteristics of a surface into color, bump, opacity, specularity, reflection, refraction, and luminosity. Not know what any of that means? Then stop reading a chapter on *creating textures* in Photoshop. There are a few other books out there dedicated to explaining texturing, and I recommend learning what texturing is before learning how to use Photoshop to create texture maps.

This chapter does *not* have any tutorials on how to create realistic-looking (insert *wood /stone/old metal* here) textures. You can find plenty of tutorials like that on the Internet; they always annoyed me. They are never really photorealistic and almost never usable in the VFX world.

From the viewpoint of a Photoshop user, a texture painter creates two types of maps: color maps and grayscale maps (a Zen-like simplification). This chapter deals with the considerations and techniques used to attack creating color texture maps. Chapter 7, "Bump Maps and Grayscale," deals with the specifics of creating grayscale maps.

Color Map Versus Matte Painting

The main goal for a texture painter when creating color textures is to portray the color characteristic in the absence of light. "What?" you ask. "How can you do that, when color is simply the reflection of unabsorbed light?" With artistic creativity is my only answer, and that is what separates the good texture painters from the great ones. An orange color map, for example, can be a flat orange color if the dimpled look of dark spots with light highlights is rendered by the bump map. Figure 6.1 is an example.

Texture Mapping Terms

Texture mapping terms can be confusing to beginners, especially since different studios and 3D programs may refer to their texture maps with similar but different names.

For example, it is common to interchange within the industry the diffuse map, the Kd map, and the color map. Usually the diffuse map is a color map, but what if you were creating a texture for a black and white checkerboard? Then the diffuse map is actually a grayscale painting. In addition, there are other maps that can be in color: specular maps, reflection maps, and glow maps, to name a few. To make things worse, in Lightwave, for example, the color map and the diffuse map are *not* the same thing; Lightwave uses the term diffuse map to refer to what others may call the subsurface map. But wait! It doesn't end there. If you said you were creating a color map, it is also possible for someone to think that you are creating a guide for converting colors—a color index!

The following names are commonly used interchangeably in reference to texture maps:

- Color Map, diffuse map, Kd map, main texture map
- Bump map, displacement map, extrusion map, grayscale maps, B maps, texture map
- Opacity map, transparency map, translucency map, Ko map, holdout map, opacity matte
- Specular map, shininess map, Ks map
- Glow map, illumination map, light map
- Reflection map, environment map, map for refractions, dome map
- Mask, matte, alpha, holdout, gobo
- Subsurface map, diffuse map, scatter map, layer map

Before you start the long e-mail to inform me about the differences between a transparency map and translucency map, remember that this table exists because there are those out there who do not know the difference and use these terms interchangeably.

To reiterate, the terms listed here are not necessarily synonyms, but knowing the common intermingling of these terms can help you form the right questions to ask: When you say you need diffuse maps, do you mean subsurface maps or Kd maps? The deadline for the main texture maps— is that for color and bump or for color only? Since this is a chrome shader, when you asked for a texture map only, you meant a displacement map, right?

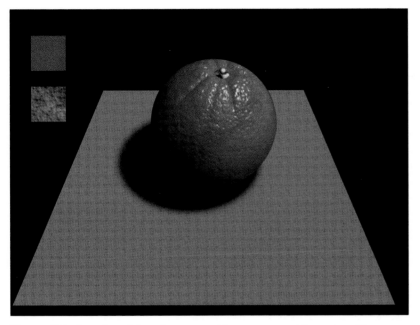

Figure 6.1 A section of the color map and bump map used to create a 3D orange.

A texture painter may also have to create a color texture that is not the true color of an object, but what the color should be in regard to how the color will be rendered in a 3D program. The white lampshade in Figure 6.2, for example, may be painted as a warm yellowish color that is darker in denser areas because the Lighter who is using the texture map uses it as a self illuminated or glowing object.

Making the UV Test Map

Before creating any maps, the texture painter should check the UVs of the 3D object. UVs are referring to the u and v coordinates that are used as texture coordinates, as opposed to the x, y, and z coordinates used in the Cartesian 3D modeling coordinates.

You are going to create a basic map that I use to test UVs. I simply apply it to every material and take a look at the model to see if everything is copasetic. Most people still use the checkerboard pattern to check for UVs, but as you can see in Figure 6.3, it does not give a detailed enough portrayal of the UVs.

Figure 6.2 The actual prop had a cream lampshade, but the 3D model uses a yellowish color map.

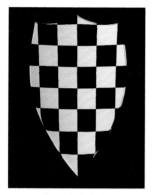
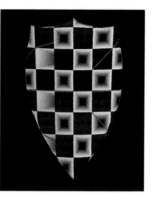
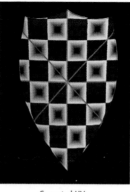

Test with Standard Checkerboard   Test with UV Test Map   Corrected UVs

Figure 6.3 The left figure looks okay, but when you apply my UV test map, you can see that the standard checker masked some problems.

Go through the steps of making this map and either use the map as it is or modify to suit your needs. This is also a not-so-subtle way of reviewing some basic Photoshop maneuvering. Pretty tricky, sis....

1. At the menu bar, choose **File > New** to bring up the dialog box shown in Figure 6.5.

2. Name your canvas **UVTestMap** and set the dimensions to 1000×1000.

3. Download the pattern libraries from the book's companion web site.

    You can save the pattern library anywhere. However, if you place the library file in the Presets/Patterns folder inside the Photoshop program folder, the library name appears at the bottom of the Pattern pop-up palette menu after you restart Photoshop. Of course, you could create the patterns yourself, but why go through all that trouble if they're available free?

This map has a gradient in every square, so you know if there is a disconnect or if the UVs are warped. The lines show where the center is so you can get a general idea of how the UVs are laid out and what part of the map you are looking at. Also, I make the textures in a hard 1K and hard 2K, meaning that it is 1000×1000 and 2000×2000 pixels, respectively. This way I know that when looking at the model, each square represents 100 pixels and I can determine whether that is enough resolution for the task at hand. You can see the full UV test map in Figure 6.4.

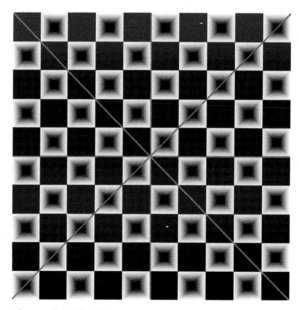

Figure 6.4 The UV test map.

Notice anything?

The astute may have noticed a change in the look of Photoshop in Figure 6.5. That is because this chapter uses screen captures from a Windows OS PC, rather than a Macintosh! The difference is minimal, but I thought I'd give Photoshop for Windows a little face time too.

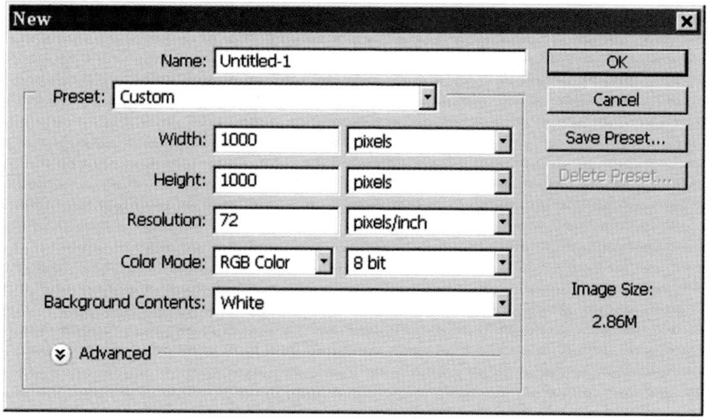

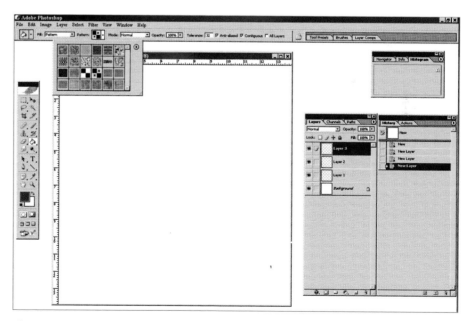

Figure 6.5 The New file dialog box.

4. Create three new layers by clicking the New Layer button at the bottom of the Layers palette three times.

   The blank layers appear in the Layers palette with the names Layer 1, Layer 2, and Layer 3.

5. Press G to select the Paint Bucket tool and switch the Fill mode to Pattern.

   You see the newly loaded patterns at the bottom of the pattern palette.

6. Choose the CheckWhtGrad pattern shown in Figure 6.6.

7. Click the top layer, Layer 3, and fill it with this pattern.

   Since your canvas is 1000 pixels wide, there should be 10 squares across. You can see the appropriate number of squares in Figure 6.7.

Figure 6.6 Choose the white gradient checker pattern.

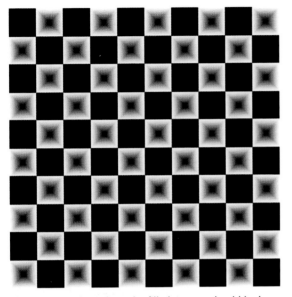

Figure 6.7 This is how the filled pattern should look.

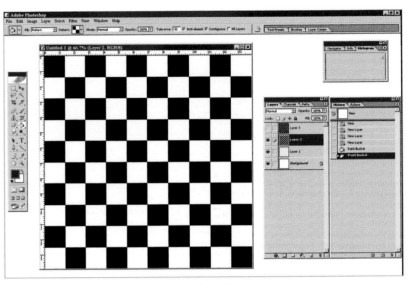

Figure 6.8 The next layer down should look like this.

8. Hide the layer by clicking the Eye icon next to the layer.

9. Activate Layer 2 by clicking it. Fill this layer with CheckBW, which you can see in Figure 6.8.

10. Hide that layer and click to the empty Layer 1.

11. Switch to the Gradient tool by clicking Shift+G.

12. Choose the Yellow, Violet, Orange, Blue gradient, making sure you have selected the Linear gradient.

13. Drag from the top to the bottom of the canvas to fill it in.

    Figure 6.9 shows the results. Now comes the fun part.

14. Click the black and white checkered layer above to activate and make it visible at the same time.

15. Change the Layer Blend mode to Screen and see what happens! Figure 6.10 reveals just what happens.

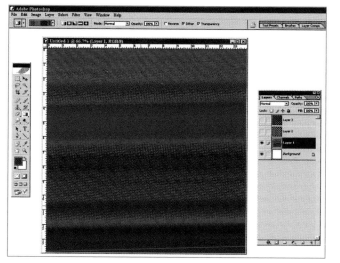

Figure 6.9 Your bottom layer gradient should look like this.

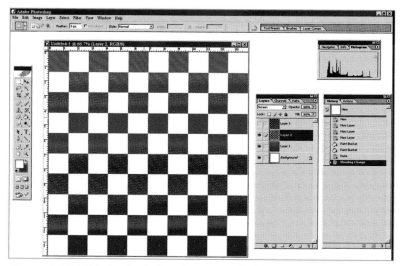

Figure 6.10 With the checkerboard to screen, the black squares reveal the gradient and the white remain white.

16. Click the white checkers above to activate and to make it visible.

17. Go to **Select** > **Color Range** to bring up the Color Range dialog box and click a fully black square to choose pure black as the selection.

18. Bring the Fuzziness setting level to 1 and click OK. This should select only the full black squares of the pattern.

19. Press Delete (Win: Backspace) to delete the black squares and change the Layer Blend mode to Darken.

    Now you have the checker base for your map! Figure 6.11 shows you.

20. Select the Line tool. Make your thickness 8 and your color a pure green (0,255,0).

21. Drag while pressing Shift to create a perfect horizontal line through the middle of the map. With the same method, create a perfectly vertical line that divides the map into four even sections. See Figure 6.12.

    If you hold down the Shift button before you click, the second line is added to the same shape layer as your first line. Continuing to hold it forces your line to be restricted to 45-degree angle increments.

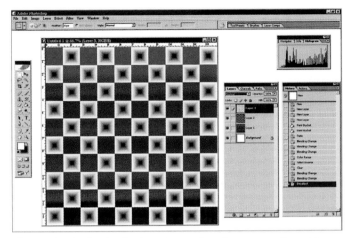

Figure 6.11 The checker base is complete, but you need to add lines that help distinguish different areas of the map.

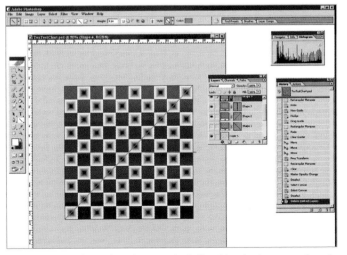

Figure 6.12 If your line does not look like this, check your tool settings against those displayed here.

22. Make diagonal lines that cross from one corner to the next, creating an X across the canvas.

    It is still the same green as the other lines, but you want it to be another color. I chose a purple color like that in Figure 6.13, but you can make it any color that stands out. Simply go up to the color swatch in the tool options bar and change the color. Your map is complete! Just one more step.

23. Flatten the image by going to the Layers palette and selecting Flatten Image. See Figure 6.14.

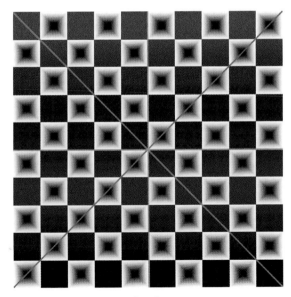

Figure 6.13 Your completed map.

Figure 6.14 You can save your PSD for future modifications, but you need to save out a copy if you do not flatten it.

Now take a look at Figure 6.15. The image on the left is the plain model, the middle image is the application of the standard checkerboard map, and the right image is your custom UV test texture application.

The whole point of testing the UVs is to make sure nothing needs to go back for UVing. Make sure that the UVs are properly taken care of before you start painting. Otherwise, you just waste your time painting, not to mention the frustrations and delays that all that costs.

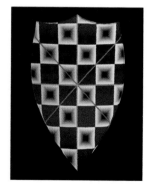

Figure 6.15 Oh what a difference!

Diffuse Maps

Now that you have checked your UVs, you can start off with your diffuse map.

I usually start with one of two methods—projection or base tiles. I definitely start with projection for objects that have to match an existing live prop or character. The base tile works for very specific cases, usually objects that are layered, patterned, or simple surfaces. Of course, there is the third method—start painting on a blank canvas. Let me go over each of these ways to start.

Base Tile Method

Many people associate this method with cheap and cheesy characters, but in actuality, this is a great way to start for any model that has a general texture associated with it. For example, I used this method to start when I was working on an Ent (a tree-like creature) for Weta, and for both a boar and an early version of a minotaur for Rhythm and Hues Studios. I have used the base tile method on occasion for texturing human characters, and the results are far from cheesy. (Though really, I think it unfair that such a noble food as cheese should be used to denote such subpar stature.) Take a look at a base tile example in Figure 6.16. Here you have a tree stump that needs texturing.

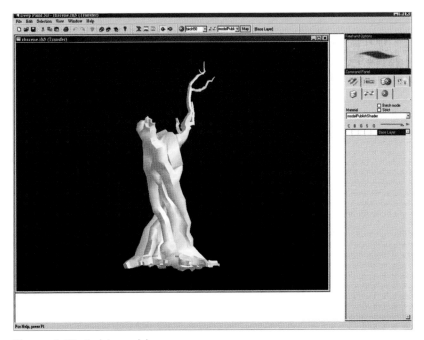

Figure 6.16 A plain model.

1. Create your canvas by going to **File > New**. Make the texture 2048×2048.

2. Press G to select the Paint Bucket tool.

3. Using the Bark pattern, fill in the entire map.

   The Bark pattern in Figure 6.17 is part of the pattern library available free from this book's web site.

4. Apply this map in your 3D paint program and touch up the color map to give it variation, dirt, and so on, like the one in Figure 6.18.

The base tiled texture made this job a lot faster and easier and the finished color map in Figure 6.19 looks more complex than it was to create.

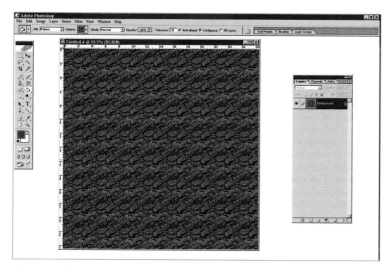

Figure 6.17 Flooding the texture with a base tile texture gives you a base to start with.

Figure 6.19 The rendered image.

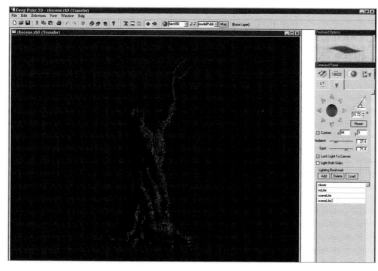

Figure 6.18 The tree stump in Right Hemisphere's Deep Paint 3D.

Tip

I often use the base tile method for skin. In the pattern folder that you imported, notice several skin tiles. These skins are used more often for animals that have fur, but still need to show some skin. (Now, now…you know what I mean by that.)

Projection Method

Projection is probably the most common method for starting textures in the VFX field. The concept is to line up the model (see Figure 6.20) with a reference photo of the object and project the image through to the model. This method is crucially necessary when an exact match is dictated (such as a *digital double*, a 3D duplicate of an actor). I used this method on just about every project I have ever worked on. Unfortunately, there is no way you could do this with Photoshop alone. A 3D paint program such as Right Hemisphere's Deep Paint 3D is necessary to pull off a projection.

1. Using a 3D paint program such as Right Hemisphere's Deep Paint 3D, line up the model to the reference photo.

   As you can see in Figure 6.21, the reference photo doesn't have the same dimensions as the model. Since you know the model's dimensions are approved, you have to warp the image to look like the model. Although it is possible to do this with Deep Paint 3D, I think Photoshop has better controls.

2. Export a snapshot of the projection wireframe and bring it into Photoshop; see Figure 6.22.

Figure 6.20 Here is a model that you texture with the projection method.

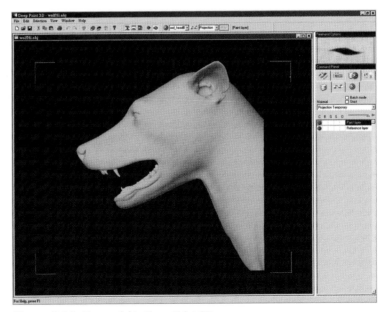

Figure 6.21 The model in Deep Paint 3D.

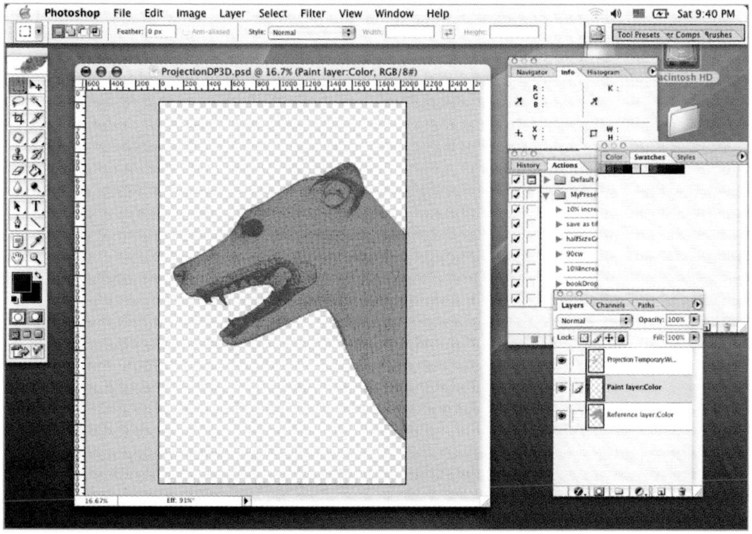

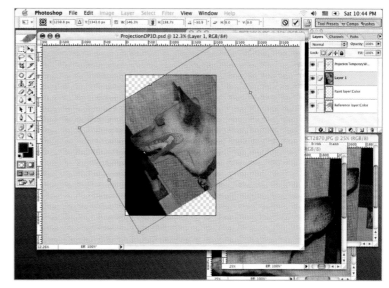

Figure 6.22 The exported PSD file from Deep Paint 3D.

6. Reduce the top layer's opacity to 50 percent with the Opacity slider in the Layers palette.

7. Press Command+T (Win: Ctrl+T) to get into the Free Transform mode and resize the image closer to the model size in Figure 6.23.

   Take a look at the different parts. You need to cut and work with quite a few pieces.

3. Open the reference photo that you want to use to create the projection for the dog. In Photoshop, press L and drag your cursor to lasso the area of the reference photo that you want to line up for projection for the model.

4. Press Command+C (Win: Ctrl+C) to copy the image.

5. Click over to the projection file and press Command+V (Win: Ctrl+V) to paste in the selection.

   Photoshop puts that image on a new layer above the existing one.

Figure 6.23 Transforming to make it a closer match.

8. Using the Lasso tool, select the areas you want to add and use the same method in Steps 1 and 2 to place your pieces.

   Keep in mind that you want to work beyond the edges of the wireframe to make sure that entire object is covered, like you see in Figure 6.24.

Note

If you need to use several different pictures to get all the pieces necessary for your projection, you are likely to run into issues of the reference photos having different exposures or color casts. Go to Chapter 12, "Matte Paintings from Pictures," and Chapter 13, "Quick Fixes for Common Problems," for the tutorials for equalizing the images.

9. Click the New Layer button on the bottom of the Layers palette to create a transparent layer above all your other painted layers.

10. Click the Clone tool (or press S to select the tool) and set the Clone tool options so that the layer is not aligned and using all layers as source.

11. Hold the Option button (Win: Alt button) and click to choose a clone source area.

12. Paint with the Clone brush to fill in any holes and integrate the transitions between the different pieces that create the projection.

    Don't worry about overspill; whatever is outside does not affect the textures much. See Figure 6.25 for the painting. Notice how the areas around the corner of the mouth and the chest, among other things, have been cleaned up to allow for a clean projection.

Figure 6.25 The completed projection painting.

13. Once the projection painting is done, make sure you have it at full 100 percent opacity and save it out.

14. Bring it into your 3D paint application and project it onto your object. You can see the results in Deep Paint 3D in Figure 6.26.

Figure 6.24 The Franken-projection image so far.

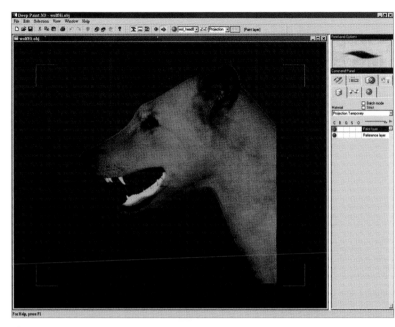

Figure 6.26 The model after projection.

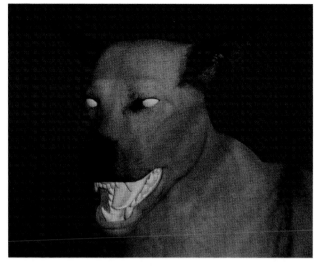

Figure 6.27 In this case, one projection and a bit of cleanup is all that is needed.

You may need to project several times from different angles depending on the model, and you may have to clean up all the streaking or messy parts or parts that need to be asymmetrical. See Figure 6.27 for the cleaned color map on the model in Deep Paint 3D. In both of these cases, you start with a base and then you paint on top of that in a 3D paint program. Are there appropriate times to just start painting in Photoshop? Absolutely.

Painting on Unwrapped Wireframe

UV maps can be represented as a wireframe on a 2D plane. Each vertex on the model is plotted and represented on the canvas. When the wireframe is recognizable in the texture, you can start by using the wireframe as a guide. Depending on the object, you may be able to complete the texture all in Photoshop!

1. Take a look at the unwrapped wireframe in Figure 6.28.

2. Press B to select the Brush tool and paint in the mask area of the map.

   You can change the color of the paint by double-clicking the foreground color swatch and selecting a color from the dialog box. See Figure 6.29.

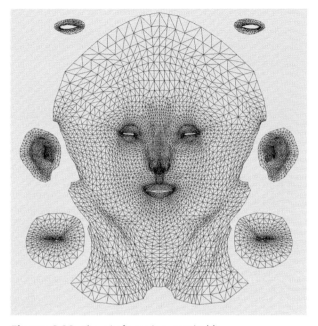

Figure 6.28 The wireframe is recognizable.

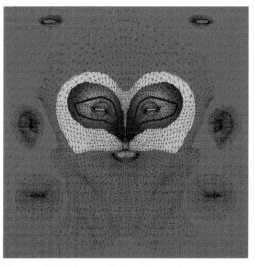

Figure 6.29 Start painting the mask.

3. Cut and paste some eyes into the mask like you see in Figure 6.30.

   Use the same method that you used in the projection mapping and lasso the areas that you want to add to your texture map. Paste them onto a separate layer in your texture map.

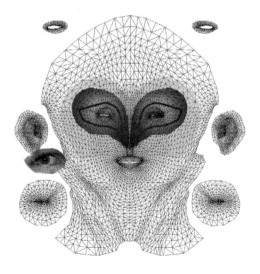

Figure 6.30 I put the layer below the painted mask so the mask hides the rough edges of the eyes.

4. Choose a custom brush.

   I have a custom brush that I use for skin. You can download this brush from the book's web site or make your own. Chapter 8, "Custom Brushes," shows you how to make a custom brush.

5. Make sure your color is similar to the colors that you used in the eye area and paint the rest of the map. It should look similar to Figure 6.31.

Since none of the seams is visible in the use of this model (the model will not get too close to the camera or take off her cowl and show the seams), you are done with this particular texture!

Figure 6.32 The rendered image.

Figure 6.31 Your map so far.

That's not photoreal!

You probably looked at Figure 6.32 and said to yourself, "I've seen better textures."

I have to admit, I was torn about this chapter. On one hand, I really wanted to put in some good examples of textures. On the other hand, this book isn't about the art of texturing—it is about using Photoshop to accomplish particular goals. To go into details of what kind of textures to make for the creation of a photorealistic human character is a book in itself. A photorealistic object of any kind—organic or inorganic—is not just about textures. It is about modeling, lighting, and compositing, too. And that is if you are creating a still image! If you want a moving 3D object to blend into a live-action background, you have to involve many more talents: animators, trackers, and riggers, all who can make or break the illusion of reality.

With the wonders of Photoshop, I could have made any mediocre still image look passably photorealistic. However, I wanted to show in this chapter what the color texture alone would do. All of the models used in this chapter have simple materials applied with a color Kd map and no more than two auxillary maps (usually bump or spec). I think it an important reality check to see how these quick textures look on a simple render. Too many books give a 15-minute tutorial and show a finished render that probably took three days to complete to the shown standard. If you want something to look good, you have to put in the time. Photoshop (and any other program) does not make a texture or matte painting with a few pushes of a button. Okay, I'll step off of this soap box now.

CHAPTER 7

BUMP MAPS AND GRAYSCALE

As a texture painter, the things you want out of grayscale are different from a photographer or a matte painter. Generally, you want to make bump maps, opacity maps, and specular maps. These things are intrinsic and distinctive to texture painters.

Bump Map

A *bump map* is a grayscale image used to simulate surface texture on a 3D object, giving more surface detail than what is actually modeled. To put it simply, a bump map's white areas tell the surface to stick out and the black areas tell the surface to depress inward. In this case, I want to make a bump map—something that I can assuredly say a photographer generally doesn't try to do. Oftentimes people in 3D work make bump maps by using their desaturated color map. For most cases, and especially in film, you need a little more finesse and a lot more control. Beyond the interpretation of color and light, you may be asked to make a bump map with values between 80 and 20 percent gray with 50 percent gray being *flat*, or neutral. Before you start finessing, take a look at how it's generally done.

Desaturating: Tolerable on Occasion

The common way of making a bump map is to convert it to grayscale.

1. Open the brick wall color texture map Brick.tga provided at this book's companion web site.

2. Go to the menu bar and choose **Image** > **Adjustments** > **Desaturate** or press Shift+Command+U (Win: Shift+Ctrl+U).

   Figure 7.1 is what you get. This won't do for a bump map, especially since by standard conventions of the way a bump map is processed the mortar will be sticking out and the bricks will be sinking in. The Lighter using your maps may be able to reverse the effect, but again by convention, you should invert it.

3. To invert your image press Command+I (Win: Ctrl+I) or go to **Image** > **Adjustments** > **Invert**. See Figure 7.2.

Figure 7.1 This is how your brick tile looks with standard desaturation.

Figure 7.2 The map is inverted, so the mortar goes in and the brick is raised.

Does it work? Yes, it works. That's why so many people stop here—but look at the image values. You need to set up your Info palette options to show HSB.

1. Go to the drop-down menu in the Info palette and choose Info Options.

2. Change the Second Color Readout Mode from CMYK to HSB Color and click OK.

3. Press I to choose the Eyedropper tool, make sure your Info palette is visible, and take a look at the mortar.

If you hover or slide the tool over mortar areas you see that the values displayed in the Info palette under the B section of the HSB area are all under the 50 percent mark, averaging around 30 percent brightness according to my guesstimation. Now take a look at the brick. The values are averaging 55 percent brightness. One brick is even around 47 percent and is therefore displaced inward.

Many would ignore the numbers, clean this up, and turn it in. This renders decently on a sample. The problem may arise, however, that this texture butts up to another texture and any difference in values between the two maps are obvious.

In other words, too often this method of just desaturating does *not* work. If objects are supposed to be flush to your displaced texture, then the values in the bump map you just created will not work; if the brick wall has to look photorealistic and a camera will be close or focusing on it, the bump map you just created will not work. Each of these sample situations calls for a more sophisticated grayscale bump/displacement map.

Channel Mixer: A Better Way

I really like using this method to create a bump map. It lets me interactively blend all three channels to get the type of grayscale I want. Start with the same brick color map, which is shown in Figure 7.3.

1. Go to **Layer > New Adjustment Layer > Channel Mixer**.

   Alternatively, you can go to the bottom of the Layers palette and access the adjustment layer there. You could go to the Image menu, but that restricts your ability to go back and edit at a later date. See Figure 7.4.

Figure 7.3 Make a coordinating bump map.

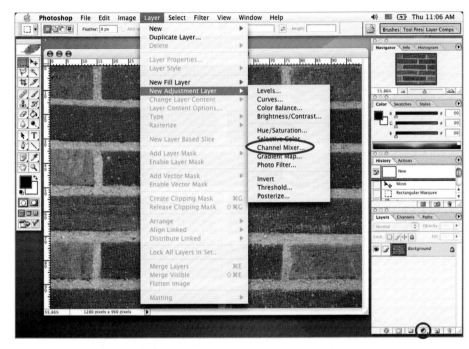

Figure 7.4 Creating a Channel Mixer layer from the menu bar or from the Layers palette are both equally valid.

4. Use the Eyedropper tool to check your values as you do your adjusting. Hover the tool over an area and look at the HSB B value in the Info palette for feedback.

Setting negative values in the Channel Mixer's source channels seems to subtract its values from the composite, but does not invert. (You can't invert a channel using this.) Once I had the basic look that I wanted, the Eyedropper info indicated the values were a little too dark overall, so I increased the constant by 15. You can see the values I applied in Figure 7.5.

2. Click OK to accept the name and default settings in the New Layer dialog box. The Channel Mixer dialog box appears, using RGB mode by default.

3. Go to the bottom of the dialog box and select the Monochrome checkbox to display the layer in grayscale.

The output channel at the top of the dialog box reflects the change by switching to Gray. You can play with the sliders to get the look you want.

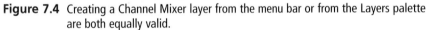

Figure 7.5 You don't need to use the same values I have here. You do want to make sure your mortar is darker than your bricks and that no highlight/bump in the mortar is higher than the brick value levels.

5. Click OK to accept your settings; take a look.

Note

One of the advantages of channel mixing is that if you need to tweak the values, you still have the adjustment layer with all its controls. For example, if you are asked to bring it down overall just a tad, you can reduce the adjusted constant. You can do this to extremes without degrading the image and having to start from the original.

Beyond ease and control, look at the quality. Compare the results of the two different methods of grayscaling.

You can see that in Figure 7.6 that the right image is superior in that the bricks are more even and the dirt/grime coloration incorporated into the left figure has been greatly reduced. Also, if you look in the mortar area, white spots would have jutted out far beyond the level of the bricks in the left image. This is no longer an issue with the image on the right created with the channel mixer.

Desaturate Method

Channel Mix Method

Figure 7.6 The bump map you made in the previous section on the left and, on the right, the result of channel mixing.

Grayscale

So now you have a richer grayscale bump map image. How do you make it meet the numbers? What if the Powers That Be want you to raise the midpoint by 10 percent and keep the range out of the extreme 10 percent on either end? Occasionally, specular maps, opacity maps, and bump maps have to hit certain numbers. It may be because of how the rendering program interprets the gray values, or it may be that different people are working on various maps that have to be cohesive in the final product. If you are told to make sure that 50 percent gray is

the *base*, or flat area, and that the edges *must* be flat, then you *cannot* have 49 percent or 51 percent gray passing as flat—it must be exactly 50 percent! This can seem daunting when the map has to be soft and gradated and you're painting it by how it looks— not by some value assessment.

With a little understanding of how Photoshop's Levels dialog box works, you can calculate exactly how your image is processed and say with confidence that you raised the midpoint by exactly 10 percent or that the range is definitely between 10 percent and 90 percent brightness.

Simple Range Adjustments

Create a gradient that goes from pure black to pure white to represent your bump map.

1. Click the Gradient tool or press Shift+G until it cycles to the Gradient tool (instead of to the Paint Bucket tool).

2. Create a new file (**File** > **New**) in the resolution of your choice and drag within the canvas to create a gradient.

   See Figure 7.7. Make sure to choose a black and white gradient. It does not matter for this tutorial whether you are still in RGB or grayscale mode, nor if you go from black to white or vice versa. Just make sure that you have the full range of black, white, and grays in your image.

   Before you start adjusting the values, create a few markers to help keep track of the numbers. The Color Sampler tool allows you to set up to four markers.

3. Choose the Color Sampler tool from the toolbox by pressing I or choosing Shift+I.

4. Make sure the Sample Size is 3×3 Average in the options bar and click a spot that shows up as 50 percent gray (or 128, 128, 128 in RGB settings). See Figure 7.8.

   Don't worry if your marker doesn't hit the spot when you first lay it down. If you place the mouse pointer over the marker and it changes to a triangle, you can drag it to a better spot.

5. Create a marker for the two extremes: the 0 percent and the 100 percent gray (black and white). Click what reads as pure white to set marker #2, then click pure black to set marker #3.

   This allows you to consistently track the changes you make. See Figure 7.9.

Figure 7.7 Your gradient is an example of a bump map that is difficult to adjust within the needed range.

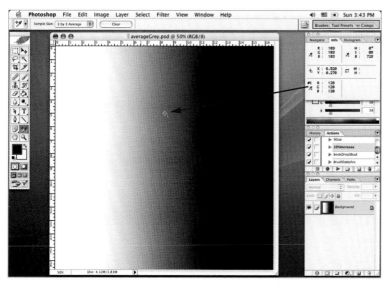

Figure 7.8 This is your 50 percent gray marker. This is the point that is flat, neither going up nor down.

Say that your bump map is perfect, except that you can't have the values go within the 10 percent range of either end of the grayscale. In other words, your bump map has to be within 10 percent and 90 percent gray. The general relation to itself is perfect as is. If you tried to paint out just the nine percent gray and below, for example, the overall bump map values would not have the same relationship, resulting in a flattening out at either end, as the top image of Figure 7.10 shows. The lower figure is the result of adjusting the bump to keep the relative relationship of the values.

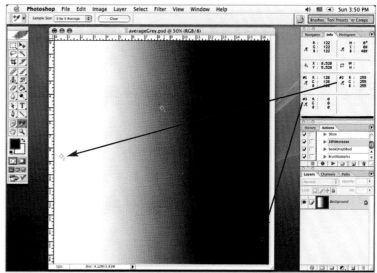

Figure 7.9 Your markers don't have to be in the same place as mine, but your values should read the same.

Figure 7.10 How you adjust your bump map affects how it is rendered.

What you really want is to squish the values that you have right now within 10 percent and 90 percent gray. Luckily, the solution is easy.

1. Add a levels adjustment layer by going to **Layer** > **New Adjustment Layer** > **Levels**.

2. Click OK to Accept the default settings and name in the New Layer dialog box.

3. In the Levels dialog box, change the Output Level slider from 0–255 to 26–230.

    That's roughly 10 percent of 255 and 90 percent of 255. Take a look at Figure 7.11.

4. Click OK and take a look at your gray level values by looking at the values of your color markers.

As you can see, your midgray (50 percent flat mark) is unaffected, but your extreme ends have been brought in between 10 percent and 90 percent. This simple method works as long as you bring in the range evenly on both sides.

Advanced Range Adjustments

What if you need your gray values to be between 10 percent and 85 percent? The range is correct if you enter 26–217 in the Output Level box, but your 50 percent gray is shifted to 122 (48 percent). This won't do for something like a bump map, which must use 50 percent as a neutral point.

What you need to do is first take everything below the 50 percent mark and compress it to go between 10 percent and 50 percent. Then take everything above the 50 percent mark and compress it between 50 percent and 85 percent. Luckily, I happen to know an ancient Chinese secret that solves this problem. (Well, maybe it's not really ancient…or Chinese…and if I tell you, I guess it won't be a secret either…)

1. Hide the levels layer with which you were just working by clicking on the eye icon next to the layer in the Layers palette.

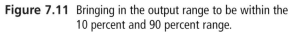

Figure 7.11 Bringing in the output range to be within the 10 percent and 90 percent range.

2. Create a new threshold adjustment layer by either going to **Layer > New Adjustment Layer > Threshold** or clicking the Create New Fill or Adjustment Layer button on the bottom of the Layers palette and choosing Threshold, and accept the default name by clicking OK in the New Layer dialog box.

3. In the Threshold dialog box, enter **128** for the threshold value if it is not already so.

   This is, in effect, a mask for the areas that have a brightness greater than 50 percent. See Figure 7.12.

4. Click OK to accept and close the Threshold dialog box.

5. Switch to the Channels palette. Since this is a black and white image, all the channels should look the same.

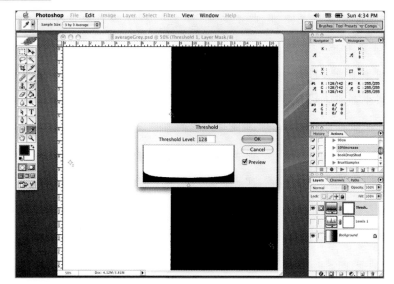

Figure 7.12 The black/white demarcation should go right through your #1 marker.

6. Duplicate one of the channels for calling on later: Click a color channel, click the triangle button to open the Channels palette menu, and choose Duplicate Channel. See Figure 7.13.

7. Give your channel a name—preferably one that is descriptive—and click OK.

You see your new channel, called an *alpha channel* or *holdout mask*, on the bottom of the Channels palette, as in Figure 7.14.

8. Click the RGB composite channel.

9. Click the Layers tab to bring forth the Layers palette. Hide the threshold adjustment layer by clicking the Eye icon next to the layer's name. See Figure 7.15.

10. Go to **Select** > **Load Selection** on the menu bar.

11. In the dialog box, choose your recently made alpha channel from the Channel pop-up menu, make sure this is a new selection, and click OK.

This loads the left (light) side of the image as a selection. Figure 7.16 points out the desirable settings.

Figure 7.13 I chose the blue channel, but the R and G channels would have been fine, too.

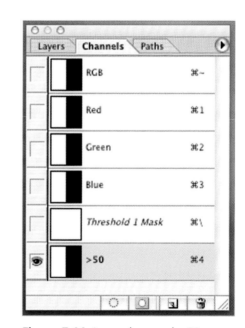

Figure 7.14 I named my mask >50.

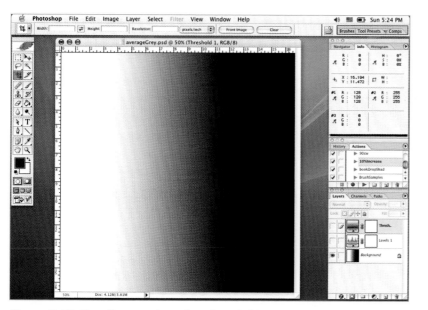

Figure 7.15 The adjustment layers have been hidden and now you can see your original gradient.

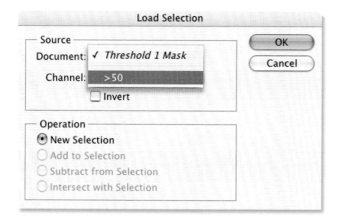

Figure 7.16 Load your alpha channel.

12. With the selection still active, create a new levels adjustment layer by selecting **Layer > New Adjustment Layer > Levels.**

13. Name your layer and click OK.

    In the next dialog box, you see the histogram in the middle is chopped off. That is because you only have half of the values selected.

14. Ensure that the upper limit for the Output Levels is 217 (85 percent).

    Notice in the Info palette that the values change in the #1 and #2 markers when you input that value. The #2 marker is perfect at 217, but the #1 marker should come back up to 50 percent.

15. Slide the triangle under the left side of the Output Level slider slowly toward the center, until the #1 marker in the Info palette reads 128. Click OK and see Figure 7.17.

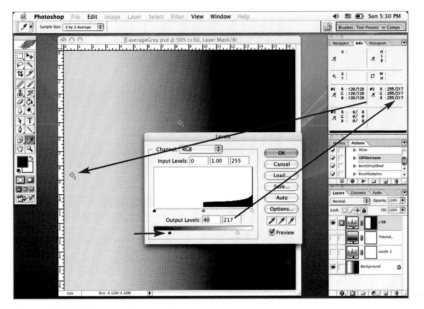

Figure 7.17 The secret numerology.

Great. Now that you have the upper (lighter) range fixed, do the same for the lower (darker) range.

1. Load the same channel map selection by choosing **Select > Load Selection**.

2. Invert the selection by pressing Shift+Command+I (Win: Shift+Ctrl+I) or by going to **Select > Inverse.**

3. Now that you selected the other half, go through same methods you just did for the upper half but apply the methods to the lower half, shown in Figure 7.18.

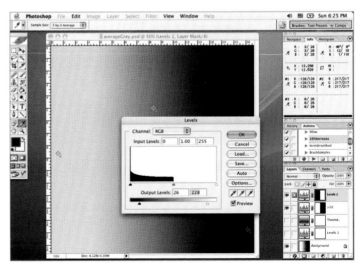

Figure 7.18 Do the same technique to bring up the lower sections.

This time look at marker #3 and bring in the range from 10 percent to 50 percent by sliding the right slider in.

Voilá! Your bump map is now complete. Check out Figure 7.19. Your middle, flat areas are still at 50 percent and your range is between 10 percent and 85 percent gray. Bravo!

Using these techniques, you can squash and stretch any grayscale image to the values that you need. The more you do it, the more intuitive it becomes.

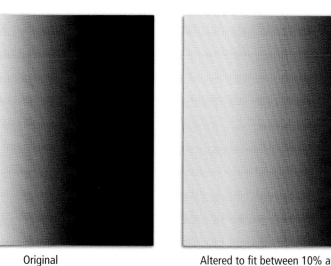

Original   Altered to fit between 10% and 85% gray

Figure 7.19 The same gradient altered to fit the numbers.

CHAPTER 8

CUSTOM BRUSHES

Chapter 2 covers the details of working with the brush options. Now you learn how to save out your favorite brushes and create some specific brushes that come in handy in the VFX world.

Getting Dirty

You know how just about everyone had acne as a teenager or how just about every baby eats dirt at some point? The same kind of idea holds true here: Just about every digital painter creates a dirt brush. One of the most common brushes you use as both a matte painter and a texture painter is a dirt brush. A *dirt brush* is an organically shaped brush that makes it easier to paint on any type of grime, wear, or dirt, much like the way do-it-yourself people use a sponge to give a textured or aged look to walls and furniture.

Creating the Brushes

The following steps show you how to make a couple of custom dirt brushes.

1. Create a 200×200 blank white canvas by going to **File** > **New** in the menu bar.

2. Click the New Layer button at the bottom of the Layers palette to form a new transparent layer.

3. Using black, create a smudgy, dirty blob like the one I have created in Figure 8.1.

   Don't worry about going to the edges; you clean this up later. Since this is going to be a brush, it needs to have an organic shape. Any part that goes to the edges will end up giving a tiled, hard edge look. You may not even notice or see the edge, but even a 10-percent opacity shows up when you try to use your brush.

4. Use the Lasso tool to cut away at the edges, making sure not to have any minute smudges going to the edge, as shown in Figure 8.2.

5. After cutting away to clean edges, soften the edges by running an eraser over the edges at 40 percent opacity.

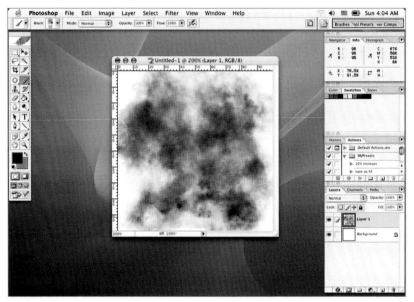

Figure 8.1 Use whatever brushes work for you to create a similar blob.

Note

Although it may seem that a 200×200 image is pretty small, that is a pretty large brush. In the old days of Photoshop custom brushes, you had to manually make different sizes of the same brush and save each one separately. Since this is no longer the case, you can jump into making this map into a brush. Figure 8.2 shows the softened edges.

6. Select the entire layer by way of one of these methods:
   - Marquee tool
   - Option+a (Win: Alt+a) shortcut

7. Go to **Edit** > **Define Brush Preset**. A dialog box asks you to name your brush.

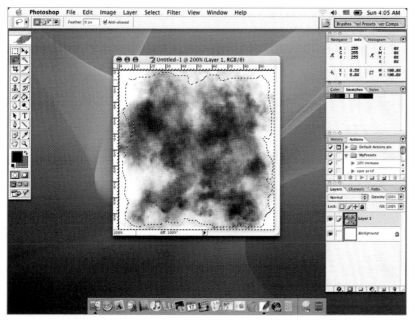

Figure 8.2 Use the lasso to ensure that you have no stray pixels outside of the brush.

Note

Photoshop uses the entire active canvas to determine the brush preset, but it's safer to make a selection to ensure that the proper image is used to create your brush. Also, if you want to use part of the image to create a brush, you only have to make the selection around the area that you want to use. Photoshop creates the brush preset from your selection.

8. Give your brush a descriptive name.

Since I think this looks like a mouse hiding in grass, I call this dirt brush gardenMouse. See Figure 8.3. The brush is now saved to the brush presets, and by default is all the way at the bottom. You can see it in Figure 8.4.

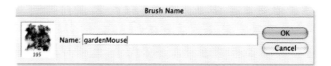

Figure 8.3 Give the brush a name that helps you remember it—preferably a name that others understand.

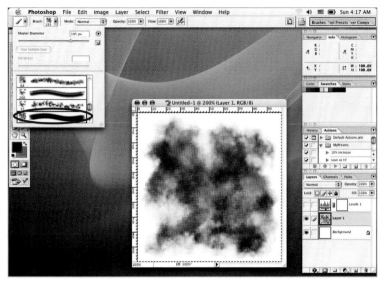

Figure 8.4 You can see your new brush is already available in the Brush Tip palette.

9. Hide the layer you created your first brush map on and create a new transparent layer.

10. Do the same steps you just did and make another dirt brush.

    This time, give it a distinct irregular shape. Again, give it a descriptive name. My friend Brian is highly irregular, so I named this brush after him, as evidenced in Figure 8.5.

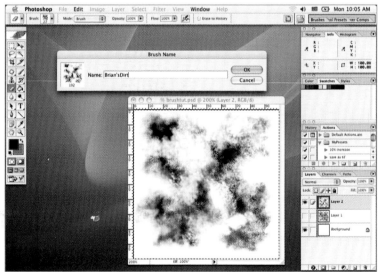

Figure 8.5 Since you don't know Brian, I suggest using another name that makes sense to you.

Adjusting the Settings

Now you're going to go to the brush options to give these two brushes the proper dirty variations characteristics. That way it won't look like a bad sponge-on type of dirt. I had you make two brushes so you can blend the two for more variation.

1. Choose the first brush you made in your brush presets.

2. Open the Brushes palette in the palette well.

3. Start with the Brush Tip Shape options, increasing the spacing so the brush details can be seen more.

    Don't let it become so far apart it looks like a stamp. Figure 8.6 is an example of good spacing.

4. Turn on shape dynamics. Go to the options and jitter everything (see Figure 8.7) to break up any repeating patterns.

5. Go to Scattering and play with the settings.

    These settings change the number and placement of brush tips to a stroke. Everything in this dialog box is as intuitive as the previous dialog box, except for that little Both Axes checkbox on the very

top. As you select and deselect the checkbox, you are witnessing the difference of scattering the brush tips in a radial direction from each spacing point or in a perpendicular direction to the tangent of the path. Again, there is no right answer: Slide the sliders, select the checkboxes, and find a combination that you like. Figure 8.8 shows my settings.

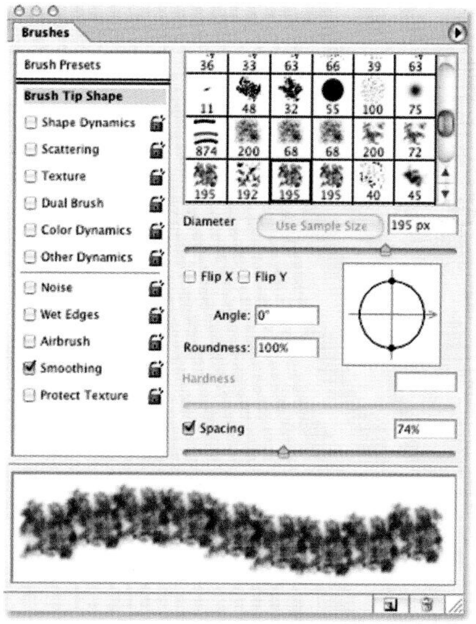

Figure 8.6 To get the dirt brush to start looking better, give the brush some space.

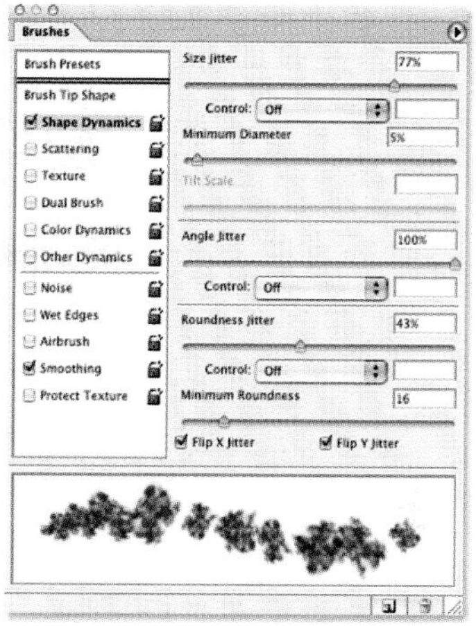

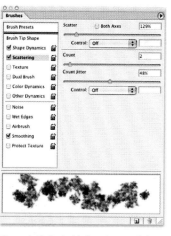

Figure 8.7 Don't be afraid to go wild with the controls. You can always change them later if they don't work.

Figure 8.8 I think I changed this setting about four times before settling on this one.

6. Go to the Dual Brush options and find your other brush tip in the thumbnails.

   Now comes the play of your two brushes. Unlike the Brush pull-down menu, the tips may not necessarily be at the very bottom. In my case, they were in the middle.

7. Choose a blend mode (at the top of the dialog box). This determines how this second brush interacts with your main brush.

8. Play with the sliders at the bottom of the dialog box until you find a good setting. See Figure 8.9.

9. Continue onto Color Dynamics and Other Dynamics, playing with the sliders.

   I also like turning on Smoothing and Airbrush, but that is not necessary for a good dirt brush. See Figure 8.10 for another look.

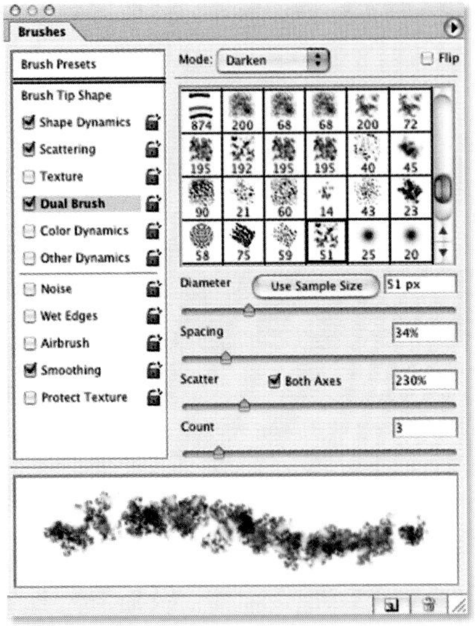

Figure 8.9   Once again, this is all about eyeing the preview window and finding a good setting.

Save! Save! Save!

Great! You have a wonderful dirt brush. Before anything happens, save the brush.

1. Go to the Brushes palette's pull-down menu and choose New Brush Preset, as I did in Figure 8.11.

   This saves the brush as a separate and different brush, but you can either delete the old one or keep them both.

   Another option is to save the settings as a new tool preset. This way your brush remains as you first saved it in the Brushes palette, but you can access the brush with these specific settings in the Tool Presets palette.

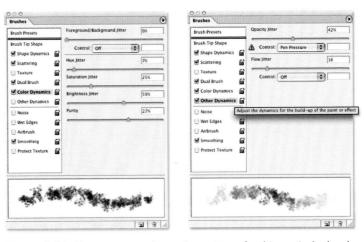

Figure 8.10   Here are some of my other settings for this particular brush.

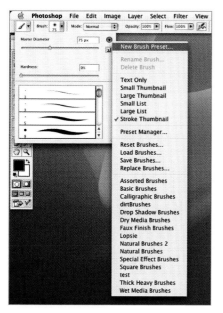

Figure 8.11 The settings are not associated to this tip until you save it as a brush preset.

To do this, make any adjustments you wish to the settings, then go to the Tool Presets palette in the upper-left corner of the options bar. (See Figure 8.12.) Press the New Tool Preset button; a dialog box appears in which you should name your brush. Alternatively, instead of pressing the New Tool Preset button, you can access the same command in the Tool Presets palette's pull-down menu.

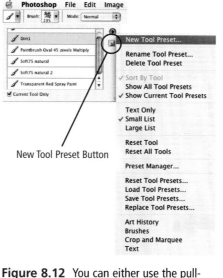

New Tool Preset Button

Figure 8.12 You can either use the pull-down menu or the button.

2. Since the tool preset name is listed in the palette, give it a very descriptive name (such as dirt scattered 75 percent opacity color) that gives some details to remind you of your settings.

The new tool preset is placed above the preset you have highlighted at the time of your save. See Figure 8.13.

3. Last but not least, save your brush and tool preset libraries.

Under each palette's pull-down menu, you find a Save Brushes or Save Tool Presets option. You can see the options in Figure 8.14. Use one!

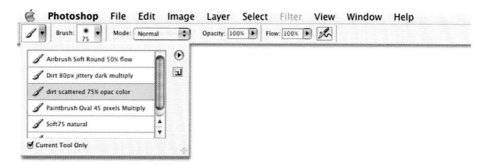

Figure 8.13 The Tool Presets palette lists the names; therefore, it is more important to give a descriptive name.

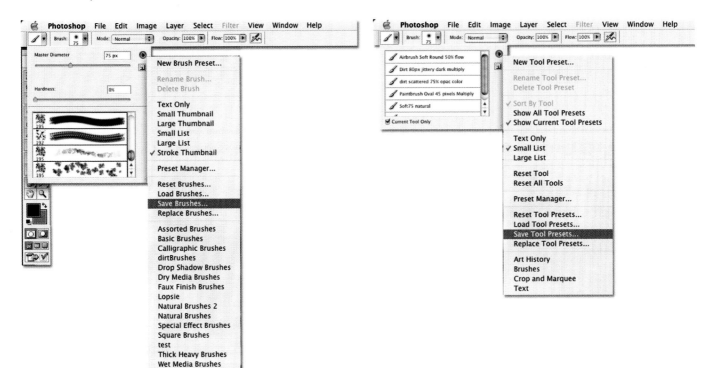

Figure 8.14 Save your libraries!

Natural Color

When I paint textures, I like to use my special custom brushes that have a certain amount of hue, saturation, and brightness variations built in. This gives a more natural look, especially to solid color objects. Without these variations, the objects tend to look flat, computer generated, or fake. The following steps create one of the brushes I use often.

1. Grab a soft brush as I've done in Figure 8.15. I chose a 75-pixel-wide soft brush with 0 percent hardness.

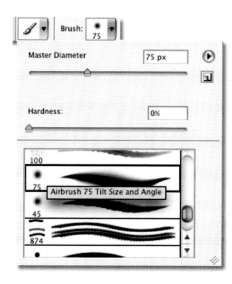

Figure 8.15 You can make a custom brush from one of the existing presets.

2. At the Brush Tip Shape options, increase the spacing a bit. Aim for a spattered look like you see in Figure 8.16.

3. Select Shape Dynamics and give a bit of size jitter to your brush. See Figure 8.17.

   This ensures that the variations you add don't look as mechanical, since the brushstroke's size variation masks any color pattern.

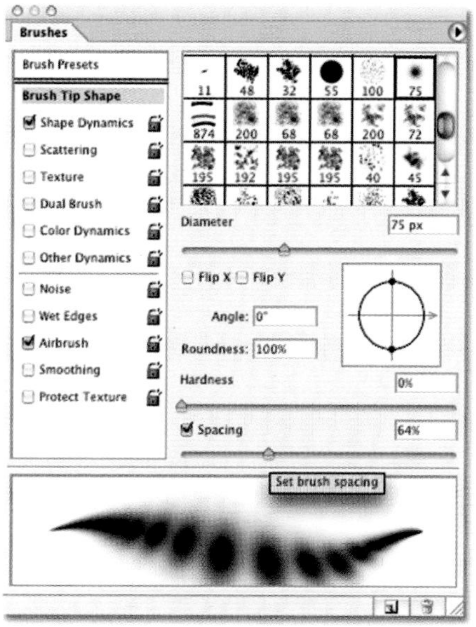

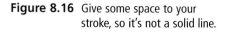

Figure 8.16 Give some space to your stroke, so it's not a solid line.

4. Go to the Scattering options and give the brush a bit of scatter.

   This allows the different colors and sizes to show up more, because the brushstroke isn't confined to a single vector. Now comes the really nice stuff. This is a function I used to love Painter for and always complained about Photoshop for lacking.

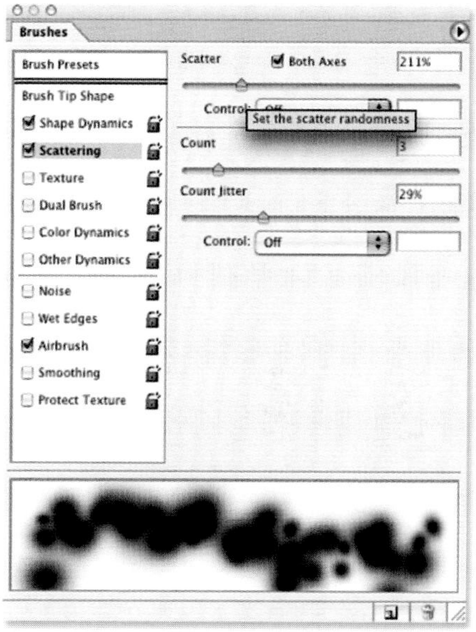

Figure 8.17 The size jitter, spacing, and scattering break up the stroke so it looks less uniform.

5. Select the Color Dynamics Options and play with the Hue, Saturation, and Brightness Jitter settings you see in Figure 8.18.

   The goal is to have a setting that doesn't create a calico (bright and multicolored) effect, but subtly varies the color enough that it doesn't seem flat.

6. Now that you have a setting that is nice, save it the same way you saved the dirt brush.

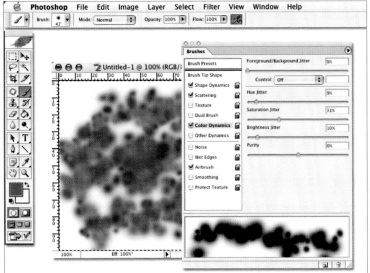

Figure 8.18 This is what gives an organic effect to your brush.

7. Go to your tool presets and click the New Tool Preset button.

8. Give your brush a descriptive name and click OK, as shown in Figure 8.19.

Now take a look at how this particular brush makes a difference in a finished render. Notice in Figure 8.20 how flat the solid colors look in the left image? See how much more natural the right image looks? The only differences between the two are the color maps.

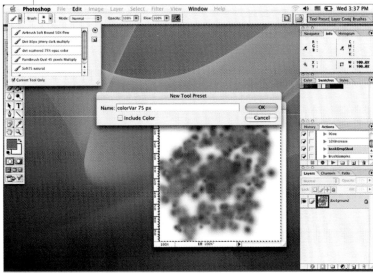

Figure 8.19 You lose all your settings unless you make a point to save your brush as a new tool preset.

Figure 8.20 The left has solid painted color maps. The right is the same but with color maps that were painted with your brush.

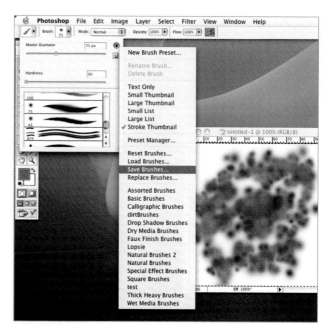

Figure 8.21 If you don't save your library, you chance losing all your custom brushes.

You'll be amazed at the variety of uses you can find for this brush—and this is just the tip of the iceberg! You can scan a leaf and create a leaf brush or make a fish brush or produce a brush that paints cats' paw prints over everything. Your only limitation is your imagination!

Brush Libraries

Now for the part you've been waiting for: how to make sure you don't lose all your beautiful brushes.

Caution

Even though the brushes appear in the Brush Preset pull-down menu, if anyone resets the brushes to factory settings (as you did at the beginning of this book), you are out of luck—brushes lost. It's best to save a brush library that can be loaded when you wish.

1. Choose Save Brushes (shown in Figure 8.21) from the Brush palette menu or Brushes palette menu.

   Photoshop should automatically take you to your preset brushes folder.

2. Enter a name for your brush library and click Save.

Note

This saves *all* the brushes currently in the Brushes palette. After you restart Photoshop, your new brush library name appears at the bottom of the Brush palette pop-up menu (accessible by right-clicking the canvas while using the Brush tool) and Brushes palette menu (accessible by clicking the small triangle on the right side of the tab when the Brushes palette is selected). You can see all my library's titles in Figure 8.22.

Now that you know the general way to save a library, save just the newly created dirt brushes as its own library.

As you create more brushes, you may find yourself getting more particular about the brushes that are available in the palette. Unused brush tips become a hassle that clutters up your workspace. You can manage this library or any other saved preset with the Preset Manager:

1. Go to **Edit** > **Preset Manager** to bring up the dialog box.

2. Make sure your preset type is set to Brushes, as in Figure 8.23.

3. Click one of your dirt brushes.

4. Hold Command (Win: Ctrl) and click any other brush you wish to include in the library.

5. Press the Save Set button and give your library a name in the ensuing dialog box.

Figure 8.22 This is the name for all the brushes that are currently in my palette.

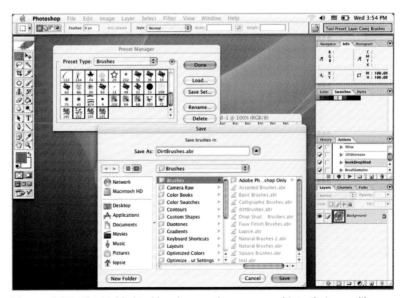

Figure 8.23 The highlighted brushes are the ones saved into their own library.

CHAPTER 9

Tiling and Transformations

Tiling and transformations is more than just a clever alliteration for a chapter heading. You generally have to use transformations to get a photo ready to be turned into a repeatable tile. In addition, you can create a type of painting short-cut by creating a repeatable tile, using it as a pattern, and then transforming the image to give it perspective. Are you lost yet? The best way to explain is to go step by step through a few examples.

Basic Tiling

First, the basic concept of *tiling*: The goal is to take an image and make it repeatable in x and y. (That's geek talk for horizontally and vertically, respectively.) Ideally, for a tileable color texture, you should start with an image that is flatly lit and shot straight on, with no perspective. Take a look at BasicBrick.tga, which is in Figure 9.1. You can download this image from the book's companion web site.

Figure 9.1 This is a great reference photo in that it is straight on and has flat lighting.

Preparing the Image

Although you could, technically, create a tileable image from the image in Figure 9.1, for the sake of the Lighter implementing your texture, you need to straighten out the image before making it tileable.

1. Open BasicBrick.tga.

2. Make a duplicate of the background layer by pressing Command+J (Win: Ctrl+J).

3. Drag out some guides to line up against. Take your cursor to the edge of your window where the rulers are and click and drag out from them.

   If your rulers are not visible, go to **View** > **Rulers**. You should see a dotted line drag out with your cursor.

4. Place the guide alongside one of the bricks.

   When you release, the line turns into a solid cyan line.

5. Get a couple guides set for your vertical guides and a couple set for your horizontal guides.

   The horizontal guides come down from the top ruler and the vertical guides come out from the left ruler.

6. Press V or go to your Move tool to move your guides.

   For this to work, you have to get your cursor right over the guide and see it change to the guide cursor. I created four guides, as you can see in Figure 9.2.

7. Making sure that you have extended your window to just beyond the scope of the image, press Command+T (Win: Ctrl+T) to bring up the Free Transform guide box.

8. With your cursor just outside of the box, click and drag to rotate the image so that the bricks line up against the guide, as in Figure 9.3.

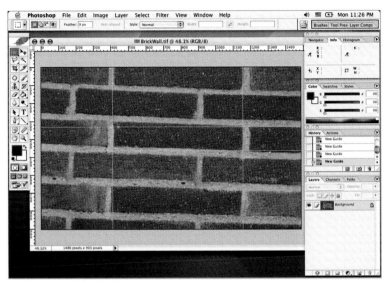

Figure 9.2 I tried to place the guides in alignment with that one center brick.

9. When you are satisfied with the rotation, press Return (Win: Enter) to apply the transformation.

Tip

Should your transform nodes rotate out of your viewable area, simply press Command +0 (Win: Ctrl+0—that is zero, not the letter O). The window widens to frame your transform nodes.

10. Drag out a few more guides to double-check your alignment, as shown in Figure 9.4.

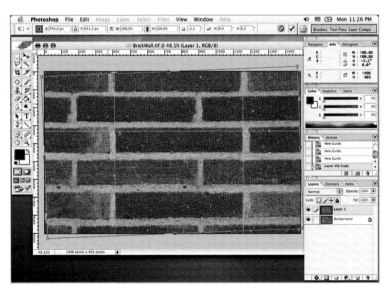

Figure 9.3 Rotate the duplicated layer to line up to the guides.

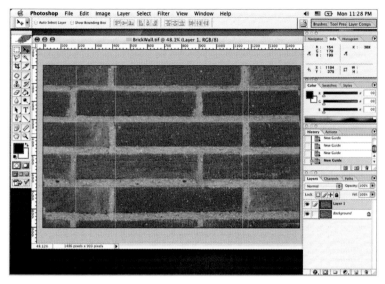

Figure 9.4 Move the guides around and check the alignment of other parts of the image.

Offsetting the Image: Horizontal

Now you're going to do the offset that makes this tileable.

1. Go to **Filter > Other > Offset**.

   A dialog box pops up, with sliders for the vertical and horizontal offset. See Figure 9.5.

2. Slide your image horizontally until the seam is somewhere around the middle of your canvas.

3. Select Preview so you can see the feedback from using the sliders and select Wrap Around for the undefined areas. Keep the vertical slide at 0 for now.

4. Click OK.

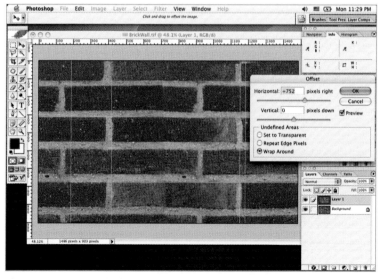

Figure 9.5 Notice the break in the middle of the image as a result of the offset.

Cleaning the Seams

The next step is to clean up the seams. Use the Clone brush and the Patch/Healing tool to get rid of the obvious offset demarcation.

1. Press J to switch to the Healing tool. See Figure 9.6.

   For inside the bricks or the middle of the grout, use the Healing tool and make the pattern seamless.

2. Move your cursor to the center of a good brick that is similar to the brick you're trying to heal and press Option (Win: Alt) down while clicking the area.

3. Move your brush cursor to the seam and brush away.

Do you prefer to do chunks at a time?

1. Press Shift+J until the Healing tool rotates to the Patch tool.

2. Use the patch's lasso-like behavior (shown in Figure 9.7) and define an area that you would like to heal.

3. Drag the patch to an area that has the look you want.

   You see the original area update to show you how it looks there.

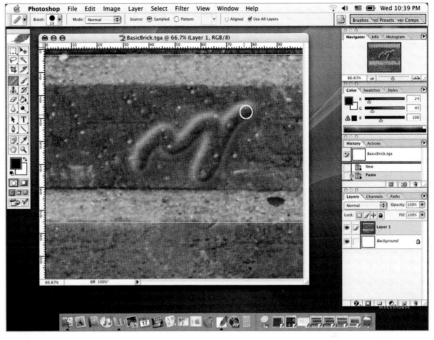

Figure 9.6 The Healing tool's toolbar icon is a bandage—completely apropos for the way it works! The brush effect has been digitally augmented for better visibility.

4. Release the mouse button to set the patch. When you are done with the Patch tool, press Command+D (Win: Ctrl+D) to deselect the patch area.

   When you are all done, the seam is no longer visible.

Note

If you try to use the Healing brush for the brick edge, you lose your sharp edge. You can see that effect in Figure 9.8. Use the Clone tool to paint a smooth or natural edge to the brick. Make sure that your Clone tool is within the top 10 percent opacity (90–100 percent; I generally like to use 100 percent for the best detail). The Clone tool's effect is clear in Figure 9.9. A more opaque brush may make the cloned areas soft and mushy. Good for oatmeal, but not for images.

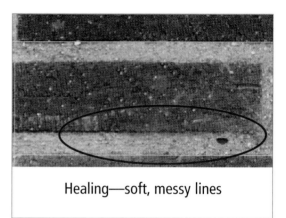

Healing—soft, messy lines

Figure 9.8 This is what would happen if you tried to use the Healing tool on this area.

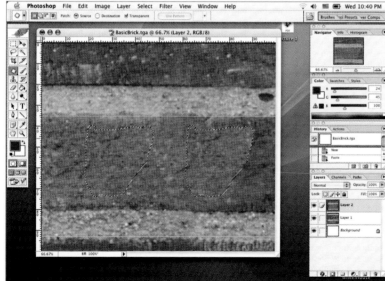

Figure 9.7 The Patch tool is good for healing big sections all at once.

Clone—cleaner lines

Figure 9.9 Using the Clone tool gives you the detailed edge that you want.

Shifting the Image: Vertical

Your image should look similar to Figure 9.10. Now you need to check how it looks when the image is shifted vertically.

1. Go to **Filter > Other > Offset** again.

2. This time make the shift vertical.

   I shifted the image vertically 337 pixels. You can see in Figure 9.11 there's a bit of a problem. This isn't just a matter of healing the seam. The pattern is broken; the brick layers don't meet correctly. You need to trim the image to make it tileable.

3. Before proceeding, undo the Offset filter by pressing Command+Z (Win: Ctrl+Z).

   Of course you could apply the Offset filter again with the exact opposite of the value previously applied (in my case, 337), but why go the long route when you just applied the filter and can easily undo it?

4. Select the Crop tool and click-drag around the areas that you are going to keep.

   Don't worry if you don't get it perfectly, as the Crop tool allows you to edit before committing.

5. Adjust as you feel necessary and press Return (Win: Enter) to crop. See my work in Figure 9.12.

6. Offset again by repeating Steps 1 and 2 of this section. You can see in Figure 9.13 that it works better.

Figure 9.10 It looks like everything is cleaned up.

Figure 9.11 When you offset the tile again, you can see that your work is not yet done.

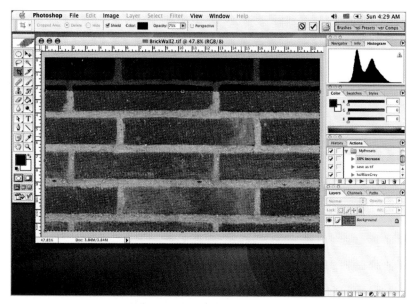

Figure 9.12 I just guesstimated where I should crop the image.

Figure 9.13 Yes, this is a definite improvement.

Tile Cleanup

You are close to finishing the texture tile. Go through the same steps you did for cleaning the seams on the horizontal shift; using the Clone tool and Healing brush. When you are done, run the Offset filter on both the vertical and horizontal shift at a different number to see if there are any new seams. If so, then clean the seams again.

Generally, you need try only one more time to clean up seams, but don't be surprised if it takes a few offsets to get it right. Figure 9.14 shows the final image. When the offset no longer shows any seams, the image is ready! Figure 9.15 shows the tiled effect.

Tip

When you have only a small sample to draw from to create a tile, even with the best of skills, you see a repeating pattern or a uniformity evident when covering a large area. In the absence of a larger sample, simply tile your small tile as shown in Figure 9.15, then use that image as a starting point for a new tile! Figure 9.16 is the same image as Figure 9.15, but with some cloning and painting to get rid of the repeating pattern.

Figure 9.14 Your final tileable image.

Figure 9.15 A sample of how it looks tiled.

Figure 9.16 Creating a larger tile from a smaller repeating tile.

Using Transformations

You used the Free Transformation tool in this chapter's first lesson to rotate and align the image. When creating seamless tiles, or patterns, you inevitably have to use the transformations to prepare your image at some point. Before you go into an example, let me go over the different types of transformations.

Types of Transformations

You can apply five types of transformations. The Free Transform option allows you to switch between any of the five types continuously. Since a transformation interpolates a rasterized image, the image loses some info each time you apply a transformation. Therefore, it is better to apply several transformations at once than to apply each of those same transformations in a separate pass.

Table 9.1 shows the difference between each of the different transformations types.

Table 9.1 Transformation Types

Type	Use	Free Transform Key	Example
Scale	Increase or decrease vertical or horizontal size	None. Simply pull a handle of the transform bounding box, as you would in Scale mode.	
Rotate	Turn an item around clockwise or counter-clockwise	None. Place cursor outside bounding box until it turns into a curved, double-headed arrow, then click and drag.	
Skew	Slant an item vertically or horizontally	Command+Shift (Win: Ctrl+Shift) and drag a side handle. The cursor should change to a gray arrow with a double-sided arrow below it.	
Distort	Stretch an item in any direction, like stretching a canvas over an odd-shaped frame	Command (Win: Ctrl) and drag any handle.	
Perspective	Apply a one-point perspective, like stretching a canvas onto a trapezoid frame	Command+Option+Shift (Win: Ctrl+Alt+Shift) and drag a corner handle. The cursor should become a gray arrowhead.	

Tip

By default, the transformation reference point is the center of the bounding box. You can move this anywhere you want—even outside of the box! Simply click and drag to where you would to place the point.

Changing Perspective

One of the most common usages for the transformation tools is to tweak the perspective of an image. Take a look at Figure 9.17.

Figure 9.17 A nice picture of a ship, but you want to sharpen the angle of the ship to the camera.

To emphasize the length of the ship, alter the image as if the ship were at a more severe angle to the camera. Can you guess which of the transform tools to use? If you didn't guess Perspective, then you have to go to jail; do not pass go.

1. Duplicate your background image by pressing Command+J (Win: Ctrl+J).

2. Go to **Edit > Transform > Perspective**.

   You should see the handles for the transformation box around your layer. If not, press Command+0 (Win: Ctrl+0) to bring the handles within view. (That key combination is a zero.)

3. Click-drag the upper-left corner handle upward and watch as it transforms your layer interactively, like you see in Figure 9.18.

4. When you have the look you want, do one of these three things:
   - Double-click within the transform bounding box.
   - Press Return (Win: Enter).
   - Click the checked box on the upper-right corner of the tool options bar to commit the transformation.

5. Reposition the layer with the Move tool for better framing.

   This is necessary because the transformation took much of the image beyond the canvas borders. In this case I reduced the layer's opacity so I could match the size and position of the original ship.

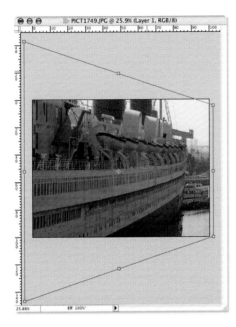

Figure 9.18 Using the perspective transformation.

6. Bring back the opacity of the transformed ship and blend in to the background.

   You can see the dramatic difference in Figure 9.19.

Figure 9.19 The before and after images.

Creating Tiles from a Non-orthographic Reference

Your assignment: Create a set extension of an elaborately tiled floor. The tile floor is very distinctive and key to blending the virtual set to the real set. If you're one of the fortunate ones, you get flatly lit, straight-on pictures of each set of tile designs, along with a wider view with the same conditions.

Alas, you are not one of the fortunate ones. Figure 9.20 is what you get.

Think Before You Act

Where shall you start? You can see no tiles straight on (*orthographically*), so if you try to use the same method you used for the brick tile earlier in the chapter, you include perspective. You know right away that you have to use your knowledge of transformation to flatten the perspective and prep the image to seem orthographic, or flat. At this point it is good to find out a few things.

These factors all contribute to determine how big you should make your tile:

- How big is the extension going to be?
- Will you see other borders or does it just follow one side?
- Does the Lighter have the ability to flip or mirror the tiles?
- Will there be a separate dirt map?

Figure 9.20 Pretty, but not optimal to the texture artist.

You may be wondering what a dirt map has to do with the size of the tile. If you have a separate dirt map, you can have a smaller tile, because the repetition or uniformity of the tile will be hidden by the overlaying dirt map. This is, of course, assuming that you can make your dirt map a different dimension than your color tile map.

Preparing the Reference with Transformations

Great. Now you have an idea of where you're going and can start cutting and transforming your image to make orthographic tiles.

1. Open TiledFloor.tif, which you can get from this book's companion web site.

2. Use the Lasso or Marquee tool to grab a section of the field that you want to start with. See Figure 9.21.

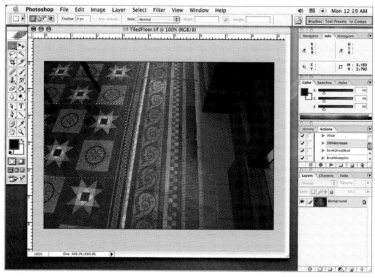

Figure 9.21 I chose this section because it doesn't have as much light shine as the closer ones, but is bigger than the far one.

3. Copy the selection by pressing Command+C (Win: Ctrl+C) and paste it to a new layer by pressing Command+V (Win: Ctrl+V).

4. Make sure the rulers are visible. If not, press Command+R (Win: Ctrl+R) to bring them up.

5. Drag guidelines out to form a small perfect square in the center of the canvas.

   To pull out a guide line, just move your cursor over to the ruler, click it, and drag into place. See Figure 9.22 for a guideline example. Now warp the tile into place.

6. Go to **Edit** > **Transform** > **Distort** to see the transform boundary with its eight handles.

7. Pull each node until the tiles look like they're lined up to your guides.

   Dragging within the transform boundary moves the selection; see Figure 9.23.

8. When you are happy with the shape, press Return (Win: Enter) to bake in (commit) the transformation.

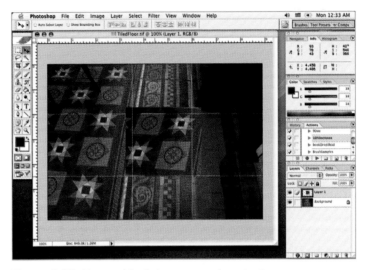

Figure 9.22 These guides help you warp the cutout.

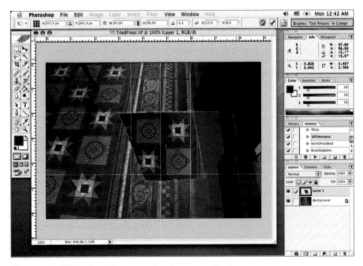

Figure 9.23 Align the cut selection to make it square.

Squaring Off the Tile

Now it's time to square off the tile.

1. Go to View and see if Snap is selected, as it is in Figure 9.24. If it isn't, click it to toggle it on.

2. Select the square marquee by pressing M or Shift+M to cycle through the marquee options until you reach the square marquee.

3. Select the excess flaps of image beyond the guidelines and press Delete.

   As you can see in Figure 9.25, a section of your tile is missing.

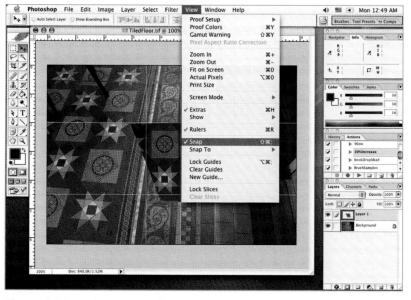

Figure 9.24 Having Snap on allows you to use your guides and makes it easier to trim accurately.

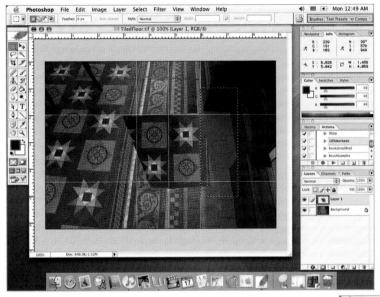

Figure 9.25 Delete the excess.

7. When you are done, press Return (Win: Enter) to commit the transformation.

8. Merge the two layers by clicking the top layer and pressing Command +E (Win: Ctrl+E).

   This is the same as going through the submenu and choosing Merge Down.

9. With your layers compacted, you can again trim away the excess using the Marquee tool.

4. Replace it by grabbing the missing area from the other star tile in your cutout.

5. Duplicate the layer by pressing Command+J (Win: Ctrl+J).

6. Click the lower layer and press Command+T (Win: Ctrl+T).

   You can now rotate, resize, and move the piece underneath until it lines up with the upper layer. See Figure 9.26.

Figure 9.26 Line up the image from underneath.

10. Zoom in really close with Command += (Win: Ctrl+=) to see the detail.

    With a pattern like this, I like to use the Clone brush to clean up.

11. Select the Clone brush by pressing S.

12. Set your source for the Clone by pressing Option (Win: Alt) and clicking the area from which you would like to pull. Brush away and check out Figure 9.27.

13. Make sure that everything for your tile is in one transparent layer—do not merge down to the background. You want the dimensions of the tile.

14. Select all by pressing Command+A (Win: Ctrl+A).

15. Copy by pressing Command+C (Win: Ctrl+C).

16. Create a new file by choosing **File > New**. The dimensions are automatically exactly the size of the tile you created. See Figure 9.28.

17. Name your new file.

18. If your tile isn't perfectly square, increase the smaller dimension to make it perfectly square and click OK.

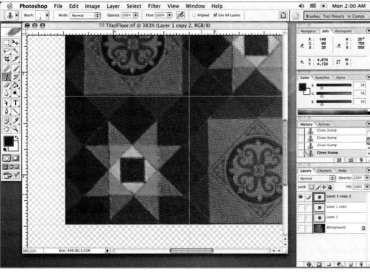

Figure 9.27 Clean up the tile.

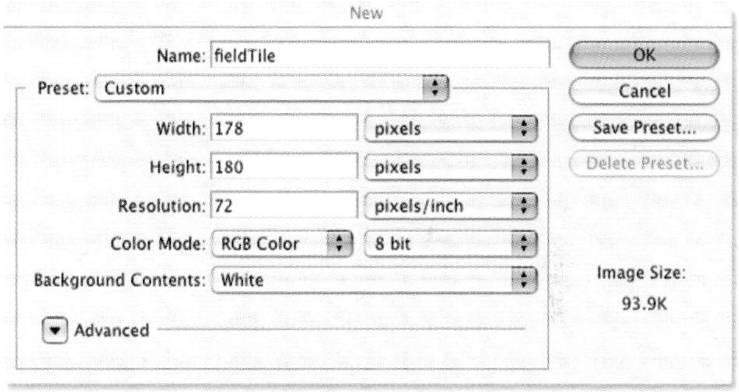

Figure 9.28 Create the file to hold the tile. My tile was 2 pixels off from being perfectly square, so I increased the width to 180.

19. In the new canvas, paste your tile in by pressing Command+V (Win: Ctrl+V).

    Upon pasting my tile in, I realized that my tile was still a little crooked, so I pressed Command+T (Win: Ctrl+T) to bring up the free transform controls and adjusted the tile to fit the canvas.

20. Flatten the canvas.

    Now you have a tile texture for your set extension. Use the same method for all the rest of the tile. Figure 9.29 shows the final canvas.

Figure 9.29 Your finished tile.

Notice that you did not need to do an off-set to create this tile. The reason should be obvious: You are making a tile of an actual floor tile. The borders do not need to blend between the tiles. That said, it is a good idea to just double check the tile with an offset to make sure there are no odd paint residue marks when the tile is repeated. Or, you could read the following section and turn your tile into a pattern to check how it looks laid out.

Patterns

You've made a tileable texture, a single image that you would give to a Lighter to place and use in a 3D environment. Customized patterns are related to this concept. You can save your tileable texture as a pattern to fill 2D areas with the Paint Bucket tool.

Making the Pattern

Take the tileable texture from the previous lesson and save it as a pattern.

1. Open fieldTile.tga (shown in Figure 9.30) if your tile is not still open.

2. Press Command+A (Win: Ctrl+A) to select the entire tile. You could also go to **Select** > **Select All** in the menu bar, if you prefer.

3. Go to **Edit** > **Define Pattern**.

Figure 9.30 Make this tile into a pattern.

4. Enter a name for the new pattern in the dialog box, as I've done in Figure 9.31.

5. Click the Paint Bucket tool, change the fill type to Pattern in the tool options bar, and look at the available patterns.

    Does the last one in Figure 9.32 look familiar? It should!

Figure 9.31 Photoshop doesn't exclude you from naming patterns with the same name. It does not overwrite.

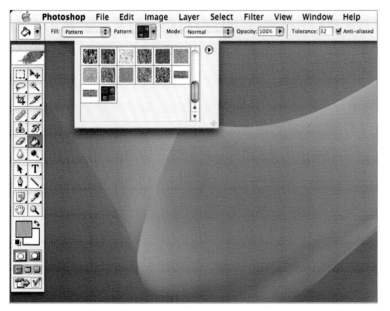

Figure 9.32 Your newest pattern is appended to the end of the pattern list.

Checking Out the Pattern

Check out how the pattern works.

1. Create a new file and make the dimensions completely square.

   In my case, I made mine 1024×1024.

2. Choose the Paint Bucket tool, making sure to switch the fill from Foreground to Pattern.

3. Apply by clicking the canvas; see Figure 9.33. That's the end of that!

Caution

Okay. I lied about that being the end of it. The pattern is there after you quit Photoshop—if your settings are set to remember your setup on closing. If you have to revert or reset, you lose your pattern forever unless you save it out to a pattern library. (You knew that was coming, didn't you?)

4. Click the Paint Bucket tool and have the fill set to Pattern.

5. Go to the Pattern submenu and choose Save Patterns, as shown in Figure 9.34.

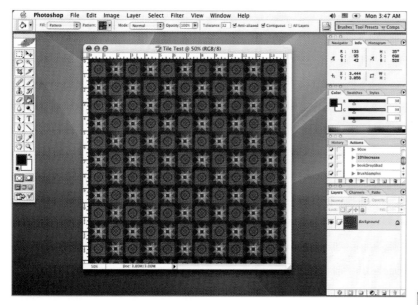

Figure 9.33 Your tile applied as a pattern.

6. Name your patterns. Remember: This saves all of the patterns as a set, not just the one pattern you created.

Enter droning, monotone language-lesson voice: This concludes your lesson on tiles and transformations. To continue, flip this page to side B….

Wait a minute! Didn't I say something at the beginning of the chapter about applying a transformation to a pattern for perspective? Ah, I'm glad someone is paying attention. You get a gold star sticker for that one!

Combining It All

Here is a quick example of how all this knowledge can be combined to make your life a bit easier. Say an art director gives the following plate, shown in Figure 9.35. She wants you to change the white plaster walls of the circled buildings to brick. Since you already made a tileable brick texture, you can use that same texture as a pattern to paint a brick wall onto these buildings!

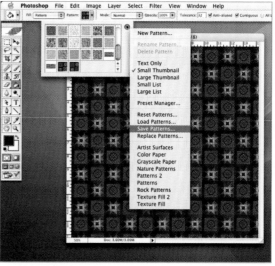

Figure 9.34 Saving all your patterns keeps you from pulling out all your hair in case you have to reset.

Figure 9.35 These two buildings need their walls changed to brick.

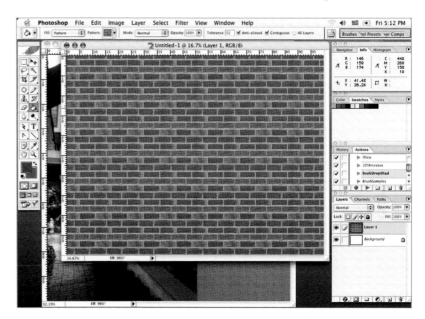

Figure 9.36 Creating a brick wallpaper to cover the plaster.

1. Open Background.tga, which you can download from this book's web site.

2. Create a new document that is 4000×3000 pixels by pressing Command+N (Win: Ctrl+N) and entering the dimensions in the dialog box.

3. Choose the Paint Bucket tool and change the fill type to Pattern.

4. Choose the Pattern pull-down menu and click the new canvas. which you see in Figure 9.36.

5. Choose the brick pattern and fill your new document with it.

6. Click-drag your new document to Background.tga.

   A new layer automatically forms for your brick texture.

7. Bring the opacity of the brick layer down so you can see the faint outline of the building you are trying to match.

8. Press Command+T (Win: Ctrl+T) and then Command+0 (Win: Ctrl+0) to see the handles for the brick's transformation.

9. Transform the layer to fit the near wall's perspective, as in Figure 9.37.

   Remember: Hold Command+Option +Shift (Win: Ctrl+Alt+Shift) to use the perspective transform. Go back to Table 9.1 if you forgot the free transform shortcuts.

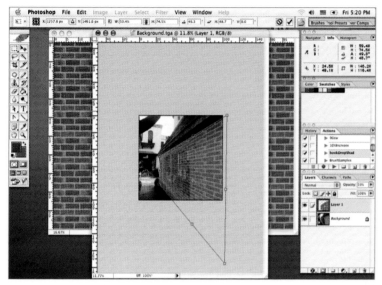

Figure 9.37 Adjusting the wallpaper to fit the perspective of the building.

12. Perform Steps 4–6 for the far building.

13. To maintain shadows and blend the texture into the wall, find a good combination of layer blend modes.

    In my case, I used a combination of Overlay and Darken. Take a look at the finished product in Figure 9.39!

10. Once you have the alignment set, press Return (win: Enter) to commit the transform. See Figure 9.38 for a look.

11. Erase the windows and the bush edges.

    Although you could use a combination of selections based on color, square marquees, and paths to cleanly erase the window and bush edges, I find it faster to do most of the work by hand with the Erase tool.

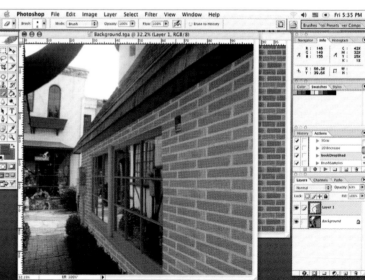

Figure 9.38 One building down, one to go.

Figure 9.39 The before and after!

CHAPTER 10

VARIATIONS

A common task for texture painters is to make variations of the same texture: Make five variations of wolves, six variations of plates, and so on. Sometimes this is used in a conceptual sense: Could you show me three variations and let me choose from them? This chapter covers some of the common tools used to create variations and the tools that help you stay organized through it all.

Snapshots

The Snapshot command is a little safety net that lets you make a temporary copy (or snapshot) of the composite image of your canvas. The new snapshot is listed at the top of the History palette, allowing you to use it with the History brush. More importantly, you can experiment with filters and other image processes, but revert to a snapshot, recovering your original state. Alternately, you can run several different tests, compare, and choose the snapshot you prefer.

Caution

Snapshots are not saved with the image, so you lose all your snapshots if you close your document.

Creating a Snapshot

Before you can fully realize the usefulness of snapshots, you must be able to create them. Luckily, creating a snapshot is, well, a snap!

1. Open your document. By default, your initial state is always saved as a snapshot.

2. Alter your image as you normally would.

3. Go to the History palette's drop-down menu and choose New Snapshot, as you see in Figure 10.1.

4. In the New Snapshot dialog box in Figure 10.2, give your snapshot a descriptive name.

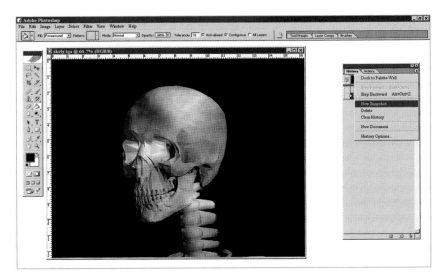

Figure 10.1 Creating a snapshot.

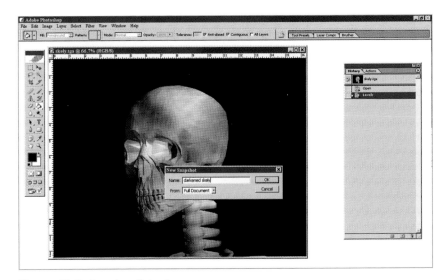

Figure 10.2 Snapshot dialog box.

5. Choose the source of its contents next. You have these choices for the snapshot's content sources:

- Full Document creates a snapshot of the composite of your document.

- Merged Layers creates a snapshot that merges all layers in the image at that state.

- Current Layer creates a snapshot of only the selected layer.

6. Click OK and continue to the next section.

Your snapshot is listed in order of creation in your History palette. To switch to your snapshot configuration, simply click the box next to the snapshot's name.

Tip

You may have noticed that when you selected a history state or snapshot from the middle of your list, the others below it dim. By default, when you select a state or snapshot and change the image, all that come after the selection are deleted. This way the History palette always displays your edits in order. If you choose to record in a nonlinear way, you can select a state or snapshot, make a change to the image, and delete just that state. The change is reflected at the end of the list.

Set a nonlinear history this way:

1. From the History palette menu, select History Options.

2. In the dialog box, make sure that Allow Non-Linear History is checked.

3. Click OK.

Using Snapshots with the History Brush

The History brush lets you paint a copy of one state or snapshot of an image into the current image window. This tool makes a copy, or *sample*, of the image and then paints with it. The limitation is that it can only paint from a snapshot to the same location on the canvas, which is actually a boon when you are trying to line things up perfectly or paint in an exact but limited area. To try using the History brush, open any file and follow these steps:

1. Open your document and apply an obvious filter to the image like the one in Figure 10.3.

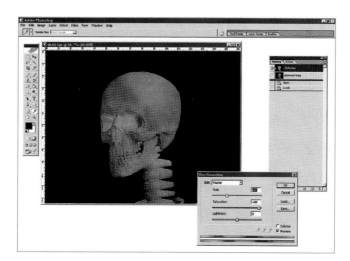

Figure 10.3 For this example, I chose to apply the Hue/Saturation filter.

2. Click the Create New Snapshot button on the bottom of your History palette.

   A new snapshot named Snapshot 1 is created.

3. Press Option+Z (Win: Ctrl+Z) to undo the filter.

4. Select the History Brush tool by choosing Y. Make sure the History Brush icon is clicked next to Snapshot 1, like in Figure 10.4.

5. Start painting the areas that you want to have the filter effect. Figure 10.5 is an example of my work.

As you can see in Figure 10.5, I have brushed into the eye area to bring in the glowing red I had created with the Hue/Saturation filter. This is a little more controllable than selecting the eyes and applying the filter to just that section, and it is easier to organize than a plethora of duplicated layers. The down side is that snapshots are lost upon closing the document. If working on an image that you know will take days to accomplish, you organize your file differently—most likely using layer comps.

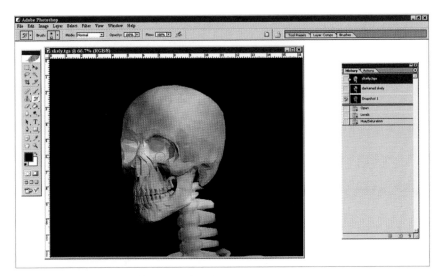

Figure 10.4 Setting up the History brush.

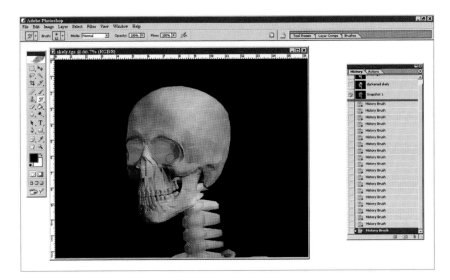

Figure 10.5 Fantastic, isn't it?

Layer Comps

This is a feature new to Photoshop CS. I used to watch in wonder at my much more organized officemates. (Nori, this means you.) They would have beautifully labeled layer sets, adjustment layers with descriptive names, and no problem recreating a session. I, whose idea of organized normally involves piles of some sort, had a hard time to say the least. But now—now!—I shall bask in the same organized glory of my officemates, as layer comps save me from my own vices.

You're probably a bit curious what exactly layer comps are. The Layer Comps feature records a layer's position and details in the Layers palette. A snapshot of the state of the Layers palette is taken and stored in its Layer Comps palette, complete with descriptions, editability, and exportability.

The best way to understand this, of course, is through example. I worked on a yellow cup. The Art Director wasn't quite sure of the color combinations that I used, so she asked me to create a green and orange cup variation for her to look at.

1. Make sure the Layer Comps palette is visible in the palette dock.

   If not, go to **Window** > **Layer Comps** to display the palette. For this tutorial, drag it out of the dock so that it is readily available. Figure 10.6 shows what this looks like.

2. Create the look you want for a color variation.

   I added a Hue/Sat adjustment layer (in Figure 10.7), but you could create your look by any means. Keep in mind, however, that the layer comp works by remembering the setup of your layers. If you simply paint green with a brush onto the same layer as your yellow cup, layer comps does not know the difference.

Figure 10.6 Drag out the Layer Comps palette.

3. When you have your desired look, click the New Layer Comp button to bring up the dialog box in Figure 10.8.

   The New Layer Comp dialog box asks you to name your layer comp, provides options, and even gives you a space for comments. If you add a comment, you see a triangle next to the layer comp name. Clicking the triangle expands the space and shows your comment.

4. Continue creating variations as I've done in Figure 10.9.

   You can add layers, use adjustment layers, and use layer effects. Photoshop remembers your configuration each time you save a layer comp.

You now have a few variations to show the Art Director. You could just click through the layer comps and show her at your desk, but wouldn't it be better to just send her each comp as a separate image? Read on to find out how you can automate this.

Figure 10.7 When you are ready to save a layer comp, you can either press the button or go to the Layer Comps palette menu and choose New Layer Comp.

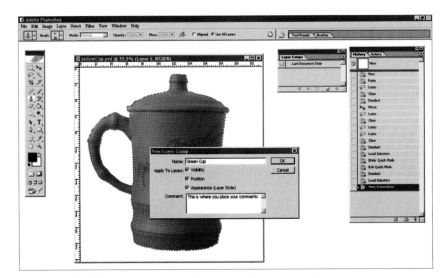

Figure 10.8 The New Layer Comp dialog box offers many options.

Caution

If you do anything that jeopardizes Photoshop's ability to recreate the layer comp, such as deleting a layer, you get an alarm icon next to each comp that cannot be restored without that layer. Supposedly, Photoshop gives a warning if you try to rotate, crop, or resize, but I did not receive any warning or errors when I took such actions on my iBook. Should you receive an alarm icon, but decide that you want to get rid of the icon and not the Layer comp, do the following: Right-click (Windows) or Control+click (Mac OS) the caution icon to see the pop-up menu that lets you choose either the Clear Layer Comp Warning or the Clear All Layer Comp Warnings command.

Figure 10.9 Create a few variations and save their configurations.

Saving Out a Layer Comp as a File

Now comes a very cool addition to using the Layer Comp function: Saving out each comp in its own file. Consider some things before you do this:

- If you want to save out only a few comps, Command+select (Win: Ctrl+select) them *before* going to the Scripts option.

- If you had a very long comment on any of the comps, you might want to reduce the comments, as the names have the layer comp name and as much of the comments as can fit.

Now onto the steps:

1. Go to **File** > **Scripts** > **Layer Comps to Files** to bring up the Layer Comps to Files dialog box shown in Figure 10.10.

2. Choose a destination and a prefix name for your file.

3. Indicate whether you want to save only selected layer comps. Choose the file type and any compression or compatibility options associated with your file type.

4. Click Run and Photoshop saves a copy of each layer comp to its own file.

   When this is finished, you receive a completion successful dialog box. Pretty nifty, eh?

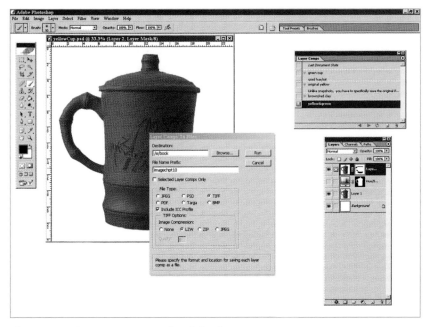

Figure 10.10 Layer Comps to Files dialog box.

Color Variations

Snapshots and layer comps are fine and dandy as organizational tools, but how exactly should you create some of these variations? There are many ways to go about creating color variations, and not all are created equal.

Color Match

Color Match is a feature added with Photoshop CS. The concept is simple: Photoshop looks at the values in a selected area and adjusts another selected area to have the same color range. In reality, I've found that this works better on fairly monochromatic images (such as a lunar landscape) and for bringing a particular area to match a selected color, but doesn't quite work for most other scenarios. Nonetheless, it is a powerful tool that is worth mentioning.

Take a look at Figure 10.11. Assume a scenario where the Art Director would like this image of a door built into a hill to have a ground color that matches three different ground pictures. You could try to color sample or eye it, but this is the type of scenario that Color Match is perfect for.

1. Press L to select the Lasso tool and draw around the ground area you would like to affect.

   You can press Shift and drag to add sections to your selection or press Option (Win: Alt) to select areas to trim away from your selection. If you don't make a selection, Match Color affects the entire layer. Figure 10.12 shows your image with the ground area selected.

Figure 10.11 Change the ground of this image to color match the three sample colors.

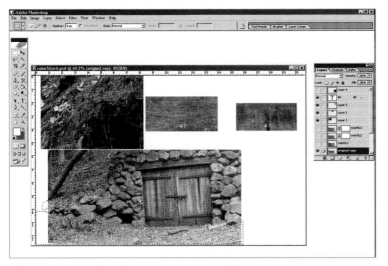

Figure 10.12 Select the area you want to affect.

2. Make sure you are on the layer that you want to affect and go to **Image > Adjustments > Match Color**.

3. In the Match Color dialog box, go to the Image Statistics area and choose the source file from the pull-down menu.

   The Layer menu becomes active (is no longer grayed out). The Match Color dialog box appears in Figure 10.13.

4. Choose Layer 1, the first ground color image that you are trying to match.

5. Go to the Destination Image area. Make sure the Ignore Selection When Applying Adjustment option is *deselected*. You want the match color to apply only to your selected area.

Figure 10.13 The Match Color dialog box.

6. Go to the Image Statistics area and make sure to follow these settings:

   ▪ Use Selection in Source to Calculate Colors: Not selected. (You use the Layer 1 in its entirety as the source.)

   ▪ Use Selection in Target to Calculate Adjustment: Selected.

   You see your canvas update in real time. You can adjust the look of the results with the three sliders available and see simultaneously how it affects your image. The Luminance slider increases the Brightness. Shifting the Color Intensity slider saturates or desaturates the colors, and moving it to its minimum value of 1 results in a grayscale image. Fade blends in some of the original unadjusted image to make the effect more subtle.

7. Once you have a look that appeals to you, click OK.

8. Take a snapshot of your result and press Command+Z (Win: Ctrl+Z) to revert to your original image.

9. Repeat Steps 2–8 and choose layer
   2 this time. Repeat Steps 2–8 again
   and choose layer 3.

   Figure 10.14 shows your three
   variations that match your
   reference images!

Figure 10.14 Your original and three variations.

Beware Variations and Brightness/Contrast

One of the features of Photoshop that I see used often is Variations. Back *away* from the keyboard…*slowly*…. Although anyone can mess up an image with just about any function, Variations is one of two features that you should stay away from. Figure 10.15 shows the offending feature's dialog box.

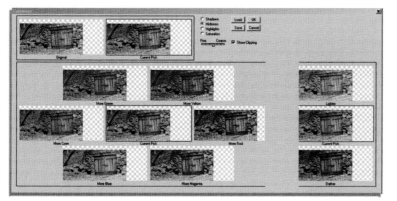

Figure 10.15 The Variations dialog box.

At first glance, the variations adjustment function seems like a good idea—a visual method of color correcting. There is one central image and you choose whether to work on the highlights, midtones, or shadows by adding any combination of green, yellow, cyan, red, blue, or magenta.

The main problem is that you have no way of finding out what exactly was done and no way to truly control it. For example, if you are working in an RGB space and add cyan to your shadows, what values are being considered shadows and what mix of RGB is cyan? In addition, all of its changes are linear, so your image tends to flatten out with too much adjusting. What's worse is that there is nothing tracking your changes; no numerical slider or other input device can help bring back a neutral, unadjusted state. Did you add cyan to the highlights or to the midtones? And how many times did you click to add cyan, three or five? It takes more than a concentration whiz to keep track of the changes and replicate them. The last little jab with Variations is that there is no way to zoom in and see details. The little thumbnails may look great, but once you click OK and see the result in full resolution, you may be in for a big surprise.

If you insist on using the Variations feature, then use it as a form of visualization, cancel out, and make the corresponding changes in Curves and Hue/Sat.

What's wrong with Brightness/Contrast? Nothing if all you need to do is to nudge the entire histogram over a bit for a final correction. The way people generally try to use Brightness/Contrast results in losing valuable tonal information; see Figure 10.16. The function makes linear adjustments and often forces some pixel data off the chart—an irrevocable loss. Brightness/Contrast shifts the histogram to the left or right for brightness, and linearly expands or contracts the histogram shape for contrast. The main point is that these adjustments don't change the *relationship* between the values; they only shift them to a different location. Proper tonal correction involves changing the relationship between the different tones in the image.

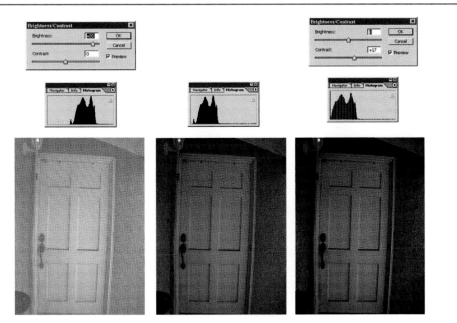

Figure 10.16 Notice how the Brightness/Contrast feature affects the histogram.

For brightness and contrast issues, it is better to use levels and curves. Not only do they give better control, but both allow for saving and loading adjustment value sets. Notice how the histogram in Figure 10.17 shows the loss of data involved with the brightness adjustment.

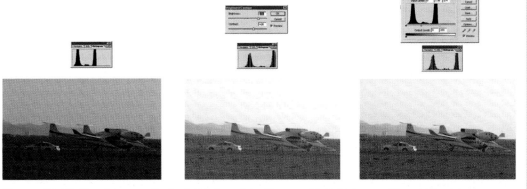

Figure 10.17 The picture on the far left is the original image with its histogram. The middle picture uses Brightness to brighten the image and the picture on the far right uses Levels to bring brightness to the picture.

Adjustment Layers

Several adjustment layers can create variations of color and tone. The draw of adjustment layers is that the original image is not touched and can be fully reverted to with no loss of data. What this means is that the effects can be reversed or tweaked and you can zoom in tightly to see the details of your changes.

The only questionable adjustment layer is Brightness/Contrast. This is an overused adjustment tool. With simple sliders that set the brightness or contrast between 100 and −100, most people think they are increasing the brightness or contrast by a percentage. This is not the case, and there are other reasons this adjustment tool should only be used rarely, if at all. Read the "Beware Variations and Brightness/Contrast" sidebar for why this is mostly a no-no.

Your mission, should you choose to accept it, is to create 15 variations for the Director before he comes by in 15 minutes. (Figure 10.18 shows your original.) Given that Hollywood is notorious for being fashionably late, you may have a few minutes more—but don't count on it. This is to be a solo mission, with the adjustment layers as your main tools. This book will not self-destruct, but if you don't get the variations done, *you* might.

Without further ado….

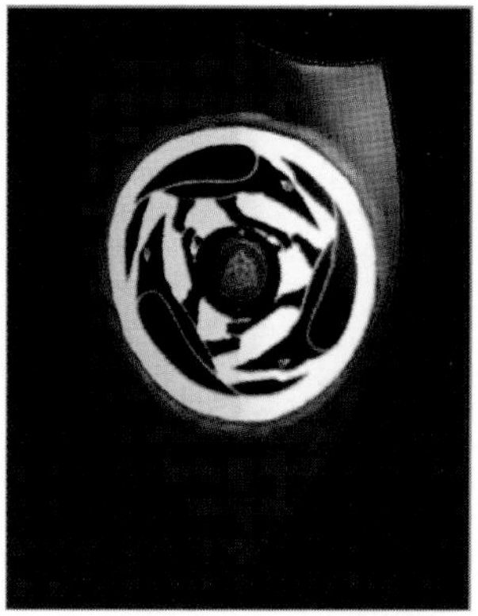

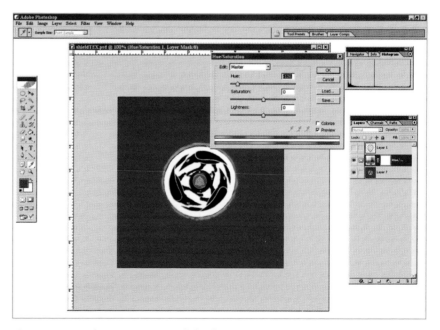

Figure 10.18 Your mission is to create 15 variations of this object.

1. Open your texture file and go to **Layer Menu** > **New Adjustment Layer** > **Hue/Saturation**. Figure 10.19 shows the Hue/Saturation dialog box

2. Reduce the saturation, slide the hue over a bit, and click OK.

3. Go to your Layer Comps palette in the palette well and save a layer comp.

4. Double-click your Hue/Sat adjustment layer to bring up the dialog box.

Figure 10.19 The Hue/Saturation dialog box.

5. Readjust the sliders, click OK, and save a new layer comp. Do this two more times to create four variations (with 13 minutes to go). See Figure 10.20.

6. Hide your Hue/Sat adjustment layer and apply a new adjustment layer. This time choose Selective Color.

7. Play with the sliders on a few colors and save layer comps for three more variations.

   You now have seven color variations (see Figure 10.21) and 10 minutes to go.

8. On top of all your layers, add a Channel Mixer Adjustment layer.

9. Select the Monochrome check box at the bottom and create a nice-looking grayscale for use as a bump map.

10. Click OK and make a layer comp of your bump map.

11. Click a layer comp that has a different contrast ratio than the image you used to make your first bump map.

12. Click the Eye icon next to the Channel Mixer layer and apply the adjustment to this other image. See Figure 10.22.

13. Make another layer comp and call it **bump map 2**.

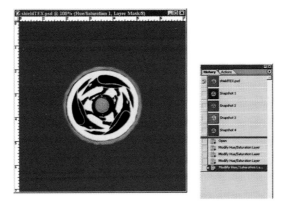

Figure 10.20 Four color variations were created and saved as layer comps.

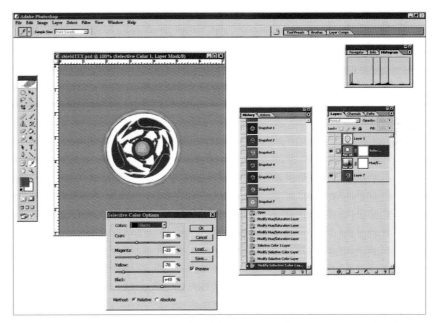

Figure 10.21 In five minutes you already have seven color variations saved in the Layer Comps palette!

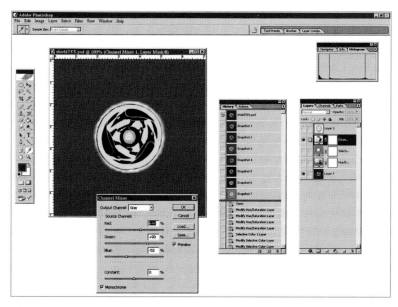

Figure 10.22 The Channel Mixer gives you two bump maps.

17. While on an active layer in the Layers palette, press Command+Shift+C (Win: Ctrl+Shift+C) to create a copy of your visible layers.

18. Go to the top layer of the Layers palette and press Command+V (Win: Ctrl+V) to put the copy of the image on a new layer.

19. Choose another layer comp that has colors complementary to the image you just pasted.

    Photoshop hides your newly created layer and shows the layer comp you selected.

20. Click the top layer, which has the copy of the previously chosen image, and click the Add Layer Mask button.

14. Create a new layer at the top of your layers and paint with a 50 percent gray brush to erase some of the bumps from the bump map. See Figure 10.23.

15. Save this as another layer comp. You now have seven colors variations, three bump variations, and seven minutes to go.

16. Choose a color variation layer comp.

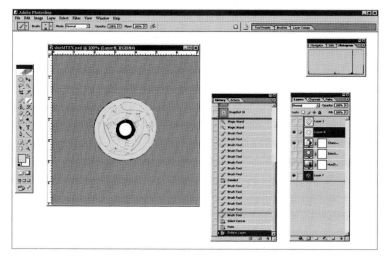

Figure 10.23 A few quick strokes of the brush give you your third bump map.

21. Making sure that you have the layer mask selected, use a black brush to reveal the underlying layers and create a combination color map like the one in Figure 10.24.

22. When you like your result, save a layer comp of it.

23. Create a new layer at the top of all your layers by pressing the New Layer button; press G to get to the Paint Bucket tool.

24. Fill the layer with the color of your choice.

25. Go to **Filter > Noise > Add Noise** and add some subtle noise.

26. Save this as another layer comp for a total of nine color variations and three bump variations.

27. Go to **File > Scripts > Layer Comps to Files** and save out your layer comps in the file format of your choice.

    Although you have enough maps to create more than 15 variations, you can also open your maps and layer one over another with a different layer blend mode and save it as another variation.

Take a look at Figure 10.25 for the 15 variation renders I created. Mission accomplished!

Figure 10.24 Use two color variations to create a third.

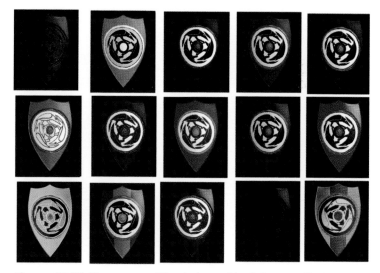

Figure 10.25 These are my 15 variations, with all the maps (both color and bump) created in 15 minutes!

CHAPTER 11

AUTOMATING
TASKS

I'm lazy. I admit it. I am a strong believer in laziness; it fuels inventiveness and creates wonderful tools such as Photoshop's Actions palette. Why reinvent the wheel each time you deal with some type of image processing? If the steps do not involve brush-strokes or necessitate eyeing something, you can probably create an action for it.

The Actions Palette

By default, the Actions palette is in List mode. By going into the palette's submenu, you can change this to Button mode, which turns each action into a button, but doesn't give you the option of tweaking the actions. See Figure 11.1 for a look at Button mode.

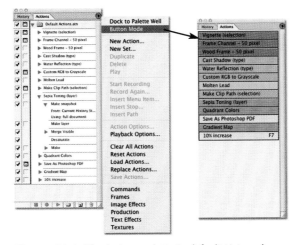

Figure 11.1 The Actions palette in default List mode and Button mode.

Defining an Action

What's an *action*? It is a set of instructions that repeats in a particular order. I had to create a few rocks for the movie *The Rundown* that needed the same treatment done to each texture map. I created an action and simply batch processed them.

How do you use these actions? More importantly, how do you make your own customized actions? And what is batch processing, anyway? Patience, young grasshopper. When you can make this paper look like rice paper, then you will be ready. Okay, enough *Kung Fu* references.

Using an Action

First you need to know what the action does. You can get an idea by looking at the Actions palette in List mode (shown in Figure 11.2) and expanding each of the action's steps. To do that, click the triangle next to the action itself and then each step.

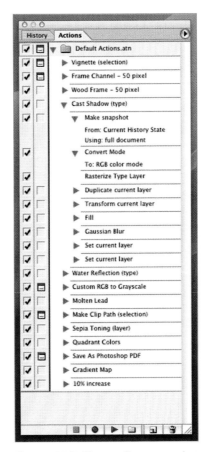

Figure 11.2 You can figure out what an action does by expanding each step.

Personally, I like to just press play and see what happens. I use two examples.

1. Open an image like the one in Figure 11.3.

2. Now try one of the default actions. Click the Wood Frame action and click the Play selection button at the bottom of the Actions palette, like I've done in Figure 11.4.

3. A dialog box like that in Figure 11.5 warns that the image dimensions must be at least 100 pixels high and 100 pixels wide. Click Continue.

Photoshop goes through the series of steps, and Voilá! You can see the results in Figure 11.6.

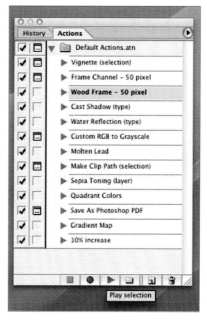

Figure 11.4 Apply an action to find out what it is

Figure 11.3 Use a copy of an image to test actions.

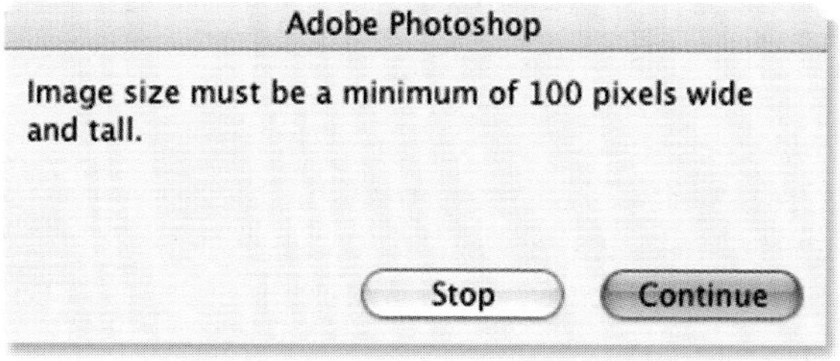

Figure 11.5 A warning embedded into the wood frame action.

Figure 11.6 The results of applying the wood frame action to the cuttlefish image.

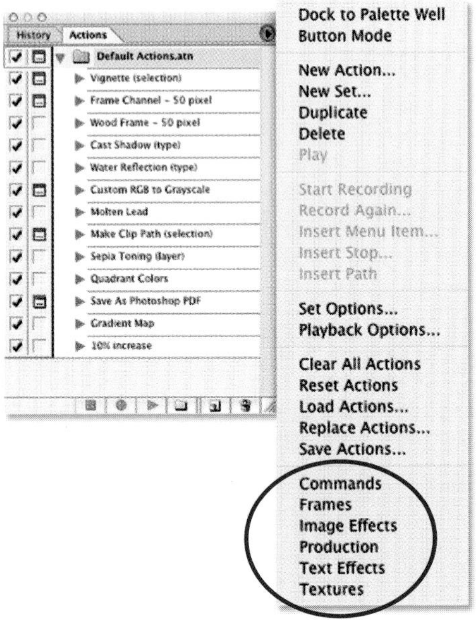

Figure 11.7 There are more action presets available and you can add your own, too.

Other Action Presets

Adobe provides you with additional action sets beyond the default actions. To load the other action sets, click the Actions palette's menu (triangle) button. You see the other presets at the bottom of the menu in Figure 11.7.

If you had created and saved your own action sets to the Photoshop Actions folder, they would show up at the bottom of this menu, too. Should you need to load a set that's saved elsewhere, use the Load Actions command in the palette menu. A Load dialog box in which you can locate and load your presets appears.

Creating Actions

Now, of course, you want to know how to make your own actions and presets. Well young grasshopper, here you go:

1. Start by making a new set. Go to the Actions palette's palette menu and select New Set. See Figure 11.8.

2. In the New Set dialog box, give your new set a new name. I called the new set MyPresets, which you can see in Figure 11.9, but you can call yours Bob if you want.

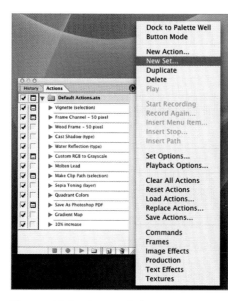

Figure 11.8 It's a good idea to create a new set to hold your created actions separately from the default actions.

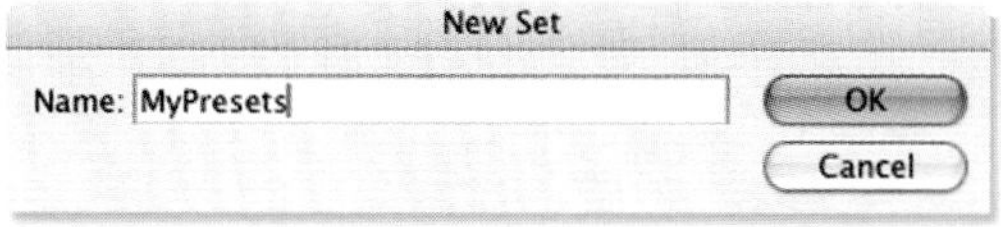

New Set

Name: MyPresets

OK

Cancel

Figure 11.9 Give your new set a name that makes sense to you.

Figure 11.10 By default, your new set comes in on the bottom, but you can click and drag it up to the top.

3. Once you click OK, your new set is located at the bottom of the Actions palette. See Figure 11.10.

4. Add an action to your set.

   As an example, make one that reduces the image to 50 percent of its size and then converts it to grayscale.

5. Open the same image you used before; go to the Actions palette's menu, and choose New Action. See Figure 11.11.

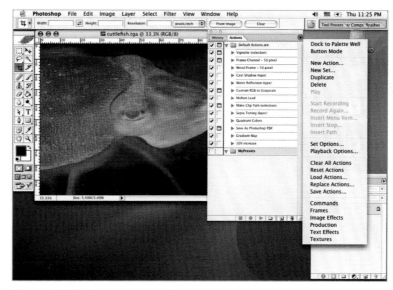

Figure 11.11 Create a new action.

6. In the New Action dialog box, name your action and make sure it's going to your new set.

   You can create a hotkey for this action by assigning a function key to it. The color helps you visually organize all your presets, so choose a color if you wish. Green is shown in Figure 11.12.

7. Click Record and you're ready to roll.

   From this point on, Photoshop records your actions until you tell it to stop recording. I go through a few example steps so you can get a feel for how it works.

8. It's recording, so go to **Image** > **Image Size**.

9. In the dialog box shown in Figure 11.13, change the units from pixels to percent. Enter 50 percent and click OK.

10. Go to **Image** > **Adjustments** > **Desaturate**, like you see in Figure 11.14.

11. Stop recording by clicking the stop button at the bottom of the Actions palette. You can see the button in Figure 11.15

Now you have your new action listed in your new set. If you change to Button mode, you see that the button for your new action is the color that you selected. Check out Figure 11.16 for the color coding.

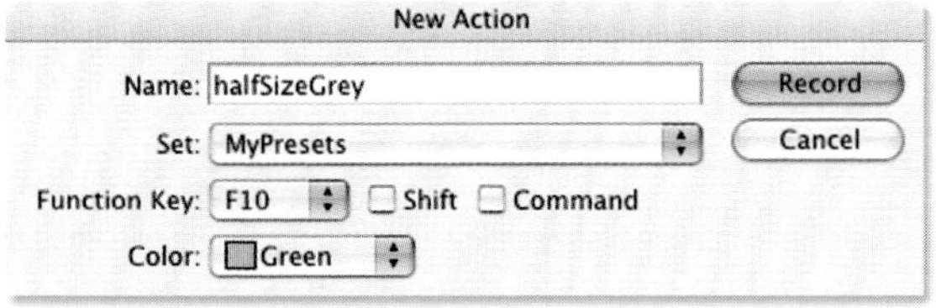

Figure 11.12 You can assign a function key keyboard shortcut and a color code to your new action.

Caution

Any shortcut you assign overrides any default assignment, and there is no warning letting you know if you are reassigning a key. The only hint is that Photoshop tries to avoid your assignment and modifies it with a Shift+ or Command+. It does not warn you if you deselect these options and overwrite another hotkey.

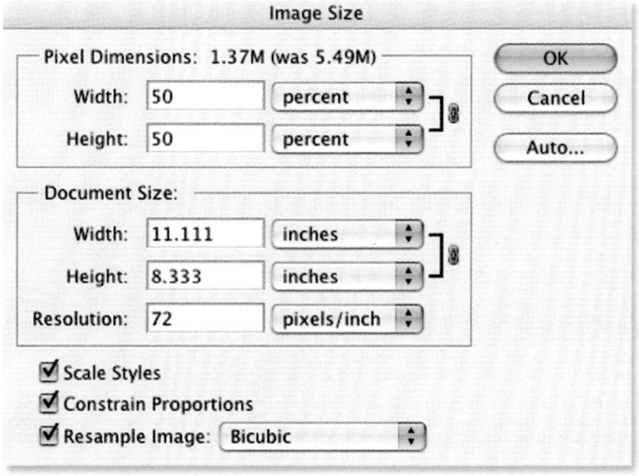

Figure 11.13 You have your action resize the image to half.

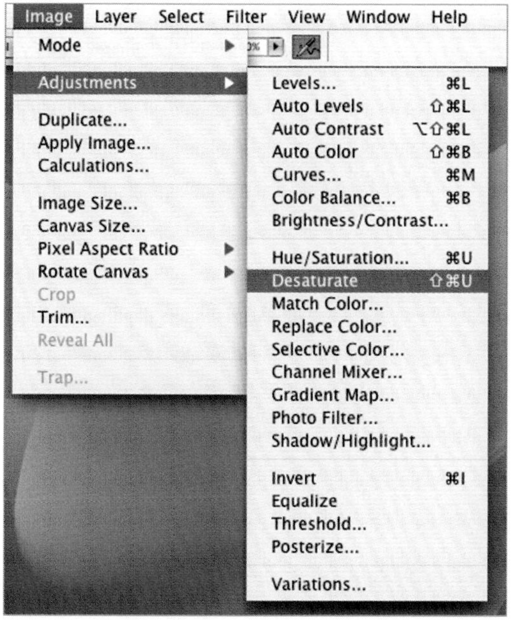

Image
Layer
Select
Filter
View
Window
Help
Mode
Adjustments
Duplicate...
Apply Image...
Calculations...
Image Size...
Canvas Size...
Pixel Aspect Ratio
Rotate Canvas
Crop
Trim...
Reveal All
Trap...
Levels... ⌘L
Auto Levels ⇧⌘L
Auto Contrast ⌥⇧⌘L
Auto Color ⇧⌘B
Curves... ⌘M
Color Balance... ⌘B
Brightness/Contrast...
Hue/Saturation... ⌘U
Desaturate ⇧⌘U
Match Color...
Replace Color...
Selective Color...
Channel Mixer...
Gradient Map...
Photo Filter...
Shadow/Highlight...
Invert ⌘I
Equalize
Threshold...
Posterize...
Variations...

Figure 11.14 An action can have many different steps. I am making the image grayscale.

History
Actions
Default Actions.atn
Vignette (selection)
Frame Channel - 50 pixel
Wood Frame - 50 pixel
Cast Shadow (type)
Water Reflection (type)
Custom RGB to Grayscale
Molten Lead
Make Clip Path (selection)
Sepia Toning (layer)
Quadrant Colors
Save As Photoshop PDF
Gradient Map
10% increase
MyPresets
halfSizeGrey
Image Size
Desaturate
Stop playing/recording

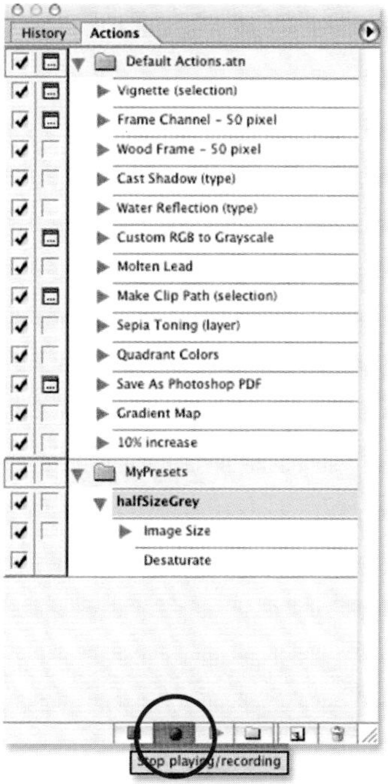

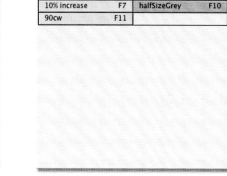

Figure 11.15 To finish recording, just click the stop button.

History
Actions
Vignette (selection)
Frame Channel - 50 p...
Wood Frame - 50 pixel
Cast Shadow (type)
Water Reflection (type)
Custom RGB to Graysc...
Molten Lead
Make Clip Path (select...
Sepia Toning (layer)
Quadrant Colors
Save As Photoshop PDF
Gradient Map
10% increase F7
halfSizeGrey F10
90cw F11

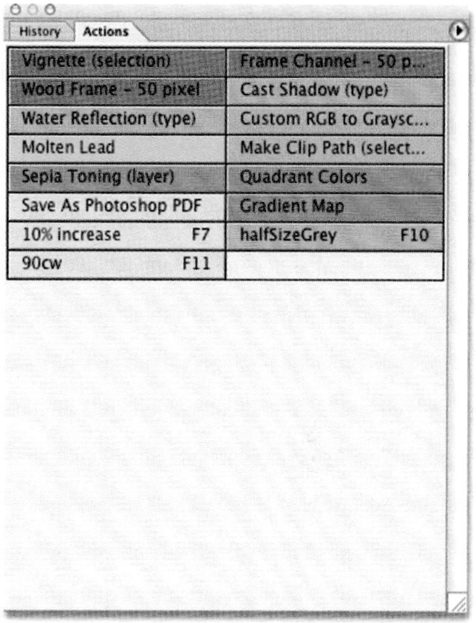

Figure 11.16 The color code you selected for your action only shows in Button mode, but this is a good way to organize your actions.

Why not change the mode to grayscale?

You may have noticed grayscale as a mode under the **Image > Mode** menu. I recommend against this; color management deals with grayscale modes and RGB modes differently. Transfer between programs, conversion to other formats, and implementation in 3D can be affected by this "simple" mode change. Unless you are working in pipelines that specifically address using the grayscale mode in their color management, stick to RGB. Advanced texture artists actually take advantage of using the RGB mode by putting a grayscale matte into each of the channels, thereby getting three mattes into the space of one!

Editing or Changing an Action

So many editing options make it easy to fine-tune any action—an action created by you or anyone else. First make sure you have your Actions palette in List mode. Then you can implement changes the following ways:

- Holding down the Option key (Win: Alt) while double-clicking an action brings up the dialog box where you can change the name, function key, and color. (This option is also available via the palette pop-up menu.)

- You can move any part of an action to another part of an action by clicking and dragging it wherever you want it. If you want to copy a step in the current action or another action, hold down the Option key (Win: Alt key), then click and drag it.

- To add steps anywhere within the action, simply click the step after which you want your new steps, click record, perform the steps you wish to add, and click stop when you are done. The new steps stay within the action where you placed them.

- Don't like a step within an action? Simply drag the step to the trash, or highlight the step and click on the Trash button.

- Like your action but want to change some of the values? Highlight the action and use the Record Again feature. The Record Again feature, which is in the Actions palette menu, runs through each step, pausing at each dialog box so you can tweak values. Figure 11.17 shows this feature.

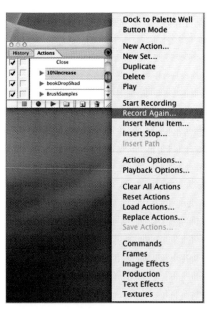

Figure 11.17 You can change input values for an existing action with Record Again.

Saving Your Set

You have these wonderful actions all under your new set. Then your brother comes by and reinstalls Adobe Photoshop. Guess what? It's all gone. Yup. Lost forever. You just have to start over.

Caution

Before you go too far, make sure to save your set. This allows you (or anyone you decide to give it to) to load the set—and it doesn't even take up much time.

1. Select the name of the set and choose Save Actions from the palette pop-up menu, shown in Figure 11.18.

2. Save the set in the Photoshop Actions folder if you want it to appear on the Actions palette menu. See Figure 11.19.

   However, you can save it anywhere as long as you remember where it is! Simple, isn't it?

Note

Adobe Photoshop remembers your newly created sets and actions, even if you do not specifically save them. The actions are there next time you open Photoshop. However, if you reinstall Photoshop without saving your new set of actions, you lose them.

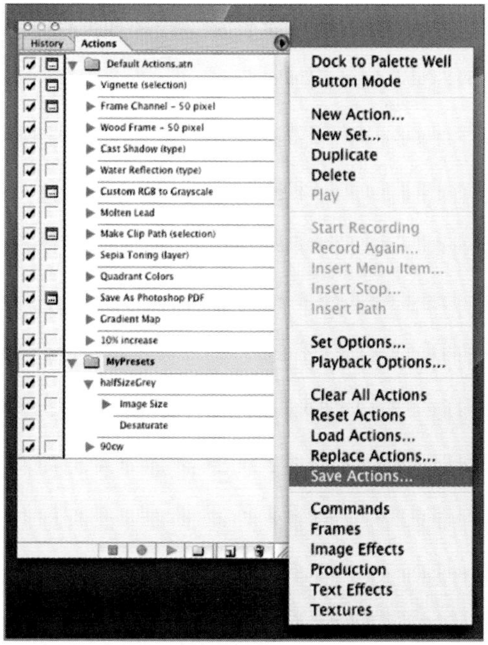

Figure 11.18 Saving your set can save you a lot of grief down the road.

Figure 11.19 Saving your action set to the Photoshop Actions folder makes access much easier.

Batch Processing

The texture artists working on the hell-hound for the *Chronicles of Riddick* had to deal with 400 scale textures! Luckily, Photoshop has *batch processing*. That is, Photoshop runs an action on a whole bunch of files for you. Go through this with me, using the example action just created.

1. Create a folder somewhere and copy a bunch of images into it.

   I created a folder on my desktop called batchSource. Personally, I like to have a destination folder so the originals in the source folder aren't overwritten. I've created one called batchResults, which you can see in Figure 11.20.

2. Go to **File** > **Automate** > **Batch**, as I've done in Figure 11.21.

Figure 11.20 Set up your source and results folders before beginning batching.

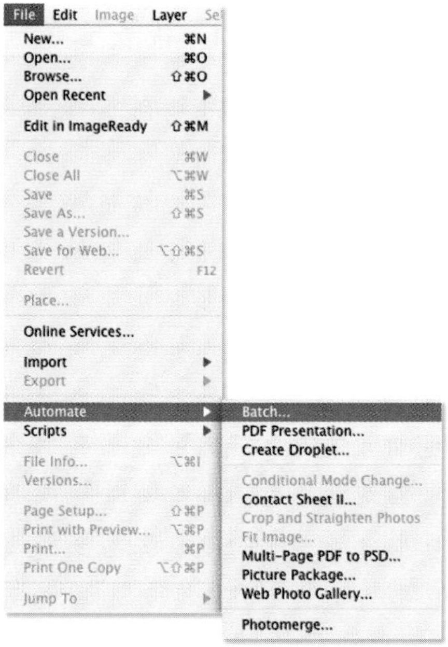

File   Edit   Image   Layer   Se

New...	⌘N
Open...	⌘O
Browse...	⇧⌘O
Open Recent	▶
Edit in ImageReady	⇧⌘M
Close	⌘W
Close All	⌥⌘W
Save	⌘S
Save As...	⇧⌘S
Save a Version...	
Save for Web...	⌥⇧⌘S
Revert	F12
Place...	
Online Services...	
Import	▶
Export	▶
Automate	▶
Scripts	▶
File Info...	⌥⌘I
Versions...	
Page Setup...	⇧⌘P
Print with Preview...	⌥⌘P
Print...	⌘P
Print One Copy	⌥⇧⌘P
Jump To	▶

Automate submenu:
- Batch...
- PDF Presentation...
- Create Droplet...
- Conditional Mode Change...
- Contact Sheet II...
- Crop and Straighten Photos
- Fit Image...
- Multi-Page PDF to PSD...
- Picture Package...
- Web Photo Gallery...
- Photomerge...

Figure 11.21 Start the batch process.

3. In the Batch dialog box, make sure you have selected your actions Set and the Action you want performed.

4. Under Source, select Folder. Use the Choose button to select your source folder. You can see these options in Figure 11.22.

5. Select any of the options that pertain to the action you are batching:

   ▪ Override Action Open Commands. If your action has an Open command, select this so the action processes the chosen images rather than the originally programmed images.

   ▪ Include All Subfolders. If you want to process folders within folders, select this option.

   ▪ Suppress File Open Options Dialogs. Select this option to have Photoshop ignore any opening dialog boxes.

   ▪ Suppress Color Profile Warnings. Select this if you want Photoshop to use its default color profile rather than any embedded color profile when running the batch process.

6. Under Destination, select Folder. Use Choose to select your destination folder.

   Should your action contain a Save As command, select the Override Action Save As Commands option. Once this is selected, you can use the boxes in the File Naming area to name the processed files. Since your action doesn't have a Save As command, the files are saved with the same name to the Batch Results folder that you created.

7. Click OK and watch the show!

Note

You cannot suppress a saving dialog box, so if you're saving as a JPG, the batch waits for you to set and okay the JPG dialog box. Since JPG is a *lossy* format (which means information is lost in compression each time is the file's saved), I recommend *against* saving any master files as JPG. That way you won't have to worry about having a semiautomatic batch process.

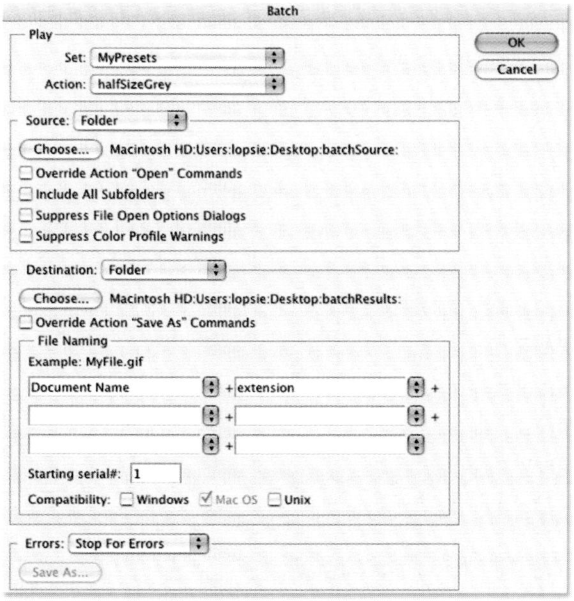

Figure 11.22 The Batch dialog box.

Figure 11.23 Any existing action can become a droplet.

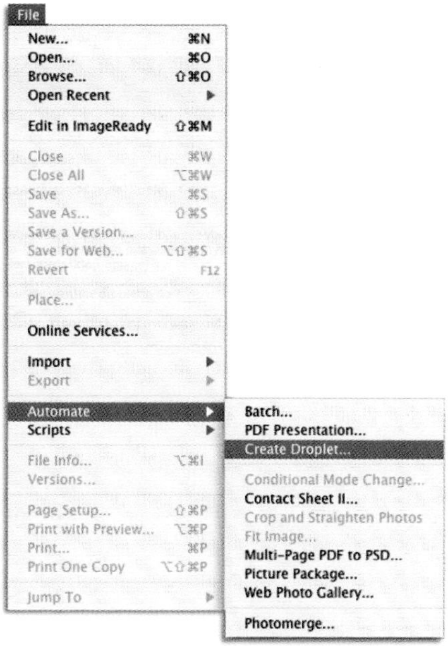

Creating a Droplet

Introduced in Photoshop 6, *droplets* are standalone *macros*, or mini-applications, that you can put anywhere (on the desktop or in a folder) and just drag and drop files onto (hence *droplet*). Standalone may be a bit misleading, because you still must have Photoshop on the computer on which the droplet is located, since it accesses Photoshop to complete its actions. Think of it more as a shortcut to a prerecorded action. The only complaint I would make about droplets is that I wish they didn't have to open the Photoshop GUI when activated. It defeats the purpose a bit.

I have a lot of photos that were taken horizontally, so I want to create a droplet to quickly turn those images. I already have an action that does this, called 90CW, but now I want a droplet that I can just drag and drop my files onto. See Figure 11.23.

1. Go to **File** > **Automate** > **Create Droplet**, as I've done in Figure 11.24.

Figure 11.24 Creating a droplet.

2. Take a look at the options in the Create Droplet dialog box; they're shown in Figure 11.25. Adjust as fits your circumstance and needs.

- **Save Droplet In.** This asks where you would like to save the droplet. You would click on the Choose button and navigate to the location of your choice. It doesn't matter where the droplet is saved to, since you can just move it anywhere that's convenient for you. I want to just save it to my desktop, so I click Choose and navigate to my desktop.

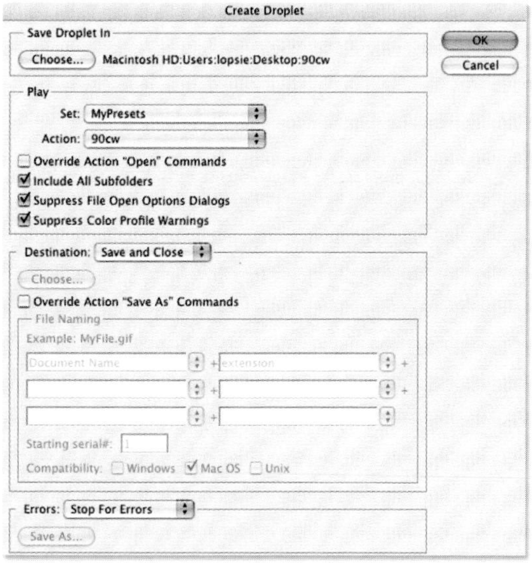

Figure 11.25 Droplet options.

- **Play.** Select the set that contains your action and choose the action for your droplet. In this case, go to MyPresets and use the 90CW action.

The next few options are for specific circumstances. If you are creating a droplet that you know you will use with folders of images, select Include All Subfolders. Take a look at the following options and see if they apply to your circumstance.

- **Override Action Open Commands.** Select this option if your action specifically calls out to open and work on a file in a specific folder. This way the action works on the files you're putting onto the droplet instead of just going to the specified folder. Since my action does not have an Open command, I won't select this option.

- **Include All Subfolders.** This option allows the droplet to process any subfolders that might be within a folder that I drop on it. I know that with the pipeline I work in this is a desirable trait for this droplet, so I select it.

- **Suppress File Open Options Dialogs.** A new option added in Photoshop CS, this option has Photoshop disregard any opening dialog box.

- **Suppress Color Profile Warnings.** If the color profile of the image being processed isn't the same as Photoshop's default profile, then a dialog box asks what it should do. Should you decide to suppress these warnings, Photoshop foregoes asking and uses its default color profile.

Note

If you have any other open commands, like opening a file to use as a matte, Override Action Open Commands negates that command.

3. Review the rest of the options in the dialog box:

- **Destination.** Options include None, Save and Close, and Folder. Destination lets you choose where your processed images will be saved. Most of the time I recommend that you save it all to a new folder to avoid overwriting the originals. But in this case, I want to chose Save and Close, since I'm just rotating the image. If my action had included a specific Save command, I would have selected Override Action Save As Commands so I could also add frame numbers or file extensions.

- **Errors.** Options include Stop for Errors or Log Errors to File. This setting choice comes down to what you consider more bothersome. If you like to have everything set to go and leave your desk, you should probably have errors go to a log file; that way all other images get processed. If you don't want the process to continue if there's an error, choose to stop for errors.

4. When everything is done, click OK. You should get a small icon that looks like Figure 11.26.

To use it, just drop a file or folder onto the icon; it performs the processes you set up for it.

Figure 11.26 You can move this newly created droplet anywhere within your computer and drop files onto it to process.

Cross-Platform Compatibility

One of the great things about a droplet is that it's cross-platform compatible. You can create your droplet on a Windows machine and share it with someone on a Macintosh, and vice versa. Of course, there's a bit of fine print here (beyond my earlier mention about having Photoshop installed).

- If your droplet was created in MacOS, you must append .exe, the executable file indicator, to its name for it to work on a Windows machine.

- If your droplet was created on Windows, drag and drop it onto the Photoshop icon once it's on a Mac. This updates and recognizes the droplet.

In both cases, once you have made it recognizable, the icon changes from an unidentified system file icon to the droplet icon, as shown in Figure 11.26.

Note

You don't need the same action set or even the action itself saved on each machine the droplet is on. It is self-sustaining in that sense.

PART THREE

MATTE PAINTINGS

CHAPTER 12

MATTE PAINTINGS FROM PICTURES

A production often goes out and takes pictures of a live area that needs to be sewn together for a matte painting. The merging of multiple pictures is referred to as *stitching pictures*. Most of the time the pictures are professionally shot with proper alignment, overlap, and exposures, and the only thing you have to worry a bit about is lens distortion and perspective tweaking. But there is always a time when the pictures are a bit skewed, and despite being set on the same exposure, the colors don't quite match up. I show you some techniques for dealing with that.

Automatic Photomerge

Photoshop has a nifty function that speeds the process of stitching pictures: Automatic Photomerge. If the images have enough overlap and the exposures are not too far off, this function does a pretty good job on getting you started. In this section you join two pictures using Automatic Photomerge.

1. Open AURocks1.tga and AURocks2.tga, both of which you can download from this book's companion web site.

   You can see the shots in Figures 12.1 and 12.2.

2. Go to **File** > **Automate** > **Photomerge**, as shown in Figure 12.3.

   The two images should show up in the source files list.

3. If you see any files you don't want included, highlight them and click Remove.

   That takes them off the photomerge list but keeps them open in Photoshop. See Figure 12.4.

4. Click OK.

   You should see the Photomerge palette, with joined previews of the two images. Figure 12.5 shows the merge.

Note

In some cases, Photoshop cannot automatically assemble the composition and put a message onscreen. No worries, for you can manually drag and arrange the images yourself. Adobe recommends having an overlap of 15–40 percent and maintaining a consistent exposure and focal length to optimize the Automatic Photomerge function.

Figure 12.1 This picture was taken from the same spot as that in Figure 12.2, with the same exposure and seconds after, but the colors and alignment are off.

Figure 12.2 Same shot, same time, but again—the colors and alignment are off in this photo.

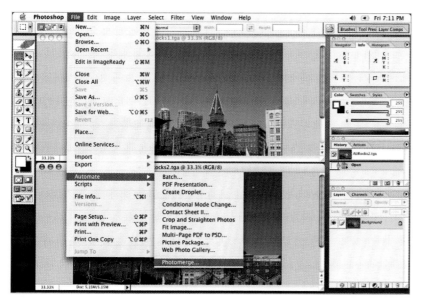

Figure 12.3 Although you could manually do this, photomerge is a nice feature that speeds your progress.

5. Set Settings to Perspective.

   You see the status in the dialog box below the work area. Then Photoshop adjusts the perspective to better align the pictures.

6. Click Keep As Layers.

   If it looks like the images are not quite lined up, manually tweak it by selecting the hollow arrow (Select Image tool) and moving the image until the steeples align to your liking.

7. Check your settings to those of Figure 12.6, then when you are ready, click OK.

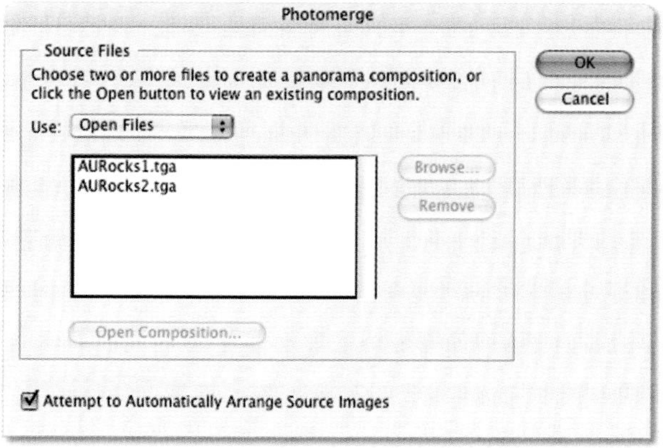

Figure 12.4 Images taken off the list are not closed in Photoshop.

Figure 12.5 The Photomerge palette has its own tools on the upper left.

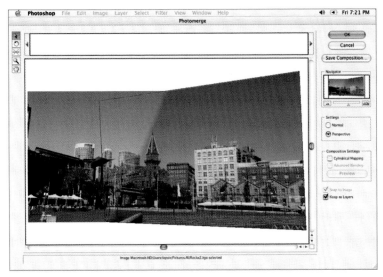

Figure 12.6 Double-check your settings against this image to make sure you haven't missed anything.

8. Photoshop generates a new file for the photomerge.

   Notice that the colors don't match up.

9. Since you kept the layers, select Australia 1's layer and then switch over to the Channels tab in the same palette as your layers and paths.

   Figure 12.7 shows the results of this step.

Figure 12.7 Make sure you have Australia 1 layer selected before you click the Channels tab. Otherwise, the following steps give you a slightly different result.

Correcting Color

In this section you get the pictures to match up in color by adjusting each of the channels independently.

1. Select the red channel.

   Your view should go to a grayscale image representing the red channel. Notice how the two skies are different shades of gray.

2. Press Command+M (Win: Ctrl+M) to bring up the curve editor.

3. Click the middle of the curve and drag it down until the grayscale matches the darker layer.

4. Raise the lower-left corner a bit by clicking the lower vertex and entering an output of 3.

   I do this because I fear having the darks too dark. Figure 12.8 shows my settings.

5. When you are satisfied, click OK.

6. Go to the green and blue channels and repeat the same steps to each.

   Match the grayscale sky via the curve and lift the shadows just a tad, as are done in Figures 12.9 and 12.10.

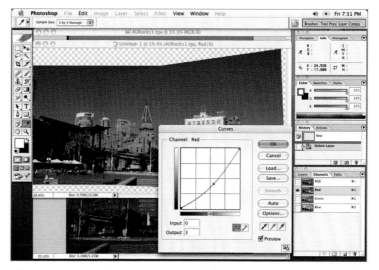

Figure 12.8 Your image turns to grayscale because you've switched to a channel layer. Your settings should be similar to the ones depicted here.

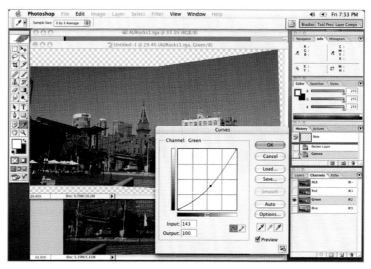

Figure 12.9 Use the same method on the green channel.

7. When you click back to the RGB composite channel, you see that not only is your image aligned, but now your colors match up! Figure 12.11 shows this.

The next steps clean it up for a final.

8. Flatten the image by going to the Layers palette menu and choosing Flatten Image, as shown in Figure 12.12.

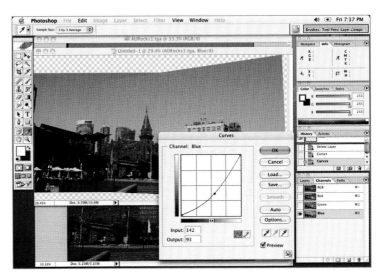

Figure 12.10 And again on the blue channel.

Figure 12.11 Bet you didn't think it would match up so well, huh?

Figure 12.12 Flatten the image.

9. Choose the Crop tool and click and drag the image to set the crop area.

   You use this area to clean up the edges. The crop area, shown in Figure 12.13, is adjustable until you commit it by pressing Return (Win: Enter). Don't commit it yet! You still need to adjust it.

10. Just drag one of the crop box's vertices to where you want it to be. When you are ready, press Return (Win: Enter).

    Figures 12.14 and 12.15 show the two original images. Figure 12.16 shows the photomerge, and Figure 12.17 shows what happens after all your hard work.

Figure 12.13 You can tweak the crop marquee until you have it just right.

Figure 12.14 Your original image.

Figure 12.15 The original image.

Figure 12.16 The photomerge results.

Figure 12.17 Your final product!

Cleaning an Image

Sometimes you have a picture that would have had a perfect background if people (or some other inconvenient thing) weren't in it. Even a plate sometimes needs cleaning. Take a look at Fiji.tga in Figure 12.18. You're going to take out the ship mast and lines that are intruding onscreen left.

The Clone, Patch, and Healing tools get rid of the unwanted sailboat parts. Although most people would use the Healing tool, it tends to bleed in unwanted colors at times. I prefer to use the Clone tool as much as possible and use the Healing tool to clean up and blend afterward.

Using the Clone Tool

The Clone tool is one of the most useful tools for painting on a photograph. The same concept that you are about to apply to erase part of the mast can be used in any other situation where you need to erase something from a picture.

1. Open Fiji.tga, which you can download from this book's companion web site.

2. Make sure you are working at around 300 percent; that way you are seeing everything.

Figure 12.18 Clean out the unwanted ship rigging onscreen left.

7. To set the clone source, hold Option (Win: Alt) and click the source area. See Figure 12.19.

   This area should be an area just right or left of the mast you're starting on; because the sky gradates vertically, by keeping your source to your immediate left, for example, your fixes blend in.

8. Be careful as you erase the mast and wires from the sky.

   As you can see in my image, a slight impression of all the lines and mast remains. You use the Healing tool to get rid of the cloning residue. Figure 12.20 shows the results.

3. Zoom in to the tip of the mast.

   You start here and work your way down.

4. Press S to switch to the Clone tool.

5. Use the left bracket ([) to make the diameter of the Clone Stamp/Brush smaller.

   You want it to be just barely larger than what you are trying to erase.

6. Make sure you have these settings:

   - Opacity: 100 percent
   - Align: Selected
   - Brush Hardness: 0%

   A lot of people like to set the opacity lower, saying that it blends easier. This is true, but it also makes the area blurry. Leaving it at 100 percent keeps the grain as crisp as the rest of the image. You use the Healing tool later to clean up any blending issues.

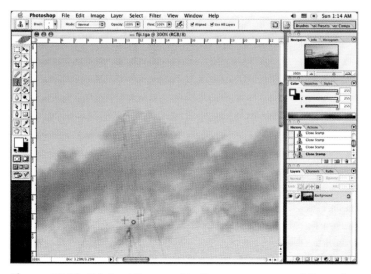

Figure 12.19 This is a bit more subjective, as you must carefully eye how you are cloning away the rigging.

Figure 12.20 There is still a ghost of the rigging. The Healing tool gets rid of it.

Using the Healing Tool

The Healing tool functions similarly to the Clone tool.

1. Hold Option (Win: Alt) and click to select a source; then paint.

   When you are painting, you see 100 percent of the source. Once you release, the colors are blended and the grain is made even.

2. Once you have the sky cleaned up, do the same thing in the grass area.

   Your painting should look like Figure 12.21.

Tip

In most cases, deleting an object from a photo with a paintbrush alone doesn't work. If the object is small or you want to use the brush, add noise and color variations to your brush. This reduces having your brush-work stand out as too flat.

Figure 12.21 The final image.

Figure 12.22 The inspiration image.

Stylized Matte Paintings

Some of the most fun paintings are those that are *stylized*. That is, they are not photo-realistic. Photoshop is obviously excellently equipped to take on such challenges, but it is impossible to cover every situation and style in one book. Although most stylized matte paintings either have a source painting or line art from which the matte painter works, some stylized looks can be derived from a photo, thereby simplifying and speeding up the process.

Pen and Ink

I can give you one example from my past. A long time ago, I did some work for a company that was trying to create an Edward Gorey series. If you are familiar with Gorey's work, it is a dark, moody, and meticulous ink-drawn style. The look was accurately portrayed—in 3D. To get the look for the textures and backgrounds that I worked on, I drew in ink and scanned it. At the time, I thought that was the fastest way. Let me show you what I wish I'd had back then.

Start by assuming there is a picture that the art director asks you to render in an ink-etch style. Figure 12.22 shows the image you start out with.

1. Press Command+J (Win: Ctrl+J) to duplicate the background layer.

2. On this new layer, run **Filter > Brush Strokes > Crosshatch**, as shown in Figure 12.23.

3. In the dialog box, play with the sliders on the right and check out the preview on the left.

You want to get some good markings for when this gets turned into a black and white drawing. Worry more about the stroke visibility than about the color artifacts. See Figure 12.24 for the idea.

4. Apply the angled strokes filter on top of the crosshatch by Option+ clicking (Win: Alt+clicking) the Angled Strokes filter in the Filter Gallery.

If you have already pressed OK and closed the Filter Gallery, you can just go to **Filter** > **Brush Strokes** > **Angled Strokes**.

5. In the dialog box, play with the sliders to get a stroked look that breaks up the uniformity of the crosshatch.

Again, don't worry about color artifacts. See Figure 12.25. Now it's time to get rid of the color.

6. Go to **Image** > **Adjustments** > **Desaturate**.

Figure 12.23 Apply a filter to a duplicated layer.

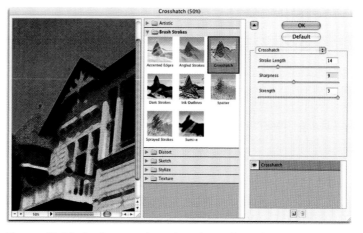

Figure 12.24 Don't worry about the color artifacts showing on the preview. You switch this to grayscale anyway.

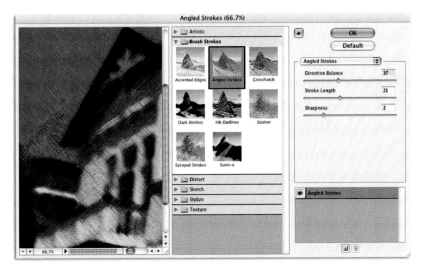

Figure 12.25 Use the angled strokes filter over the crosshatch to break up the uniformity of the previous filter.

You can get this done alternate ways:

- Press Shift+Command+U (Win: Shift+Ctrl+U).

- Look at and copy one of the channels.

- Go to **Image** > **Adjustments** > **Channel Mixer** and select the Monochrome checkbox at the bottom of the dialog box.

- Press Command+U (Win: Ctrl+U) to bring up the Hue/Sat dialog box and drag the Saturation slider all the way to the left to 0 percent.

Figure 12.26 shows the slight differences between the different options.

Desaturated   Red Channel   Green Channel   Blue Channel

Figure 12.26 The leftmost image is a straight desaturate and isn't bad. I decided to use the green channel, however, because of the sky tone balance and the etchy style.

7. If you use one of your channels as your grayscale base, select the channel in your Layers palette and press Command+A (Win: Ctrl+A) to select all, then press Command+C (Win: Ctrl+C) to copy it to your clipboard.

8. Click on the RGB composite channel before returning to your layers and pressing Command+V (Win: Ctrl+V) to paste it on a new layer.

   As you can see, the crosshatch and angled strokes still look like a processed photo and can't pass as an ink illustration.

9. Press Command+J (Win: Ctrl+J) so you have a copy of your layer.

10. With the topmost layer selected, go to **Filter > Stylize > Trace Contour**.

11. Play with the slider and edge options until you get something that appeals to you and click OK.

    Notice that the filter's actual effect is more detailed than the preview. It might take a bit of undoing and retrying to get a look that you like. Even with all the different settings that you try, it may not be enough to get the look you want. I chose Figure 12.27.

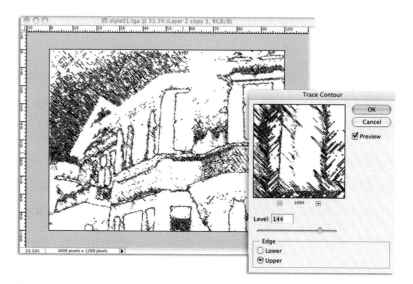

Figure 12.27 I chose this setting because I like the way the sky came in.

In this case, I liked the setting I chose, but wanted to have dark windows. That's why you created a copy of the desaturated image.

12. With the original desaturated image still selected, press Command+J (Win: Ctrl+J) with the layer selected to create a copy.

13. Either drag this new copy above the previously processed layer or hide the processed layer by clicking the Eye icon on the left.

14. Now you can apply the Trace Contour filter to this layer. See Figure 12.28.

To merge the two images I have created, I set the top layer (the one with the dark sky that I liked) to the Darken Layer Blend mode. Since the images are black and white, the white doesn't affect anything and the dark "ink" is layered on top. The effect was a bit too much, so I brought the opacity down to 57 percent. Last but not least, I touched up the image with a few small brushstrokes on a new layer. Figure 12.29 is the original and Figure 12.30 shows the finished product.

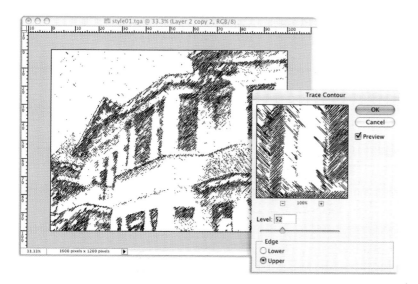

Figure 12.28 I played with the setting to give me the dark windows I wanted.

Cartoon

I have a picture of where I was sitting in my local Starbucks, and I think it would be perfect for a contemporary cartoon type of look.

Custom Swatches

You keep swatches of colors used in this image in a custom set. To do that, you have to first clean off the current palette. Unfortunately there is no New Swatch Palette button (don't ask me why), so you have to delete everything that is there to get a clean slate.

Figure 12.29 Your final image's picture source.

Figure 12.30 Your final image.

The standard way of deleting a single swatch color is to simply drag the swatch to the trash icon. But that can be a drag (no pun intended) if you have to do that to each and every swatch. Here is the secret shortcut. Remember, I'm a proponent of laziness:

1. Open coffeeChair.tga, download-able from this book's companion web site.

2. Select the Eyedropper tool, hold down the Option key (Win: Alt), and click the swatch.

   You see the cursor become a pair of scissors; each click cuts away the swatch. As far as I know, you can't select them all and cut once, but this way is pretty fast.

3. Sample a color from the picture.

   Since your palette is clear (see Figure 12.31), don't go to the Swatches palette menu and choose New Swatch.

4. Click the empty area of the Swatches palette. The Color Swatch Name dialog box pop up.

5. Name your swatch as I've done in Figure 12.32.

   As you work on the image, you save colors to your personalized Swatches palette. For organizational purposes, I like to pick and save the color as I go along, defining an area with the Pen tool.

6. Press I to make sure you are on the Eyedropper tool. Select the color you think best represents the coffee cup.

7. At the Swatches palette pull-down menu, choose New Swatch. See Figure 12.33.

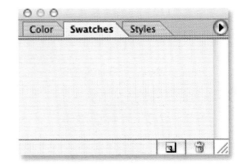

Figure 12.31 The empty Swatches palette.

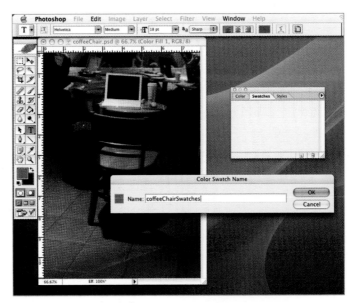

Figure 12.32 You can go through the palette menu or simply click an empty section of the Swatches palette.

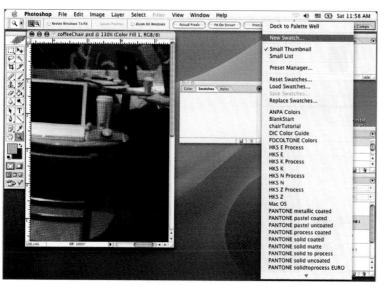

Figure 12.33 Add the current foreground color as a new swatch.

8. In the dialog box, give your color a name that makes it easy to find later on.

You can see the name I bestowed in Figure 12.34.

The Pen Tool

Now that you have the color of the coffee cup, define the area in which the color is used.

1. Switch to the Pen tool by pressing P.

   You see your cursor change to a pen with an x near its tip. This means that you are starting a new path.

2. Before you put down that first vector point, ensure your tool is set to Shape Layers (not Paths) in the tool options bar at the top of your screen.

Figure 12.34 Name the color swatch with a descriptive moniker.

3. Zoom in close on the coffee cup and start outlining the cup by clicking around it.

   The moment you start, you see a new Shape layer appear. The mask reflects the path you are creating. Figure 12.35 shows the cup.

4. As you place your second point, drag to see your Bezier handles appear.

   These handles are tangent to the point. You can adjust one or both of them to change the curvature of the lines coming in and out of that point. If you want a hard corner, click without dragging; the lines come into that point at a hard/straight angle.

   Continue tracing around the cup until you reach your starting point. Because you are doing this as a filled shape layer, you can see your outline filling in with the color you chose for the cup.

Tip

To have a bit more control, you can break the handles so they can be manipulated individually. Hold down the Option key (Win: Alt) to temporarily bring up the Convert Anchor Point tool and move the anchor point or handles.

Figure 12.35 Starting to create the cup shape.

5. After placing your second to last vector point, bring your Pen tool to the first vector point.

   You see an O appear near the tip of the pen. This indicates that clicking that point closes the curve.

6. Click to close the curve and take a look at your coffee cup in Figure 12.36!

7. Repeat the same steps, but this time for the mouse pad.

8. Pick and save the color to the swatches. Create a filled shape based on the outline of that color on the mousepad.

9. Do the same thing for the mouse.

   Now use a slight cheat for the mouse.

10. Outline the mouse as usual, but only do the light section.

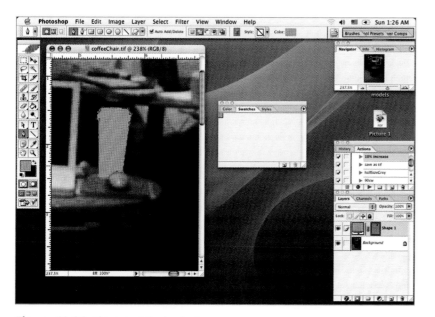

Figure 12.36 This is just the beginning.

14. Continue using the same method for all of the objects on the table.

    Your work in progress should look something like Figure 12.38.

    Do the table top a different way. You could use paths on this also, but use the circular Marquee tool since it is an oval.

15. Press M to switch to the Marquee tool, then press Shift+M to switch to the circular marquee.

11. Click the Layer Effects button on the bottom of the Layers palette. Add a drop shadow.

    The dialog box, which you can see in Figure 12.37, appears.

12. Adjust the angle and lower the opacity to match the photo's look.

13. Once the shadow looks good to you, click OK to accept the settings.

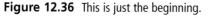

Figure 12.37 Have Photoshop do the shadow for you.

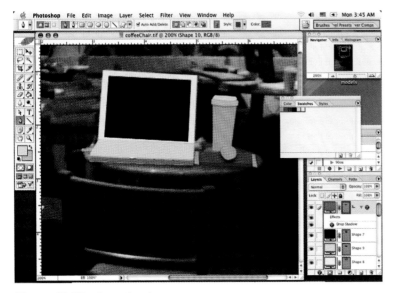

Figure 12.38 It's getting there.

16. Hold the Option key (Win: Alt). Click the center of the table and drag out to the approximate length and width of the table.

    Notice that the table is at a slight angle, and your marquee is not. Never fear—you can adjust your selection.

17. Go to **Select** > **Transform Selection**.

    Transformation handles appear. You can rotate, squeeze, or deform your shape. See Figure 12.39.

18. Once the shape fits the table, press Return (Win: Enter) to accept your selection transformation.

19. Give your shape a color fill: Go to **Layer** > **New Fill Layer** > **Solid Color**.

20. Select a color that represents the table top and click OK to accept it.

21. Click-drag the table-top color layer down until it is below all the computer and coffee layers.

    This moves the layer down so you can see the objects that are supposed to be on top of the table. Figure 12.40 shows your work.

Figure 12.39 Transforming a selection.

Figure 12.40   Your work in progress.

When you have taken care of each element, give your setting a background.

23. Choose a color from the ground near the front.

24. Press X and choose a dark color from the background.

    This switches your foreground/background swatches.

25. Press G or Shift+G until you have selected the Gradient tool.

26. Make sure the options are set to Blend from Foreground to Background.

22. Make sure to save your table-top color in your swatches; you use this color for all the highlighted wood.

    Now you get the basic idea and can do this for the chair and its shadows, saving colors and making paths. The process is pretty forgiving. You can choose which details contribute toward your painting and which ones you can gloss over. I left some of the edges rough; they did not follow the outline of an object exactly. It adds to the contemporary print feel. Your image should look similar to Figure 12.41.

Figure 12.41   All that remains to be done is the background; the image on the right is the same as the left, but with the source photo hidden.

27. On a new layer right above the source photo, create a gradient to fill the entire canvas, as shown in Figure 12.42.

28. To give a little more interest, reduce the opacity so hints of the background are barely visible.

The final product is an interesting modern graphic shown in Figure 12.43.

These stylized images are just examples of the possibilities that Photoshop offers. It shows what a little ingenuity can do. Your imagination is your palette, and the world is your canvas. Don't you feel so empowered?

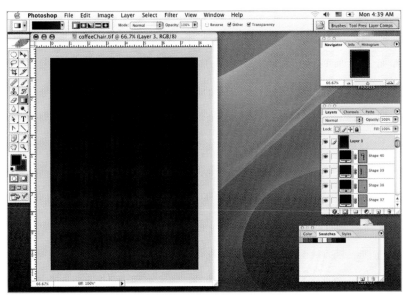

Figure 12.42 Creating a gradient backdrop.

Figure 12.43 Fit for a poster!

CHAPTER 13

QUICK FIXES FOR COMMON PROBLEMS

Y ou've been working on a matte painting for weeks. Everything is picture perfect and then the Art Director comes by and says "If you can just…." I have had to deal with my share of fixes in the film VFX industry. Here are the most common.

Looking Sharp

Ah, if only they had asked you to blur it, losing detail would be easy. But doesn't *sharpening* mean bringing in more detail? Not really—it is the perception of detail brought about by crisper differentiation within the image. Take a look at Figure 13.1. You can download this image from the book's companion web site.

Check out the image at 100 percent on a Mac by double-clicking the zoom icon in the toolbox or pressing Command+Option+0; press Alt+Ctrl+0 if on a PC. (Those are zeroes in the key combinations.) Going to **View** > **Actual Pixels** in the menu bar also results in the same thing. The window's title bar should indicate that the image is at 100 percent.

Figure 13.1 This is similar to some work I did on the tornado sequence for *X-Men 2*.

You want to see it there so you can see the true results of your sharpening. Figure 13.2 shows the image at 100 percent.

You can sharpen an image in so many ways: Switch to Lab mode and sharpen the lightness channel, selectively sharpen one or more RGB channel, apply the Unsharp mask to the image, among others. I go over two methods I like because they work for a wider range of sharpening with fewer artifacts.

Unless you have a very large screen, you are only seeing a part of the image when you have it zoomed up to 100 percent.

Figure 13.2 Double-clicking the zoom icon resizes your image to 100 percent.

Method 1: Using the Unsharp Mask Filter

This is a good, solid, simple method to sharpen an image and works under most circumstances. I usually start with the Unsharp Mask filter to see how far it can go and to determine whether I need additional sharpening techniques. Although it may seem counterintuitive to use something called the Unsharp Mask filter to sharpen an image, this term has its roots in the photographer's dark room, when a blurred version of the image was used to sharpen a photograph.

1. Select the entire image by choosing **Select** > **All** or Command+A (Win: Ctrl+A). If you are not using the image provided and have multiple layers, make sure you have the layer you want to sharpen selected.

2. Copy the image to the clipboard by pressing Command+C (Win: Ctrl+C) or choosing **Edit** > **Copy.**

3. Go to the Channels palette shown in Figure 13.3. Create a new channel by clicking the Create New Channel button at the bottom of the palette.

Make sure you are on the Channels tab

Figure 13.3 Creating a new channel.

4. Paste your image by pressing Command+V (Win: Ctrl+V). It automatically becomes grayscale, which you see in Figure 13.4.

5. Choose **Filter** > **Stylize** > **Find Edges.** Your new channel now looks like Figure 13.5, which is a crude drawing.

6. Choose **Image** > **Adjustments** > **Levels** or press Command+L (Win: Ctrl+L) to bring up the Levels dialog box.

Blue highlight indicates that we have this channel selected.

Because we are in the Channels palette, our image shows as grayscale.

Figure 13.4 Although you copied a color image, it becomes grayscale when you paste it into a new channel layer.

Look at the color image by clicking over to the composite RGB channel and switching back over to the Layers palette, which is shown in Figure 13.7.

9. Choose **Filter** > **Sharpen**> **Unsharp Mask** to bring up the Unsharp Mask dialog box.

10. Play with the three sliders to get a setting that works to your satisfaction.

Figure 13.5 Find Edges shows where there is the most contrast. The dark lines are where there's already high contrast.

7. Drag the Input Levels sliders that are at both ends toward the middle to clean up the lines. Click OK. See Figure 13.6.

8. While pressing Command (Win: Ctrl), click the channel to load it as a selection.

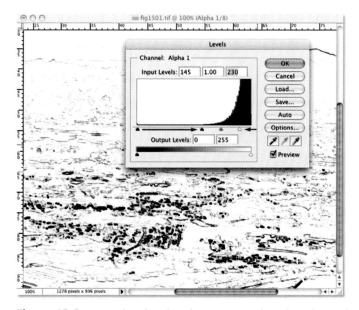

Figure 13.6 Remember that the white areas are the selected areas later.

After loading the channel as a selection, click on the RGB composite to switch back to color.

Then click on the Layers tab.

The Selection Marquee indicates that we have a selection.

Figure 13.7 Use the channel as a selection to sharpen the color image.

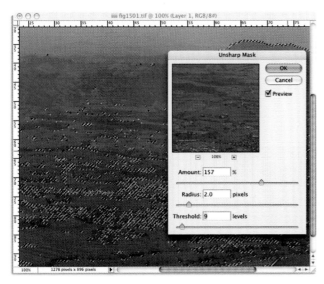

Figure 13.8 Watch for the introduction of noise (if Threshold setting is too low) and use the real-time feedback as you adjust values.

11. Make sure that the Preview checkbox is selected, so you can see the real-time feedback.

    If you click the Preview checkbox in the dialog box, you can toggle between the before and after. See Figure 13.8.

    - Amount determines the amount of contrast added to edge, or *boundary*, pixels.

    - Radius determines how many pixels from the edge will be affected by the sharpening.

    - Threshold sets a minimum difference value to how different pixels must be in order to be considered an edge. The bigger the value, the more different the values must be in order to be considered a different color.

12. When you have a setting you like, press OK. Press Command+D (Win: Ctrl+D) to deselect all. Here you are, in Figure 13.9, a bit sharper.

Before   After Method 1

Figure 13.9 The Before and After using the Unsharp Mask filter for sharpening.

But wait—the client wants to work with you on getting just the right level, so try it a different way.

Method 2: The High Pass Method

This method allows for easy tweaking and a more extreme sharpening without affecting the color too much.

1. Open Fields01.psd, which is available at the book's web site.

2. Duplicate the Background layer onto a new layer by pressing Command+J (Win: Ctrl+J).

3. Rename the layer from Layer 1 to **High Pass**.

4. Run the High Pass filter by choosing **Filter > Other > High Pass**.

5. The dialog box gives you a Radius slider that you can play with. Enter **4**. Generally, small values work best in most cases. The maximum entry is 250. Your image looks gray with some colored edges, like Figure 13.10.

6. When you have settings that you like, press OK to accept the settings.

7. Go to **Image > Adjustments > Levels** or press Command+L (Win: Ctrl+L) to bring up the Levels dialog box.

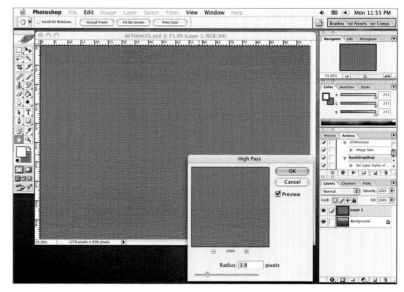

Figure 13.10 The High Pass filter removes low-frequency data in an image, resulting in an edge detail effect. This filter can also be used to create line art.

8. Bring in the outer Input Levels sliders in the Levels dialog box to the outer edges of the histogram to bring up the contrast and click OK.

   See Figure 13.11. You use this layer on top of the original image by changing the layer mode.

7. See which layer mode is better: Overlay, Hard Light, Linear Light, or Vivid Light.

   The layer blend modes are located at the top of the Layers palette. Make sure you have your layer selected, and choose a mode from the drop-down menu.

8. Keeping your zoom at 100 percent so you can see the details, rotate through the different layer blending modes to find the one that works best.

   Compare the differences between these modes, each of which is shown in Figures 13.12 through 13.17:

   - High Pass
   - High Pass at 100 percent Overlay
   - High Pass at 100 percent Hard Light
   - High Pass at 100 percent Vivid Light
   - High Pass at 100 percent Linear Light

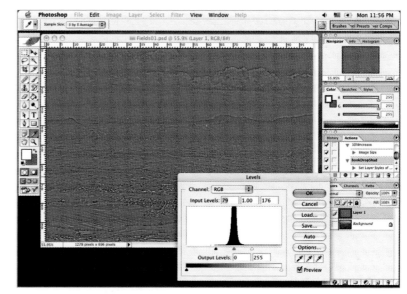

Figure 13.11 Bring up the contrast a bit.

Figure 13.12 This is the original painting.

Figure 13.13 This is the High Pass layer that you created above the original at 100 percent normal blending mode.

Figure 13.15 This is with the High Pass layer at 100 percent Hard Light. This is too noisy and the sky is a bit too crisp and crunchy.

Figure 13.14 This is with the High Pass layer at 100 percent overlay. This gives good sharpening, but it is still a bit crunchy.

Figure 13.16 This is with the High Pass layer at 100 percent Vivid Light. Way too crunchy, but this is one that a lot of beginners choose because it is so noticeably different from the original.

Figure 13.17 Speaking of too much noise, this looks like a bad print job from the 70s. Setting the High Pass layer to 100 percent Linear Light is out of the question.

Figure 13.18 Compare this original to Figures 13.19 and 13.20. Notice the subtle differences that make a big impact and all without reducing the overall sharpening effect.

It looks like Overlay is the best layer blend mode for the original photo, which is shown in Figure 13.18. I have reduced the High Pass Layer Opacity to 70 percent in Figure 13.20 to get rid of the halos (look closely at the mountain and cloud edges in Figure 13.19) and to reduce the popping whites of the buildings on the ground. For production, I would go further and reduce the noise and mute the bright baseball diamond-like dirt. See Chapter 15, "Noise and Grain," for more information on reducing noise.

Figure 13.19 100 percent overlay.

Figure 13.20 70 percent overlay.

Tip

Most beginners would have tried to first increase the contrast. The following images show you that although the image is sharper, changing the contrast has shifted the values, given the image a different tone, and blown out the clouds. This wouldn't be so bad with the exception of the clouds, but often when working on a film the client doesn't want to see such a big change.

Figure 13.21 The original is leftmost and the tutorial should result in what you see rightmost.

The center image is the original with the contrast increased to emulate a sharper image. Compare this to Figure 13.21's original (leftmost) and the results from this tutorial (rightmost), and you can see how much truer to the original your version is.

Color Change

You are on a production and the director wants very colorful buses in the background for a particular shot—but the second unit shot this with a plain yellow and white bus center frame. The director asks that since this is a locked-off shot (there is no camera move, so a matte painting can be substituted for the background plate), can you change this to a yellow and purple bus? Oh, and he would prefer you to make the yellow parts purple and the white parts yellow.

Life never is easy, is it? Luckily, this isn't hard to accomplish. Take a look at the background image in Figure 13.22, which you can download from the book's companion web site.

1. Attend first to the purple parts. Add a Hue/Saturation layer on top by going to **Layer > New Adjustment Layer > Hue/Saturation**. Figure 13.23 shows this step.

2. Accept the default layer name by clicking OK in the New Layer dialog box (see Figure 13.24).

3. Play with the sliders in the Hue/Saturation dialog box to get the purple you want.

   Don't worry about any other part of the picture; just get the yellow parts to the color purple that you like. See Figure 13.25.

4. Click OK

Figure 13.22 The director wants a different color bus center frame.

Figure 13.23 This gives the same effect as going to **Image > Adjustments > Hue/Saturation**, but allows more editing freedom.

Figure 13.24 You can give the layer any name, but I accept the default naming convention.

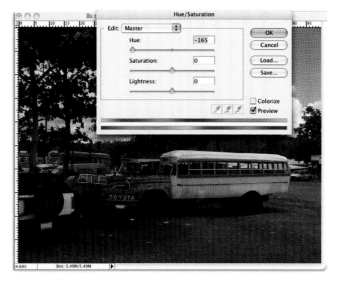

Figure 13.25 Don't worry about any color other than the purple.

5. Click the Default Foreground and Background Colors icon and press X or click the Switch Foreground and Background Colors button to switch the foreground color to black.

   Because you are on an adjustment layer, the colors are switched to reflect the default colors for masking. That is why you have to press X, shown in Figure 13.26.

6. Press Option+Delete (Win: Alt+ Backspace) to fill the Hue/Saturation mask with black. The layer changes should disappear in your main canvas window. See Figure 13.27.

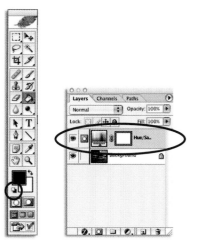

Figure 13.26 Normally, the default colors are black foreground with white background.

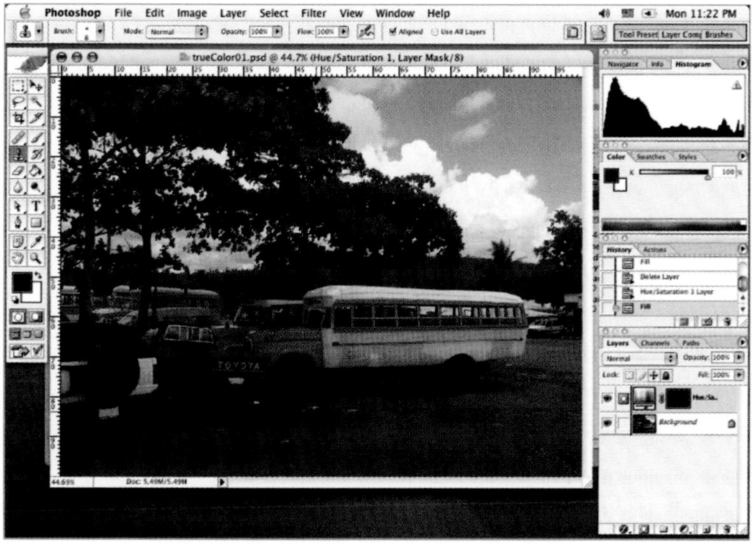

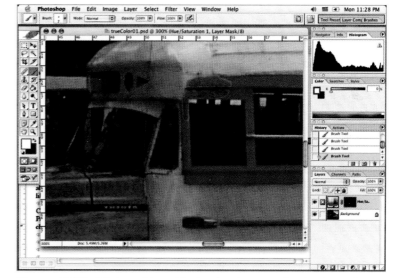

Figure 13.27 The Hue/Saturation layer is still there, but is masked out so you only see the original image underneath it.

7. Press X again to switch to white, click the Brush tool, and choose a brush in the options bar. I chose a small soft brush at 100 percent opacity.

8. Carefully brush away the yellow to reveal the purple.

    The white and black parts stay white and black. If you try to paint in the white areas, you see no results. See Figure 13.28 for the results you want. Now you have the purple parts; Figure 13.29 shows them in all their glory. You already saw that the Hue shift doesn't work on white, so how are you going to make the white parts yellow?

Figure 13.28 Painting with a white brush paints onto the Hue/Saturation mask and reveals the purple.

9. Choose the Magic Wand tool, set Tolerance to 20 in the options bar, and click the white part of the bus that you want to change.

10. Hold Shift and continue clicking until you have most of it selected, which is shown in Figure 13.30.

    If the wand goes outside of the white area and you want to subtract it, hold Option (Win: Alt) and click the area you want to subtract. Don't worry if it is not exact; you clean it up after you have most of the white areas selected.

11. Click the Quick Mask mode button and use a brush to clean up your selection. When you are done, click on the Standard Mode button. Figure 13.31 shows what's going on.

12. Now you're ready to add a new color fill layer. Go to **Layer > New Fill Layer > Solid Color**.

13. Accept the default name by clicking OK in the New Layer dialog box. Choose an appropriate yellow in the Color Picker dialog box (see Figure 13.32) and click OK.

Figure 13.29 Purple parts accomplished!

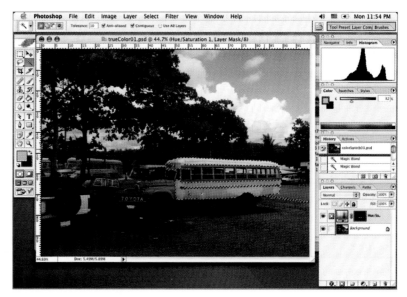

Figure 13.30 Selecting the white areas of the bus.

Quick Mask
Mode

Masked out areas
have a red overlay.

Use your paintbrush to
clean up your selection.

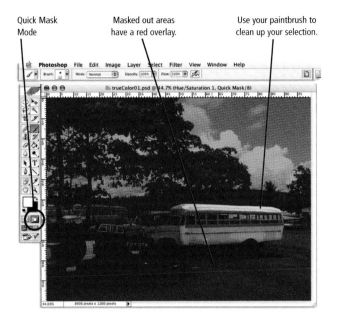

Figure 13.31 Similar to what you did with the purple parts, you are defining the area you want to affect with the Quick mask.

14. The added layer looks flat and odd. Change the blend mode for the layer to Overlay and it looks much better. See Figure 13.33.

    You're almost finished. Just tone down the colors a bit, as they are much more saturated than anything else in the plate.

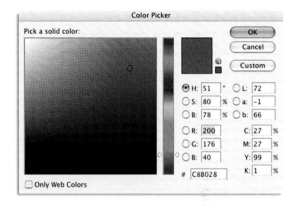

Figure 13.32 Choose a yellow that you think would look good in the picture.

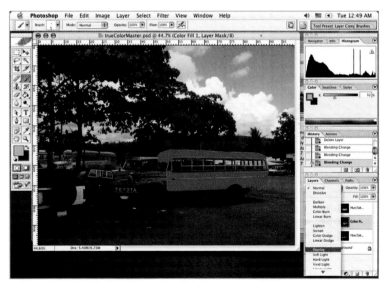

Figure 13.33 Changing the layer's blend mode to Overlay gets rid of the yellow paint's graphic look.

15. Holding Command (Win: Ctrl), click the layer mask thumbnail that defined the purple areas.

16. Holding Shift+Command (Win: Shift+Ctrl), click the layer mask thumbnail that defined the yellow areas to select both the yellow and purple areas.

17. Add a Hue/Saturation adjustment layer by going to **Layer** > **New Adjustment Layer** > **Hue/Saturation**.

    Since you had a selection in memory, the adjustment layer comes in with the selection as its matte.

18. In the Hue/Saturation dialog box, adjust the Saturation and Lightness settings to blend in with the rest of the plate, pressing OK when you are done. Then compare the before and after in Figure 13.34.

Tip

Whenever you are changing colors or adding anything to a scene, make sure that your highlight value, shadow values, tone, and saturation match up with the rest of the plate.

| Before | After |

Figure 13.34 Here are the results! I have hand painted back the patches into the modified bus as an added detail.

Neutralizing a Color Cast

In this example, the VFX supervisor originally asked you to paint the image with a blue cast to match the color-corrected plates received from the client. Once you were done, he thought it was perfect. Despite that, the client doesn't like the blue cast that the movie has been working with and is trying to eradicate it. Rather than starting over from a neutralized plate, can you work with your painting and just get rid of the cast?

Of course you are wincing inside, thinking of how hue shifting causes all kinds of unwanted colorations, how putting in an overlay or doing too much image processing flattens the image's color range; a litany of hurdles bombard your mind. Then you smile and say "Okay." You remembered this particular chapter! I think this would be called grandiose delusions on my part, but if this chapter happens to save any of you, e-mail me and tell me the tale!

Placing Markers

Before neutralizing a color cast, find out exactly from where the cast is coming. Placing color markers aids your quest and gives you feedback during the process.

1. Download file CC01.psd from this book's companion web site and open it. See Figure 13.35.

2. Click the lower-right triangle in the Eyedropper tool in the toolbox. From the pull-down menu, choose the Color Sampler tool. See Figure 13.36.

Tip

Press Shift+I to cycle through the Eyedropper tools.

3. In the options bar shown in Figure 13.37, choose either 3 by 3 or 5 by 5 Average as the Sample Size setting.

For this example I choose 3 by 3. Averaging between a few pixels ensures that you don't get an off reading of the one pixel that is vastly different from the rest.

Figure 13.35 Your original painting with a heavy blue cast.

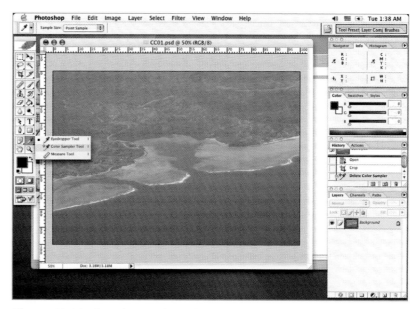

Figure 13.36 The Color Sampler tool is hidden behind the Eyedropper tool.

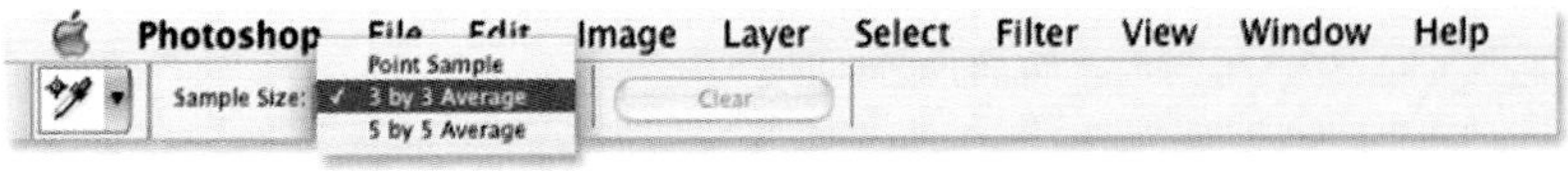

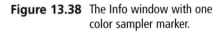

Figure 13.37 Setting the Color Sampler options to an average gives you a more accurate reading.

4. Find the brightest white point of your painting and click it with your Color Sampler tool.

   You see #1 with the average value listed in RGB in the Info palette, shown in Figure 13.38. (Choose **Window** > **Show Info** if you don't have the Info palette up already.) You see the sampler symbol with a 1 next to it, indicating from where the sample is being drawn. If you think you need to nudge it over just a bit, just place your cursor over it. When it changes into a triangle, click and drag it to where you want it.

5. Choose the darkest black area of your image with the Color Sampler tool.

   The Info palette displays this as #2. See Figure 13.39.

If you have a sudden memory lapse and forget what area you sampled, have no fear: Photoshop leaves the markers onscreen, with numbers indicating which sample is which. To clear the markers, go to the options bar and click the clear button. Figure 13.40 shows the numbered markers. Now that the markers are set, you are ready to take the first step in neutralizing the color cast.

Neutralizing Highlights

With your color markers set, first work on neutralizing your highlights. Take the neutralizing solution and spread it evenly over your head. Uh, wait. That's from my hair-streaking kit. Now you know the answer to "Does she or doesn't she?" As I recover from my utter embarrassment, take a look at the brightest points on your image as you subtract the color cast from the highlights.

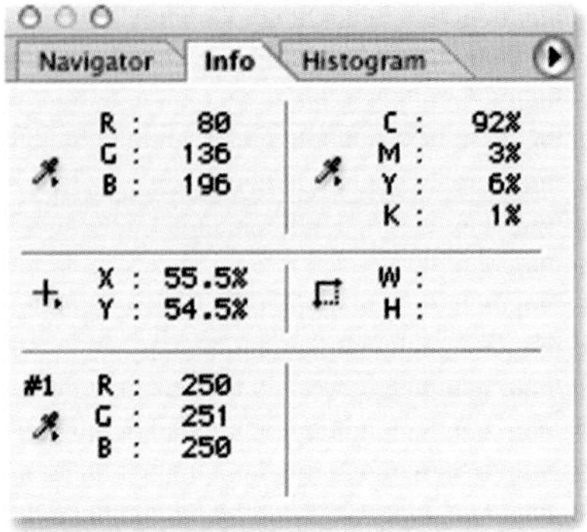

Figure 13.38 The Info window with one color sampler marker.

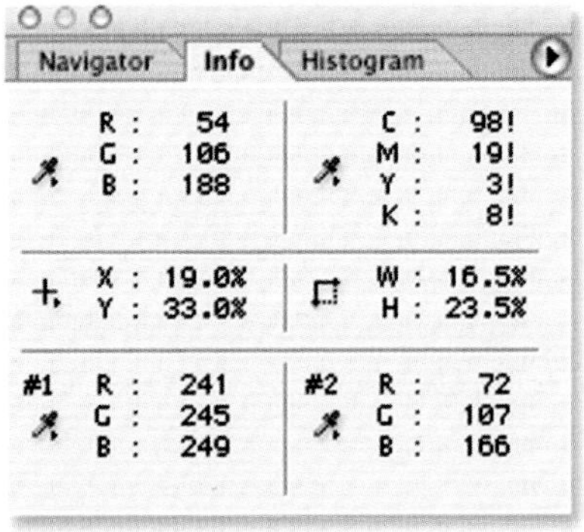

Figure 13.39 With both the #1 sample and #2 sample, the red, green, and blue channels should have a different value from each other. That is causing a color cast.

Figure 13.40 The Color Sampler leaves markers so you know where you are getting your values from.

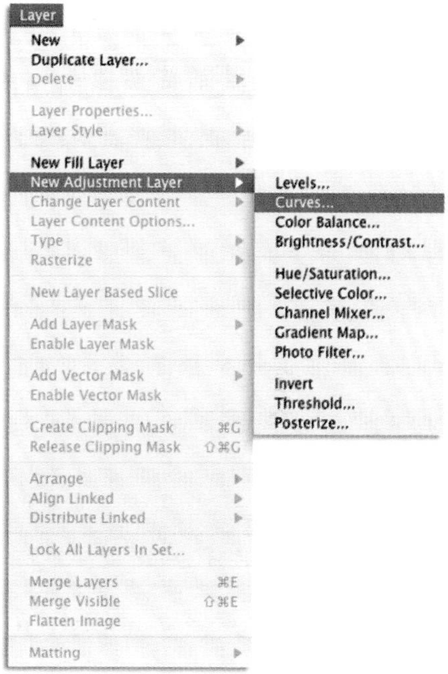

1. Add a Curves Adjustment layer to your document by clicking **Layer > New Adjustment Layer > Curves**. See Figure 13.41.

   Another way to do this: Go to the bottom of the Layers menu and choose Curves. See Figure 13.42 for what this looks like. Either gives you the same result on a separate layer. You need the flexibility of the separate layer for going back to tweak the settings.

Figure 13.41 In this case it is imperative that you use a Curves Adjustment layer instead of the Image Adjustment Curves.

Figure 13.42 You have multiple ways of doing the same thing. Click the Create New Fill or Adjustment Layer button on the bottom of the Layers palette.

2. Name your new layer any name you wish and click OK. The Curves dialog box appears.

Take a look at the values in your color sample #1 in the Info palette. Notice the highest value. In this case it is the blue channel with a value of 249.

3. From the channel choices in the Curves dialog box, choose the channel that had the lowest value.

In this example, shown in Figure 13.43, it's red with a value of 241.

4. Click the curve's upper-right node and nudge it to the left until the red value matches the highest value for the highlights—blue in this case. See Figure 13.44.

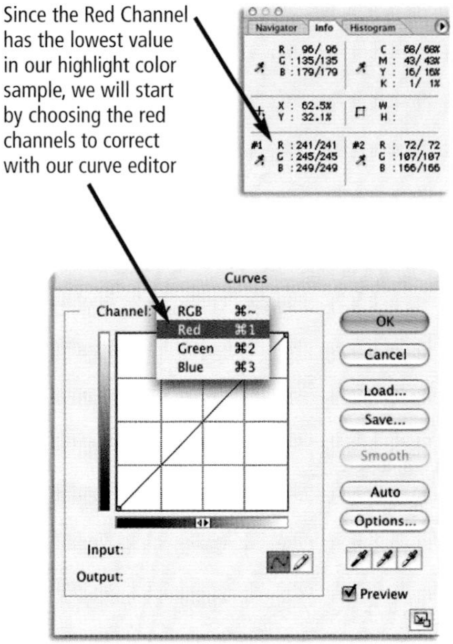

Since the Red Channel has the lowest value in our highlight color sample, we will start by choosing the red channels to correct with our curve editor

We have nudged this over just a tad bit to make the numbers match

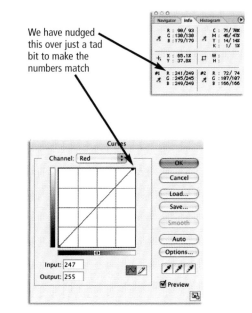

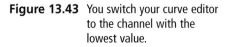

Figure 13.43 You switch your curve editor to the channel with the lowest value.

Figure 13.44 When you opened the curve editor, the sample colors were updated with a slash that divides the current and the corrected colors.

5. Correct the green channel to match, using the same methods. The highlight cast has been neutralized. Figure 13.45 shows this being done.

You have neutralized the highlights, but your image is still unbalanced until you at least neutralize the shadows. Keep working through the next section.

3. Once you have neutralized your shadows, click OK to close the Curves dialog box, and look at your image so far.

See Figure 13.47 for an example of what your image should look like.

Take a good look at the paths running through the land in Figure 13.47. See how they are tinged with green? That's because you haven't yet neutralized the midtones.

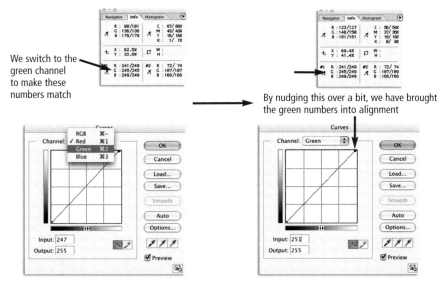

We switch to the green channel to make these numbers match

By nudging this over a bit, we have brought the green numbers into alignment

Figure 13.45 You are doing the same thing to the green channel.

Neutralizing Shadows

Before you leave the Curves dialog box, neutralize the shadows using the same method, but matching down to the lowest value.

1. Take a look at color marker #2 and find the lowest value (in this case the red channel's value of 72).

2. Adjust the blue and green channel values by moving the lower-left node to the right and bringing down the values, as you see in Figure 13.46.

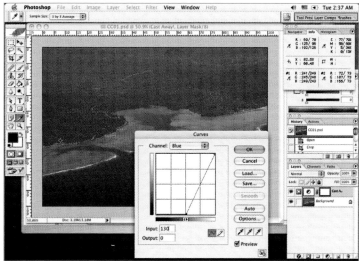

Figure 13.46 The lower-left node represents the dark shadows. You may have to make some extreme adjustments, but trust in the numbers.

Figure 13.47 Your image so far with highlights and shadows neutralized.

Choosing Midtones

The midtones are a bit trickier. Ideally, there exists a point on the image that is supposed to be 50 percent gray. In reality, that is rarely the case, and you need to determine your midpoint gray.

1. Determine what a midtone point is and choose it with your color sampler for a #3 choice.

2. Either add another curve layer or use the same one you've been using for the other adjustments.

3. Grab the center of the line to curve the values up or down. Pulling up raises the value and pulling down lowers it, which you can see in Figure 13.48.

Evening the Light

This image is looking much better, but you still need to even out the light.

1. Go to the bottom of the Layers palette and click on the New Fill or Adjustment Layer button.

2. In the pop-up menu, choose Levels like you see in Figure 13.49.

   In the Levels Dialog box, notice that the histogram is not spread across the entire range of values.

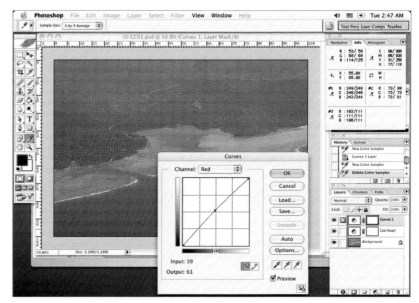

Figure 13.48 I added another curve layer for clarity, but you could have made the adjustment on the existing Curve Adjustment layer.

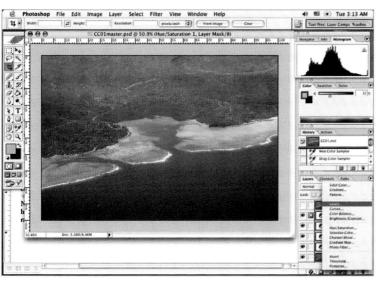

Figure 13.49 Instead of adding the Levels Adjustment layer through the Layers palette, you could go to **Layer > New Adjustment Layer > Levels**.

3. Drag the end triangles to encompass the available levels represented in the graph; this expands the image's tonal range. Figure 13.50 shows this step.

4. Click OK to accept your levels change.

Desaturating

Take a look at the image. All this processing has left it too saturated. The last order of business is to desaturate the image a bit.

1. Add a Hue/Saturation Adjustment layer by going to **Layer > New Adjustment Layer > Hue/Saturation**, shown in Figure 13.51.

2. Accept the default name in the New Layer dialog box and take a look at the Hue/Saturation dialog box.

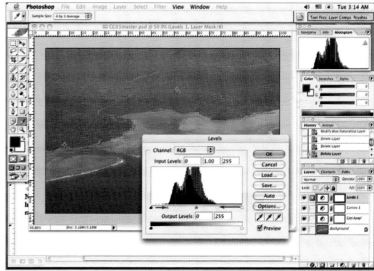

Figure 13.50 Drag the end triangles in, toward the range of the histogram, to set a new range for the image.

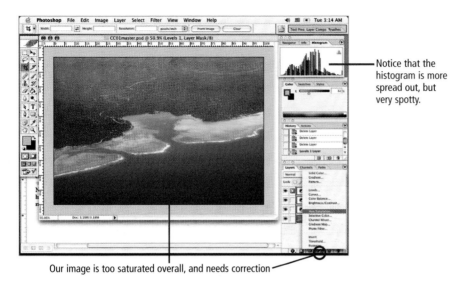

Notice that the histogram is more spread out, but very spotty.

Our image is too saturated overall, and needs correction

Figure 13.51 You're almost there!

3. Lower your saturation slowly by dragging the saturation slider to the left.

   Watch your histogram as you lower the saturation. The histogram, shown in Figure 13.52, fills in a bit and shows a fuller range overall.

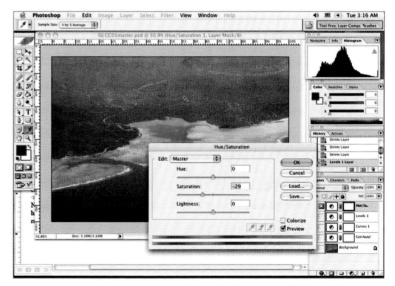

Figure 13.52 As you start to desaturate, the histogram fills in, reflecting a richer range in the image.

4. When you have something that
   you are satisfied with, click OK.

   Now you have a properly neutralized image! Figures 13.53 and 13.54
   show the before and after.

Figure 13.53 The before image.

Figure 13.54 And the after image.

CHAPTER 14

MASKS AND MATTES

One of the things you commonly have to do as a matte painter is provide a mask or matte for particular pieces of your painting. Masks and mattes are also referred to as *holdouts* or *alpha channels*. In an RGB image, Photoshop can hold up to 53 alpha channels. Hopefully, you never have a matte painting that needs that many holdouts (but in this business, anything is likely).

In alpha channels, selected pixels are white, unselected pixels are black, and anything in between is partially selected. A mask or matte defines a part of the image. Oftentimes you do this so an effect or filter can be applied, excluding certain areas of the image. Most commonly, compositors using your matte painting need masks to layer your painting's different levels and make it look 3D in the camera move.

You can go about making masks several ways, and each way works, but some are more efficient than others, depending on the situation.

The Transparency Selection Method

This is the easiest method to create a matte. If you are so lucky as to know that you will need to provide a matte before you have begun painting your matte painting, you can keep the elements that you will need to provide mattes for on different transparent layers.

1. Take a look at CanIGoHere.psd, which you can download from this book's companion web site and see in Figure 14.1.

Make mattes for the foreground and midground.

2. Select the foreground layer and go to **Select** > **Load Selection**, like you see done in Figure 14.2.

Figure 14.1 This is a Photoshop file that still has its elements on separate layers.

Figure 14.2 Make sure the foreground layer is selected before going to the Load Selection dialog box.

3. You do not have any masks saved, so the only selection that can be loaded is the layer transparency. Click OK to accept this, like you see in Figure 14.3.

   You see that you are now back out to your image and the foreground element is selected with tight crawling ants enclosing the image. You can see the ants in Figure 14.4.

4. Return to the menu bar, but this time go to **Select** > **Save Selection**.

5. Make sure that it is a new channel. Give your alpha channel a name. I called it FGAlpha for Foreground Alpha, as you see in Figure 14.5.

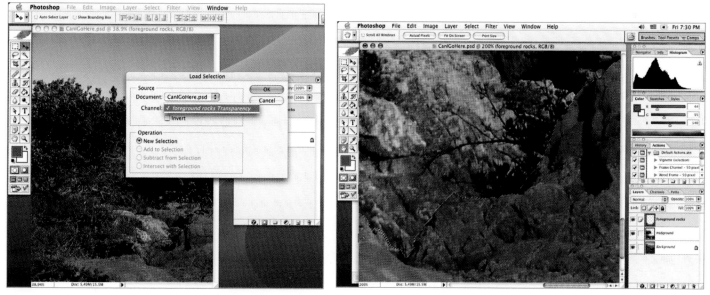

Figure 14.3 Loading the layer's transparency as a selection.

Figure 14.4 The selection enclosure is sometimes referred to as *crawling ants*.

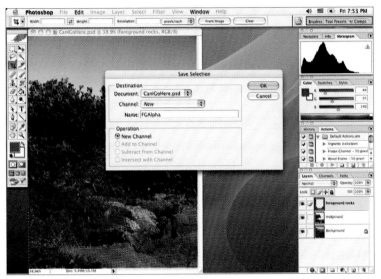

Figure 14.5 You can name your new alpha channel anything you want.

That's it. You're done. Really. If you go to you Channels palette, you see your new alpha channel on the bottom. Figure 14.6 shows this.

Try making an alpha on your own for the midground using the same technique. (No, the second matte is not called the beta channel.)

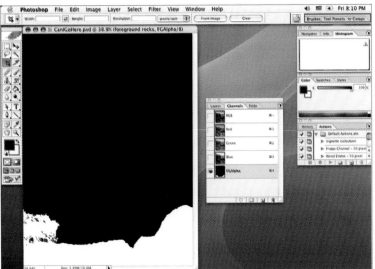

Figure 14.6 You can see the black and white alpha channel by clicking its layer in the Channels palette.

The Color Selection Method

One of the most common methods of creating mattes is to mask using a specific color selection. This is the reason for greenscreens. The green is "pulled" from the frame/image to allow easy replacement. To pull a greenscreen effectively, your subjects against the greenscreen should not have any green shades within them (unless, of course, you want to have that piece of your subject disappear). Oftentimes puppeteers do just that by wearing invisible body suits that are the same green as the greenscreen.

Of course, rarely can colors be so controlled. Even greenscreens suffer from spills and other color-contaminating issues that make pulling them less than perfect. When you are dealing with an average photo, the color selection method is rarely used on its own.

Easy Case (Read: Ideal Case)

First start with the simple ideal steps of color selection.

1. Open GreenScreen.tga, which you can download from this book's companion web site and see in Figure 14.7.

Figure 14.7 This is a perfect greenscreen, with no spills and an even green backing.

Figure 14.8 This allows you to create a mask based on a color.

Although you could put it to 0 in this case, generally I like to have at least a little bit more fuzziness to avoid aliasing and stray pixel dropouts.

5. Click OK. This gives you a clean selection of all the greenscreen areas.

6. Go back to the menu bar and choose **Select > Save Selection**.

7. Name your channel, make sure it says New in the Channel selection box, and click OK. Figure 14.10 shows this step.

2. In the upper menu bar, go to **Select > Color Range,** shown in Figure 14.8. Your cursor now looks like the Eyedropper tool when you take it out onto the image.

3. Click the green area of your image. You see the selection as a mask in the Color Range dialog box. See Figure 14.9.

4. Move the triangle under the slider down to decrease the amount of fuzziness.

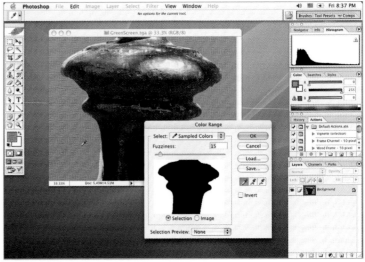

Figure 14.9 Select the green areas. The mask is previewed in the dialog box.

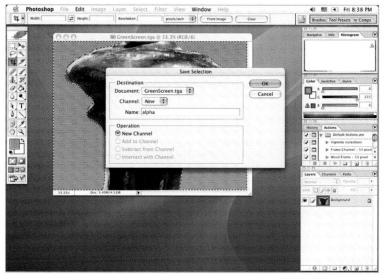

Figure 14.10 Saving your selection creates a matte.

You now have what is commonly called an alpha channel. You can see it at the very bottom in your Channels layer and in Figure 14.11.

By convention, white is supposed to be the selected area and black is the unselected area. As you can see, your matte is reversed. Invert it before passing it on.

1. Click your alpha channel in the Channels palette and press Command+A (Win: Ctrl+A) to make sure that you have the entire canvas selected.

2. Press Command+I (Win: Ctrl+I), the shortcut for **Image** > **Adjustments** > **Invert**.

   Your alpha channel should be inverted, with the greenscreen area black. See Figure 14.12.

3. Choose **File** > **Save**, which should save your image with its alpha channel.

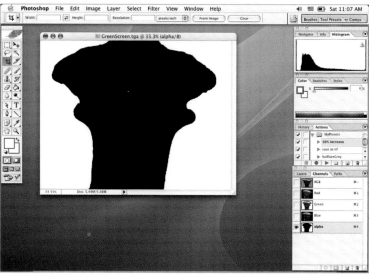

Figure 14.11 Clicking your newly formed alpha channel in the Channels palette shows it in your canvas window.

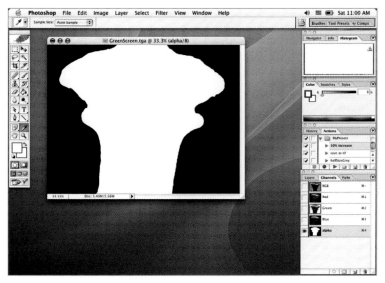

Figure 14.12 Now the alpha channel has the proper conventions.

1. Download from the companion web site and look at TongaVisit.tif shown in Figure 14.13.

   After you have finished wondering how you can get a tax-deductible vacation to a South Pacific island (be thankful that I didn't use the one of me and the…well, I'll stop there), continue on.

2. Select the Magic Wand by pressing W. See Figure 14.14.

Difficult Case (Read: Life Example)

Say you need to create a matte for a sky. It's mostly blue, and in high contrast to the island edge. It shouldn't be too hard, right? And there isn't really anything else blue in the scene…except that big body of water called an ocean. You'll get with that.

Figure 14.13 This sky needs a matte.

Figure 14.14 The results of my first click.

3. Set the tolerance to 8 and make sure Contiguous is not selected.

 You want to get all the nooks and crannies between the palm trees without having to go and select them yourself. In this case, being lazy is also faster and better.

4. Click the sky. Yes, anywhere.

 Notice that although it selected most of the sky, it didn't select all of it.

5. Hold the Shift key and click an unselected area of the sky. I click the lower-left corner.

 Ah! See, you are almost there.

Tip

Accidentally click a color that you didn't mean to select? You don't have to deselect all and start over. Holding down the Option (Win: Alt) key subtracts the selection with a click.

6. Hold the Shift key and click the cloud—voilá! The entire sky seems to be selected in Figure 14.15.

 By now you've probably noticed the little sparkles in your ocean. That would be normal for an ocean, if it weren't a still image.

Figure 14.15 Here is the selection of the sky.

7. Select the Marquee tool by pressing M.

   I like to have the window opened up a bit to show the edges of the image when I'm using the Marquee tool.

8. Since you're trying to subtract any selections in the ocean, hold down the Option (Win: Alt) key and drag around the sparkles.

9. Take a close look to see how clean your selection is. Figure 14.16 shows the image.

10. Click the Quick Mask Mode button.

11. Select the Zoom tool by pressing Z; Zoom into the section of the image around the palm trees.

    You can see some of the stuff still unselected in the sky. Clean this up while you are in Quick Mask mode.

12. Switch to your Brush tool by pressing B.

13. Choose a soft brush with 100 percent opacity and diameter of 9 pixels, like you see in Figure 14.17.

Figure 14.16 As you can see, your clean selection wasn't perfectly clean.

Figure 14.17 This is the brush I started with for clean up. You don't need to use these exact settings; it is ultimately up to you. This was to provide a guide.

14. Take a look at your swatches.

    They would have switched to black and white regardless what colors you had previously. This is because your brush is painting a virtual alpha channel to represent the selection, which is only grayscale.

15. Your foreground needs to be white, so press X until the white swatch is forward.

16. Use the left and right brackets ([and]) to increase or decrease your brush as you see fit. See Figure 14.18.

Tip

Don't forget you can fix a mistake by either pressing Command+Z (Win: Ctrl+Z) or by simply pressing X, switching to black, and painting over it.

Figure 14.18 The cleaned matte.

Whew! What started out as a simple color selection with an easy subtraction didn't turn out so simple after all, did it? In actuality, an experienced digital painter would probably not use a color selection tool on a virtually all blue image. The point is that you can still use this technique, regardless of whether it is optimal.

The Channel Selection Method

Since I considered the color selection easy, you are probably cringing at the thought of other methods for a matte.

1. Go back to GreenScreen.tga.

   Rather than just picking a color, the shorter method would have been saving a channel as a matte.

2. Now prepare yourself: Click the Channels tab.

   Does the green channel look familiar? The GATE (Gifted and Talented Education) students probably noticed in the color selection section that the resulting alpha channel looks very similar to the green channel. Without doing much, you can just create an alpha channel by duplicating the green channel.

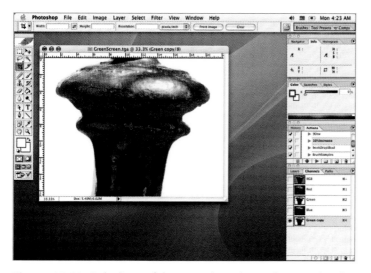

Figure 14.19 A duplicate of the green channel may give you a head start.

5. Slide the triangle under the histogram all the way to the right, as you see in Figure 14.21.

   The white areas remain white and the post's dark, grayscale image blacks out. If there are any speckles of white within the black, just paint them out with a paintbrush. That's it. Really. Figure 14.22 proves it.

Most of the time an image needs more matted than just a solid, clean color. Even in this ideal case, you had to go in with a brush and paint out little areas.

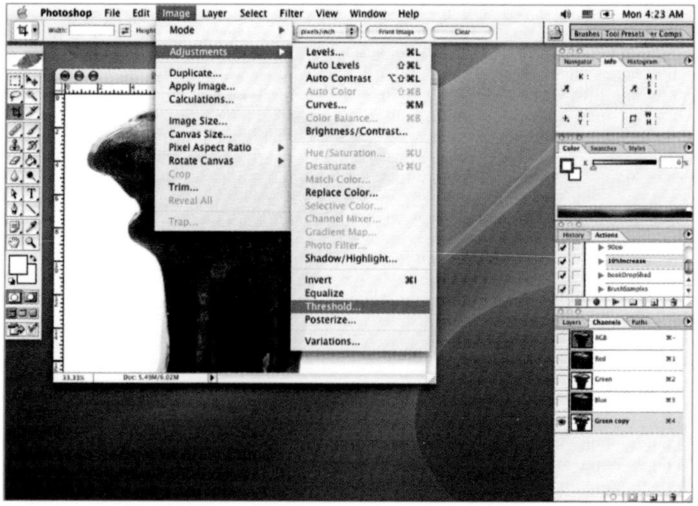

3. Click the green channel and go to the Channel submenu. Choose Duplicate Channel and name the channel in the Duplicate Channel dialog box that comes up. See Figure 14.19.

   You could also just drag the channel to the new layer icon at the bottom of the channel layer palette.

4. Go to **Image > Adjustments > Threshold**, shown in Figure 14.20.

Figure 14.20 Image > Adjustments > Threshold takes you where you want to go.

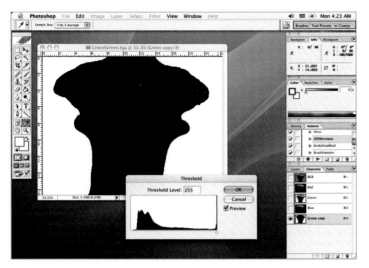

Figure 14.21 Slide the triangle to the right, as far as it will go.

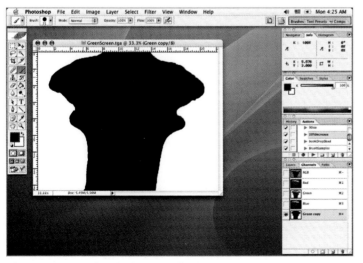

Figure 14.22 Take a look at your finished work.

The Path Selection Method

Sometimes you need to create a matte that cannot be easily selected with any of the methods I mentioned earlier in this chapter. The selection may be too complex or you may want to be able to change the matte quickly, yet maintain precision. Using paths can solve this dilemma.

Paths are vector-based Bezier curves. If you have used Adobe Illustrator or its equivalent type of illustration graphics program, you are probably already familiar with vector paths. That I use the term "dealing with" in reference to paths should alert newbies to the common perception that paths take a bit of getting used to. It may take some practice, but the results are well worth conquering the learning curve. (And really, they're not that bad.)

In this scenario you are working on a scene where a swarm of computer-generated bugs were supposed to fly across the screen. The director thought that the scene looked too flat and wants some of the bugs to go behind a few of the leaves. She circles the leaves she wants separated and e-mails the image to you. Figure 14.23 shows you the directions. No problemo.

1. Take a look at Leaves.tga in Figure 14.24, which you can download from the companion web site.

Figure 14.23 Direction.

Figure 14.24 Your image to work with.

2. Select the Pen tool or press P. Click the tip of the big leaf in the upper group.

   A small square appears where you clicked. You may want to use Command++ (Win: Ctrl++) to zoom in and the spacebar to switch to the hand to pan around to get a better look. Using these shortcuts does not affect your Pen tool.

3. Now go farther down the edge of the leaf and drag to create your second vertex. See Figure 14.25.

   Notice how the line connecting your two vertices curves as you drag. Two square points attached to your vertex look like a seesaw. These are called *handles*. They reflect and affect the curvature of your path.

4. Try creating a path partway up the leaf's edge.

5. Continue creating an outline of your intended matte.

   It takes a bit to be able to know where to place vertices based on the characteristics of the Bezier curve. Even so, you're probably wondering how this can be faster or better or even precise!

Figure 14.25 Dragging creates smooth curves. Only clicking creates straight lines between the vertices.

Figure 14.26 You can find the Direct Selection tool above the Pen tool.

6. Stop where you are and edit a few of the vertices. Hidden above the Pen tool is the Direct Selection tool, which you can see in Figure 14.26.

You can use this tool to reposition any vertices and to adjust its handles. When you are ready, switch back to the Pen tool and continue the path.

I worked all the way around one leaf, but you could have gone around the three leaves together. You can see this in Figure 14.27.

Figure 14.27 I worked around one leaf.

7. When you come back around toward the beginning of the path, click the first vertex to close the path.

   You're probably wondering where this path is being stored and how you can hide the ugly lines.

8. Click the Paths tab, which is grouped with Layers and Channels in Figure 14.28.

   You see a working path. This is a temporary path, so save it for repeat use.

9. Go to the path's pull-down menu and choose Save Path. See Figure 14.29.

10. In the resulting dialog box, enter any name for the path.

   Great. So you have a path. Now what? How does this make a matte for me? Patience, young grasshopper. You could do many things with a path. You could have Photoshop automatically stroke the path to create an outline. You could fill the closed path shape with any color. You could make the path a selection and create a matte from it. I'll take door number three, please.

Figure 14.28 The Paths tab is way down here.

Figure 14.29 Save the path, since it's temporary.

11. Make sure your path layer is selected. Go to the Path's submenu and choose Make Selection to bring up a dialog box.

12. Set the feather radius to 1 and make sure that the Anti-Alias option is checked. Click OK.

13. Now save the selection as a new channel by going to **Select > Save Selection** and giving your new channel a name in the ensuing Save Selection dialog box. Voilá! You have a matte.

Figure 14.30 What is this, the Copacabana? You work with this file.

The Extract Filter

You're probably wondering if I really know my stuff. I mean, why go through all this pain if there is an extract filter that can just—BAM!—extract it. There is method to my madness. At least that's what I tell my therapist.

Figure 14.31 Filter > Extract takes you where you need to do the work on this image.

The Extract filter rarely works as nicely as you need, and sometime one or more of the previous methods would actually be faster and cleaner. Nonetheless, this great filter has its own benefits, as you see through this tutorial. Plus, had I put this first, you may not have read the rest of the chapter!

1. Look at TropFlower.tga in Figure 14.30. You can download this file from the book's companion web site.

A color selection selects the red easily, but the flower has yellow and brown protuberances and greenish yellow tips that are difficult to distinguish from the leafy background. The channels don't give any other info and making paths around all those curves and jags just makes you sigh in resignation and paint the entire mask by hand. (Why do people always giggle when I use the word protuberances?)

2. Create a duplicate of the background layer for the Extract filter to work on by pressing Command+J (Win: Ctrl+J).

3. Go to **Filter** > **Extract**, which is displayed in Figure 14.31.

   A dialog box pops up with your image in its workspace. Figure 14.32 shows this.

4. Click the Edge Highlighter tool in the upper-left corner where the Extract's toolbox is; trace the edges of the flower like you see in Figure 14.33.

   You want to use the thinnest convenient mark, but don't worry about being meticulous. Your marker should encompass the edge, which means the marker's width should cover a bit of the flower and a bit of the nonflower areas.

Figure 14.32 The dialog box is at the ready.

Figure 14.33 The flower's edges are traced, but it's not perfection.

I repeat: You don't have to be meticulous. That is one of the filter's benefits and the reason this is faster than, say, painting the mask yourself. For the protuberances, I simply increased the brush size using the right bracket hotkey (]) and encompassed the entire thing. See Figure 14.34.

I didn't want the entire stem to be included in the mask, so I cut it off where I wanted the mask to end. See Figure 14.35.

5. Make sure that your edge marker encompasses an entirely closed space.

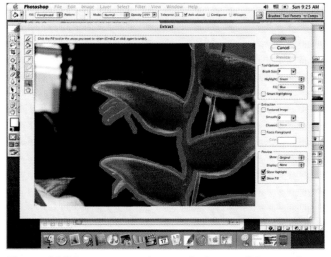

Figure 14.34 You can use the zoom hotkeys or click Extract's Zoom tool to get up close and see more detail.

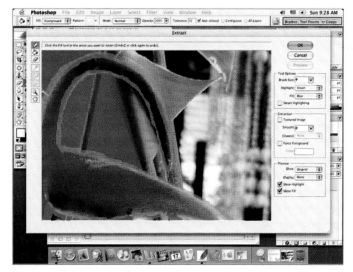

Figure 14.35 I lopped off part of a stem.

6. Click the Extract's Fill tool and fill the area that you want to define or keep by clicking the flower.

   Your flower should be covered with a blue film, like you see in Figure 14.36. If the blue cover is both inside and outside of the flower's outline, then you have a leak somewhere. Go in close and use the edge marker to paint in the gap, then try the fill again.

7. Click Preview and behold the power of the Extract filter in Figure 14.37!

8. Take a close inspection for some of the details.

   Notice how the Extract filter not only got the protuberances, but also the ragged edge of the upper-right flower.

Tip

If your extract doesn't look the way you want it to, change the view to Original instead of Generated, redraw any fixes, and Click the Preview button.

9. When you are satisfied with the result, click OK. See Figure 14.38.

Figure 14.36 I'll spare you the "feeling blue" clichés.

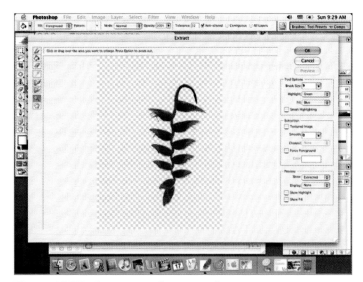

Figure 14.37 The extraction has occurred.

Figure 14.38 Take a close look at your work.

Behold the limitations of the Extract filter! All in all, it's fairly clean and you need only use whatever method you like to clean up the little details (like the dark edge included on the lower-left flower).

It did a good job getting you started and this was an almost ideal scenario in which to use it. That's kinda the advantage that I have in writing this: I get to choose what image I'm going to use. But you have to go in by hand to do the final touch up. To be fair, just about every matte requires some amount of hand clean up.

Tip

To fill in some of the gaps, try duplicating the extracted layer a few times. The areas that were semitransparent fill in. Don't do it too many times, though, or you get a thicker outline that you want for matte creation.

That's right! We were creating a matte, weren't we? And you're wondering when this extracted image will become a matte? Let's get on it!

1. Erase anything you don't like from the new layer.

2. Create the matte by going to **Select > Load Selection** in the top menu bar, as shown in Figure 14.39.

Figure 14.39 Getting closer to extraction perfection.

Fixer Uppers

Common mistakes in mattes/masks:

- The black is not 100 percent black.
- Barely perceptible smudges in the black (absent/negative) area mess up the compositing.
- The white is not completely white.
- The edges of the mask are too soft and the image is not premultiplied, resulting in a halo effect.

3. Scan the Load Selection dialog box to make sure it automatically chose your current layer's transparency to form a new channel. Figure 13.40 shows what this should look like.

4. Click OK.

5. Make sure that your background is visible and click the Quick Mask button.

6. Using the Quick Mask methods from earlier in the chapter, clean up any other edges or anything that was missed.

7. When your selection is perfect, switch back to Normal mode and save the selection as a channel.

8. Take a look at the channel and make sure the matte is clean.

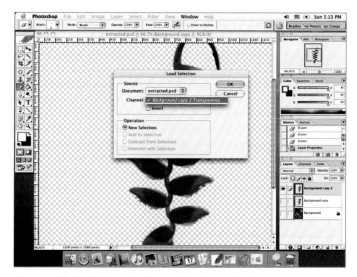

Figure 14.40 Stick a fork in you. You're nearly done.

CHAPTER 15

NOISE AND GRAIN

Noise, grain, color aliasing, high ISO noise...whatever you call it, sometimes a pebbly or dotted pattern appears in an image. This is not always bad, as a certain amount of grain feels more realistic, and is commonly introduced into 3D renders purposefully. However, starting a painting or texture with apparent grain can cause aliasing and integration problems, and can just look plain ugly. This chapter helps you eradicate or reduce the noise or grain in an image.

Explaining Grain

First let me distinguish between grain and everything else. *Grain* is usually a result of the silver halide crystals that develop the image on film. Each film stock has a different grain structure that results in different size grain and patterns. If the grain were the same from frame to frame, then this may be less an issue, but we register the grain in its movement during projection.

I refer to everything else that isn't a result of silver halide particles (or Kodak's T-grain, or an equivalent particle type) as *noise*. The patterns are a bit different—sometimes a result of compression or pixilation, sometimes due to the way a digital camera process and interprets low light situations, but always a bit different from the overall grain look that film gets.

How much grain is acceptable and how do you reduce it? Well, this chapter wasn't called "Noise and Grain" for nothing.

Show Me the Noise

Take a close look at the Ocean.tga image in Figure 15.1. This noise seems fairly mild in the composite, and it may seem unnecessary to take out the grain. However, taking out the grain is the first thing you should do before working on an image. The price you pay further down the image-editing pipeline could be tremendous otherwise.

One of the best ways to test your image for noise is to increase the saturation, give excess sharpness, and use the find edges filter. Take a look at that step by step:

1. Open Ocean.tga, which is shown close up in Figure 15.2.

   You can download the image from this book's companion web site.

Figure 15.1 It is a bit noisy; you want to reduce this.

Figure 15.2 This is a close up of a section of Ocean.tga.

2. Press Command+U (Win: Ctrl+U) to bring up the Hue/Saturation sliders.

3. Increase the saturation.

   Sometimes, this alone makes any grain or noise pop, and you can determine whether there is enough noise to warrant fixing. Figure 15.3 shows what happened when I increased the saturation.

4. Apply the Unsharp mask.

   Even if the saturation did not pop the noise, applying the Unsharp mask can show how too much noise affects your corrections and editing. See Figure 15.4.

5. To really see the noise pattern, go to **Filter** > **Stylize** > **Find Edges**.

   The Find Edges filter is applied, as you can see in Figure 15.5. Notice how the noise is represented by the overall square boxes overlaying and scattered throughout the image. If this test didn't do much, then you have a clean plate and are fine to start your image editing.

Figure 15.3 I increased the saturation by a value of 50. The grain is evident.

Unsharp Settings:

amount: 150%

Radius: 2 pixels

Threshold: 4 levels

Figure 15.4 I used the Unsharp mask with a slightly excessive setting.

N o t e

Don't set your values to anything higher than what I used here, as it makes the test less useful. If you put really excessive values in, you get weird output, even if the image were acceptably clean. The trick is to find the values that work as a limit for your pipeline.

Figure 15.5 The amount of noise is apparent after using the Find Edges filter.

Testing, Testing

Now go back to the original image and reduce the noise a little. Then run a few noise tests on it and compare it to the original.

1. Open Ocean.tga and go to **Image > Mode > Lab Color**.

   Again, you can download the image from this book's companion web site.

2. Click the Channels tab in the Layers palette to show the Lightness, A, and B channels.

3. Click the Lightness channel.

4. Run a despeckle on the Lightness channel by going to **Filter > Noise > Despeckle**, like you see in Figure 15.6.

   The result is a cleaner image. To get rid of some of the color noise, I ran a despeckle on the composite image for good measure. You can see the comparison in Figure 15.7. It may seem like there isn't that much difference between the two images, and it's easy to wonder if the plate is clean enough. You can perform three noise check points that make the noise apparent and let you know if there is too much noise.

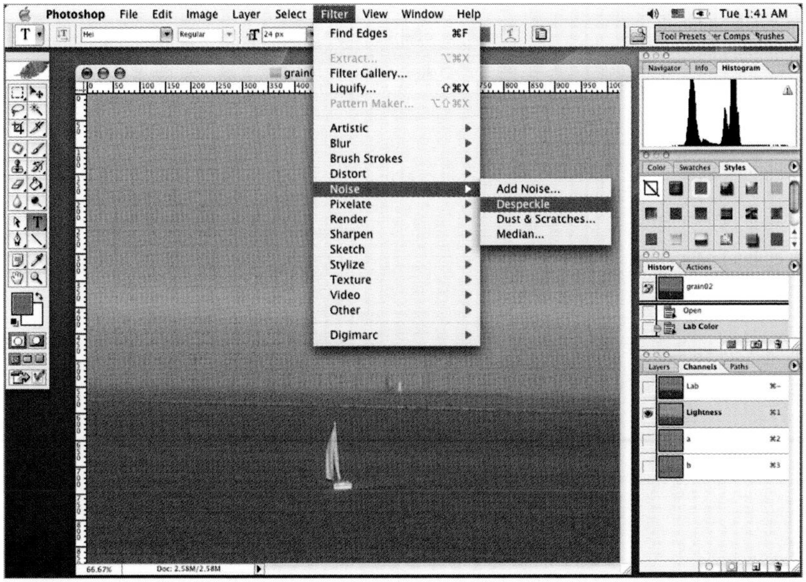

Figure 15.6 You can run despeckle on this a few times, but be careful not to over blur it.

5. The first test: Simply increase the saturation by 50.

   Take a look at Figure 15.8. You can see that this simple test has already brought up the grain in the form of a pebbly overall color. This is not always apparent to everyone, so the next step helps define the noise to those who are having a hard time seeing the noise now.

6. Apply the same Unsharp mask you did in the previous section, with these settings:

   - Amount: 150 percent
   - Radius: 2 pixels
   - Threshold: 4 levels

   Compare the two photos in Figure 15.9. Again, the original is on the right. You can clearly see the noise now, especially in the sky. Notice how spattered the original looks compared to the cleaned version on the left. Still unsure of how to determine how much noise is too much noise? The Find Edges filter helps make this crystal clear—pun fully intended!

Figure 15.7 Side by side, you can see that just that the simple despeckle worked wonders compared to the original on the right.

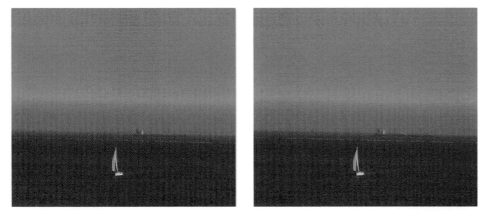

Figure 15.8 The saturation already is showing quite a difference.

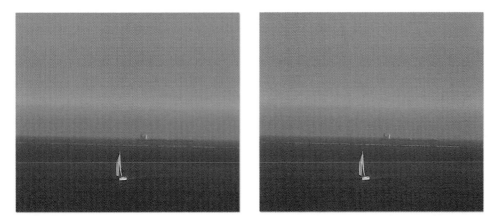

Figure 15.9 Wow, look at how the grain difference really shows with the Unsharp mask.

7. Run the Find Edges filter on your saturated and sharpened image.

   You can truly see a difference in Figure 15.10. Notice that the clean plate is not completely blank. If you were wondering how much noise is acceptable, the image on the left is a good example. The image on the right, the original uncorrected image, is a good example of unacceptable amounts of noise.

Turning Down the Volume

Between the low light and the JPG compression, the noise is hideously apparent in this image. How do you reduce the amount of noise?

1. Open Aquarium.tga, whose noise you can see in Figure 15.11.

   You can download the image from this book's companion web site.

2. Duplicate the background layer by pressing Command+J (Win: Ctrl+J).

   Applying a Gaussian Blur until the graininess is just blurred out is what you do next.

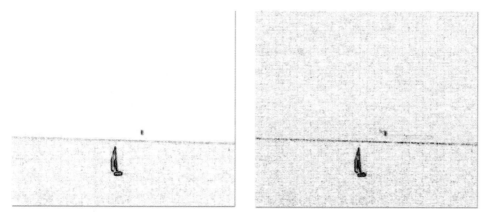

3. Make sure you are on the duplicated layer and go to **Filter** > **Blur** > **Gaussian Blur**.

4. Set the Radius to 2.4 pixels.

   You can see my values in Figure 15.12, but experiment to get a feel for the level of blur that works for you.

Figure 15.10 The Find Edges filter shows how your simple correction really paid off.

Figure 15.11 The noise in the blue background is painfully obvious.

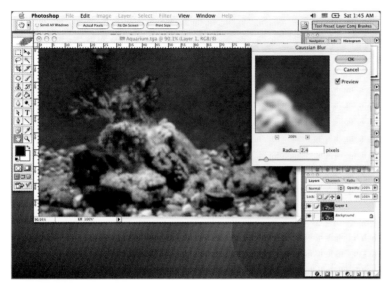

Figure 15.12 As noisy as this is, you can't blur it completely.

6. Switch to the Channels palette and take a look at the individual channels.

   The red channel, which you can see in Figure 15.14, is not too bad.

7. Click the green channel. The green channel in Figure 15.15 isn't too bad either.

5. Go to the Layers palette and switch the Layer Blend mode from Normal to Color.

   Figure 15.13 has the composite image use the luminance from the lower layer and the color info from the top layer. Quite a bit of noise still exists. Looking at the RGB channels can help you see where this is most obvious.

Figure 15.13 The noise is much reduced, but still obvious.

Figure 15.14 The red channel looks fine.

8. Click the blue channel.

Ah ha! It looks like you have found your culprit in the blue channel! Check it out in Figure 15.16. You know the culprit, but doing anything right now only applies the change to your selected layer. You want to apply it to the composite image.

Figure 15.15 The green channel looks okay, too.

Figure 15.16 It's very common for the blue channel to hold the most noise.

11. Reselect the blue channel and apply the Gaussian Blur until the painful freckles are reduced to smudges.

   Don't worry too much about its blurriness, the likes of which Figure 15.18 shows. The point is to try to eradicate the noise. Because you're only blurring one channel, you can go a little more blurry on this one.

9. Switch back to the composite image by clicking the channel layer marked RGB.

10. Flatten the image by going to the Layers palette and choosing Flatten Image. See Figure 15.17.

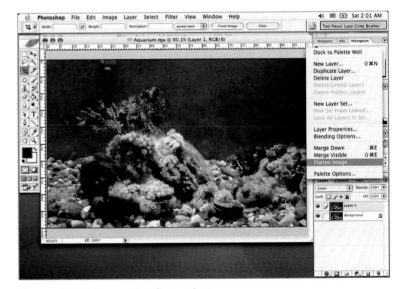

Figure 15.17 You need to flatten the image.

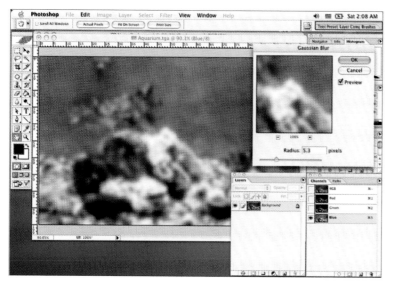

Figure 15.18 I pulled out the Layers palette to remind you to apply the blur to the flattened image.

12. Now take a look at the composite.

    Much improved—especially when you compare it to the original image! You can see it in Figure 15.19. How does this compare in noise tests?

13. Run the Find Edges filter on only the before and after.

    See how they look in Figure 15.20. The after image on the right is remarkably cleaner than the original.

Figure 15.19 Compare the before (left) and after (right).

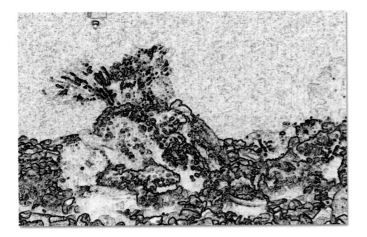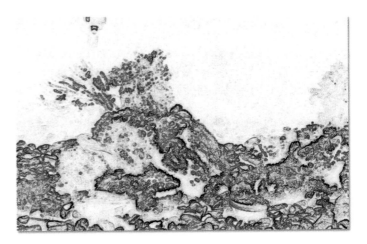

Figure 15.20 I desaturated the results so as to not be distracted by the colors. Even though you didn't run the Saturation or Unsharp masks, Find Edges shows quite a difference between the two.

CHAPTER 16

LIGHTING EFFECTS

If you've ever tried to shoot a photograph at sunrise, you know how difficult it is to capture the look of that one moment. Now imagine trying to do an entire act (with camera angle changes, multiple takes, and so on) while keeping that same light. Now try to keep continuity of light over a few days of filming. That's why movie stage environments are recreated: Huge lights emulate sunlight and gels and gobos make variations off those lights. Even with the best equipment, sometimes the light is not quite captured the way the director envisioned it, or the light has to be changed for continuity or story changes.

The harnessing of light is the matte painter's primary and most difficult task. Calculations in 3D programs are expensive in time or money or both, and a good matte painter can create the look at a fraction of the cost and with much more visual appeal.

Lighting

If you don't have a background in some type of traditional lighting (photography or stage lighting, for example), I recommend either taking a course or at least picking up a book on the subject. Most computer programs try to emulate traditional light, and most of the people that you work with in the VFX industry may give feedback in the form of traditional lighting terminology.

Don't know what a gobo is? Would it clarify it if I told you it's the same as a cookie? A gobo is just anything opaque that is put in front of a light source to emulate patterned shadows (dappled sunlight filtering through leaves, for example). What about a gel? That's short for gelatin filter—an optical filter placed in front of a light to adjust its color.

Figure 16.1 This is a fairly flat and uninteresting photo of a wine-tasting area.

The Lighting Effects Filter

The Lighting Effects filter is fun to explore when you're getting started, and can do a surprising job of emulating different types of light. The best way to get a feel for it is to do a simple and subtle effect.

Now say you want to bring attention to the far bar and wall in Figure 16.1 by making it seem as though it is a bit darker outside; you want the recessed lights shining down, illuminating the bar. One click of the Lighting Effects filter can help.

Caution

Since the Lighting Effects filter affects the original image, duplicate an image onto another layer to apply the filter. It's always safer to do so in general, but I happen to be in the know: You will need to bring back some of the original plate.

1. Open Wine.tga, which is shown in Figure 16.1.

   You can download this image from this book's companion web site.

2. Duplicate the image layer by pressing Command+J (Win: Ctrl+J).

3. Go to **Filter > Render > Lighting Effects**.

Note

Is the Lighting Effects option grayed out? Then you are most likely not working in RGB mode. The Lighting Effects filter only works on RGB images. Go to **Image > Mode > RGB Color** to correct your mode.

4. In the dialog box, change the style to Crossing Down.

5. Move the lights by clicking the white circles in the preview.

   I also brought down the intensity of one spot light. You can see an approximation in the preview window as you make changes. You can compare your settings to mine in Figure 16.2.

6. Click OK when you like the settings.

   The Lighting Effects filter gives a good result, but has put a dark shadow over the light bulb in the hanging fixture on the right. Now you must manually touch up the hanging fixture on the right to bring the light back in.

7. Use the Eraser tool to reveal the background original image.

   ■ Erase the lightbulb. You see the brighter lightbulb in the lower original layer come through.

   ■ Bring down the opacity and softly erase around the light. It should look like the area is brightened by the light.

Now take a look at your results, the likes of which are in Figure 16.3. Your eye is drawn to the bar, and for a quick pass this works rather well.

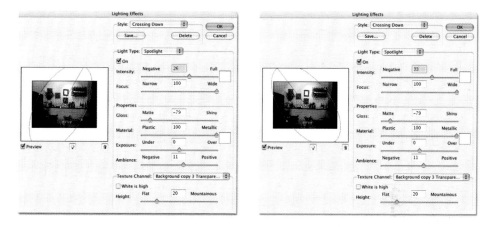

Figure 16.2 The Lighting Effects dialog box settings for each of the two spotlights.

Figure 16.3 The before and after images—a subtle but effective change.

This is definitely one of those things that you just have to play with to familiarize yourself with the possibilities. It's also a prime candidate for one of my exploded views! Check it out in Figure 16.4. The Lighting Effects filter comes with 17 presets. Table 16.1 shows an example of each of them at their default settings.

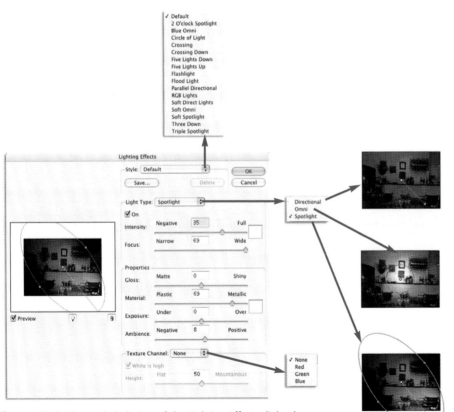

Figure 16.4 The exploded view of the Lighting Effects dialog box.

You can always choose from three types of lights:

- **Directional light.** Floods the entire image with an even, unidirectional light, much like the sun. This light is represented by a line whose angle denotes the direction of the light, and the length denotes the distance, or height, of the light. (A short line gives a brighter effect and a long line gives a dimmer effect.)

- **Omni light.** This light casts equally in all directions from the center. It is like holding a small light bulb over your image. Increasing and decreasing the size of the Omni light is like moving the light bulb closer or farther away.

- **Spotlight.** Probably the most used form of light, this light creates an elliptical beam of light with a hot spot that fades out in the distance, much like a true spotlight (hence its name). The line within the ellipse denotes the angle, and the ellipse defines the spread.

Again, the best way to learn what this filter can do for you is play with it. The next shot gives you a more dramatic use of the Lighting Effects filter. The advanced day for night shot that follows after the quick-and-dirty version creates the shot without using the Lighting Effects filter at all.

Table 16.1 Lighting Effects Filter Style Presets

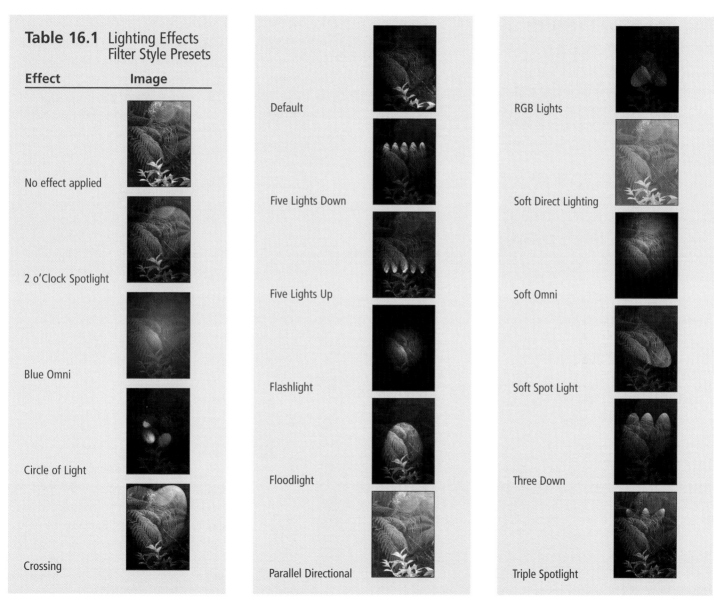

Effect	Image
No effect applied	
2 o'Clock Spotlight	
Blue Omni	
Circle of Light	
Crossing	
Default	
Five Lights Down	
Five Lights Up	
Flashlight	
Floodlight	
Parallel Directional	
RGB Lights	
Soft Direct Lighting	
Soft Omni	
Soft Spot Light	
Three Down	
Triple Spotlight	

Day for Night (Quick and Dirty Version)

When a shot is purposely shot during the day and is supposed to be a night shot, it is referred to as a *day for night shot*. Using the Lighting Effects function, you change the day shot in Figure 16.5 into a moonlit night.

1. Open NZcountry.tif, which you can download from this book's companion web site.

2. Go to **Filter** > **Render** > **Lighting Effects**.

3. Choose Blue Omni and move the center of the Omni where you want to put the full moon in the sky.

4. Play with the settings until you have something you like. Figure 16.6 shows my settings and they're here too:

   - Light Type: Omni
   - Intensity: 39
   - Gloss: 16
   - Material:14
   - Exposure: −25
   - Ambience: −11
   - Texture Channel: None

5. Click OK to accept your settings.

6. Create a new layer by pressing the New Layer button on the Layers palette.

7. Use a soft airbrush to create a glowing dot where the moon should be. Figure 16.7 shows the moon.

8. Paste on a picture of the moon and check out Figure 16.8.

Figure 16.5 Take this New Zealand countryside into night.

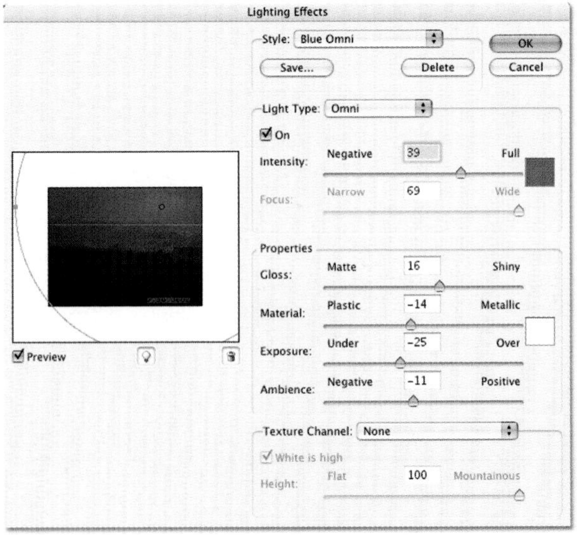

Figure 16.6 The Lighting Effects dialog box.

Figure 16.7 Creating the moon's glow.

Figure 16.8 The day for night image.

Moonless?

NASA astronomical societies have heaps of stellar pictures (pun fully intended). Follow these steps after you've found a picture of a full moon you like.

1. Use your circular Marquee tool. (Shift+M until it cycles up.)
2. Hold down Option+Shift (Win: Alt+Shift) and click from the center of your moon and drag out until the circle encircles your moon.
3. Press Command+C (Win: Ctrl+C) to copy the selection.
4. Go back to your NZcountry image and press Command+V (Win: Ctrl+V) to paste it into your scene.

The Real Assignment: Day for Night Advanced

Say that an evening scene has been added to the movie you are currently working on. Rather than take the entire film crew and actors back to the same location (which happens to be out of the country) and shoot the shot, they have decided to shoot the actors against a greenscreen. All you have to do is use one of the plates and change it from day to night. This looks deceptively simple—just darken it and add some lights, right? Not really.

You don't want the landscape to lose too much detail and have everything look completely black. You want the lights to match up with the image's general features, but don't have the time nor need to mark every window and street lamp from the day picture. (There may be times where that level of detail is necessary, but not in this case.) Using the technique you used in the preceding section wouldn't pass muster. You need a more detailed approach.

1. Take a look at Ensenada.tga, shown in Figure 16.9 and downloadable from this book's companion web site.

Figure 16.9 You take this daytime image to night.

2. Go to the menu bar and choose **Layer > New Adjustment Layer > Curves**.

   This starts you off adding a Curves Adjustment layer. You want to darken the image and bring the range of brightness to a narrower range. See Figure 16.10.

3. Pull both end vertices down and drag the middle of the curve down a bit to give it a deeper darkness. Make your curve similar to mine, shown in Figure 16.11.

Figure 16.10 You could also go to the bottom of the Layers palette and click the Adjustment Layer button to add a Curves Adjustment layer.

4. When you have a nice level of darkness, click OK.

The waterside paths and the park underneath the huge flag would probably be pretty well lit during the night, so I exclude those areas from the darkening. You could start painting with a black brush on the Curve layer right now, but it can be a bit difficult to see if the difference is subtle. Since I like to see my mask better, I went for a different tack.

5. Make sure that your Curve layer is selected and click your channel layers tab.

6. Click the Curves Mask layer and start painting the areas with your black brush.

   The masked-out areas show as red. You can see them in Figure 16.12.

Check out your final product in Figure 16.13. Keep going in the following section.

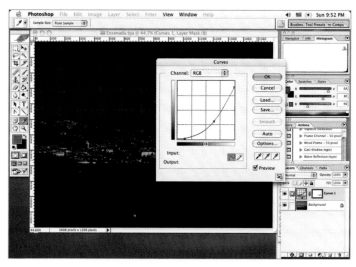

Figure 16.11 Don't worry about exact values, since this is really just done by eyeing it. The good thing about adjustment layers is that you can come back later to adjust.

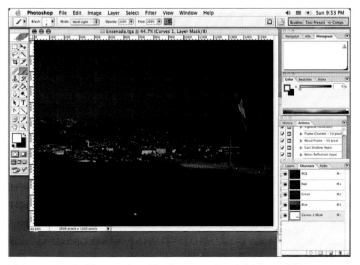

Figure 16.12 I have painted in the areas that I think would be brighter and have loosely blotted back in any bright areas that would be too bright without the curve adjustment.

Turning Dark Into Night

Now you have something that looks darker, but obviously this won't work for a night image. You can't have nighttime in a city like this, without all its accompanying lights. You want the lights to follow the general layout of the buildings and roads, but don't want to sit and paint in each window or streetlamp. I use my lazy rule and find another way.

1. Duplicate the background layer by clicking it and pressing Command+J (Win: Ctrl+J).

Figure 16.13 You can see the results of your mask in the color composite image.

2. Click and drag the duplicate layer so that it is on the top of the layer stack. See Figure 16.14.

3. Go to **Filter > Stylize > Find Edges** in the menu bar, shown in Figure 16.15.

   Figure 16.16 shows the results of applying the filter.

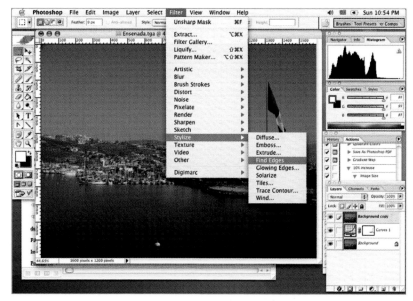

Figure 16.15 The Find Edges filter.

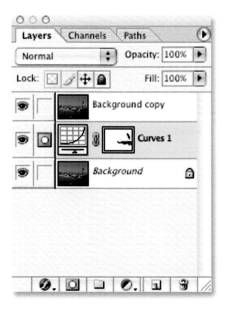

Figure 16.14 Work on a duplicate of the original image for the next step.

Figure 16.16 The result of the Find Edges filter.

4. Take your resultant image and invert it by pressing Command+I (Win: Ctrl+I).

These results are in Figure 16.17. Now you have a neon-filled city like Hong Kong and need to make it more like the suburban sprawl of Ensenada. Run the Pointillize filter on it!

5. Go to **Filter > Pixelate > Pointillize**, the effects of which are in Figure 16.18.

6. Enter your desired value in the dialog box that Figure 16.19 shows.

I have used 5, but you can enter whatever you wish. If you really want to get fancy, run this on three different layers and give three different sizes to blend together for a less uniform look.

This gives you a colorful, messy, dotty image. See Figure 16.20.

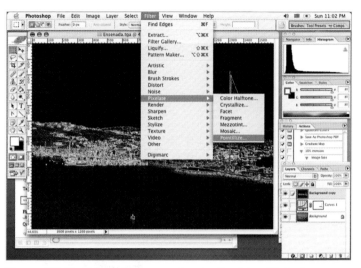

Figure 16.18 This filter gives you the star-like dots of lights for your landscape.

Figure 16.17 The same image inverted.

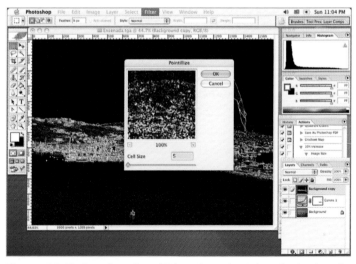

Figure 16.19 I used a value of 5 based on what I thought the size of lights would be in the middle distance.

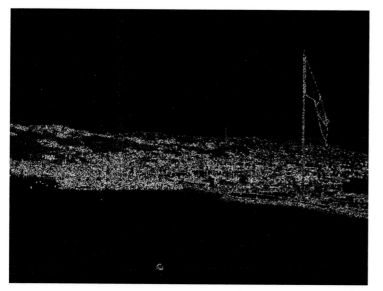

Figure 16.20 This is starting to look more like Candy Land instead of night lights.

7. Duplicate this layer by pressing Command+J (Win: Ctrl+J).

8. Change the duplicate layer's Layer Blend mode to Overlay, as in Figure 16.21.

9. Duplicate the Overlay layer several times by pressing Command+J (Win: Ctrl+J) until the black areas lose the noisy look.

10. Merge these stylized copies, including the original duplicate of the background image (but not *the* background layer).

I choose the first option here (see Figure 16.22), but you have several ways to do this:

- Link all of them and choose Merge Linked in the Layers palette submenu.

- Hide the other layers and choose Merge Visible.

- Merge down each Overlay layer to the Normal layer.

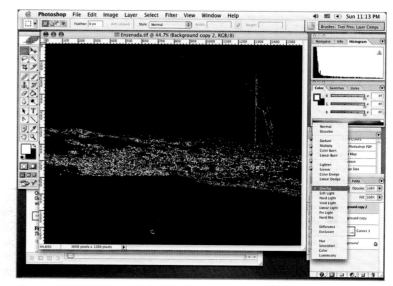

Figure 16.21 Make sure that it's the topmost layer that is changed to Overlay.

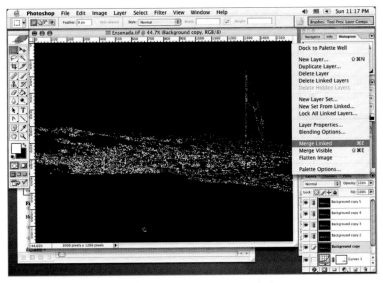

Figure 16.22 When you have a moderately sparse lightscape, merge the duplicate layers. Make sure the Normal duplicate is included with the Overlay duplicates.

11. Before you go any further, rename the layer to Night Light like you see in Figure 16.23.

   You can either right-click the image and choose Layer Properties, or click the name in the Layers palette and write in the new name.

12. Set your Layer Opacity for Night Light to 70 percent and switch your Layer Blend mode to Overlay.

   Now your picture is starting to look a bit more like night—but you're not done yet!

Fine-Tuning the Dark

Some of the obvious things that need to go are the bright dots outlining the flag and the same effect on the docked boats. You can see this in Figure 16.24.

I just took a large, soft, black brush and painted on the Night Light layer, getting rid of the offending dots. You can see the effect in Figure 16.25. Things are starting to come together, but you need some closer lights that are a bit brighter. I started marking in the dock lights.

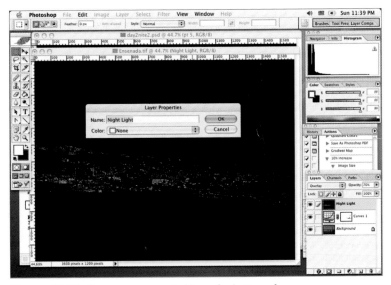

Figure 16.23 Rename your created layer for better reference.

Figure 16.24 The lights are starting to come on, but the Candy Land effect is still there because the Night Light layer hasn't been cleaned up.

1. Paint with yellow onto the same Night Light layer to get some light effects.

   Figure 16.26 shows these effects. Now try some water reflections.

2. Make some off-white and yellow squiggles on a separate layer, then run a Motion blur perpendicular to the drawn lines to get started. See Figure 16.27.

Figure 16.25 Continue painting as you feel is necessary. I think the squiggle on the flag still needs to go and I want a few places to be a bit spottier.

Figure 16.26 Roughing in some of the lights.

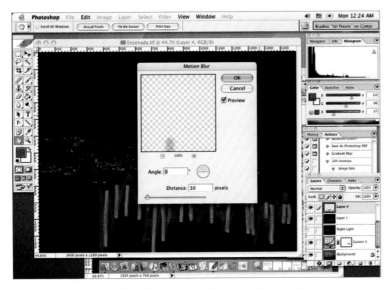

7. With the selection active, add a Curves Adjustment layer by choosing **Layer** > **New Adjustment Layer** > **Curves**.

8. Click and drag the curve to adjust your image, as in Figure 16.29.

Figure 16.27 Some directional Motion blur is applied to soften the airbrush strokes and give a bit of a watery effect.

3. Paint and erase until you get a look that you like. Figure 16.28 shows the work in progress.

4. Brighten up the sky a bit.

   With so many lights in the city, there would be a glow on the horizon.

5. Press Shift+L until the Magnetic lasso cycles up.

6. Define the horizon and select the sky, ignoring the flag.

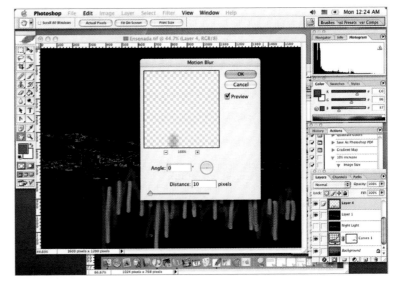

Figure 16.28 This is the work in progress as I paint and erase over it.

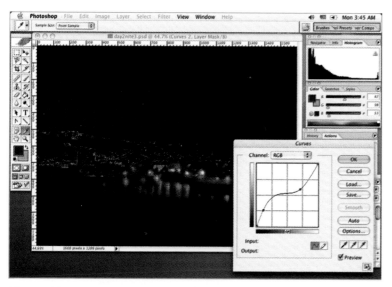

Figure 16.29 To keep the sky from looking too graphic and to create the glow effect, add more points to the curve and exaggerate the end levels.

9. Adjust your curve and click OK.

10. Make sure you are on your Curve mask and apply a Gaussian Blur to the mask so the horizon is a bit blurred.

    Figure 16.30 shows this being set up.

11. Paint out the flag in the Curve mask so that the Curves Adjustment isn't affecting it.

You're almost done. Keep going with this image in the next section.

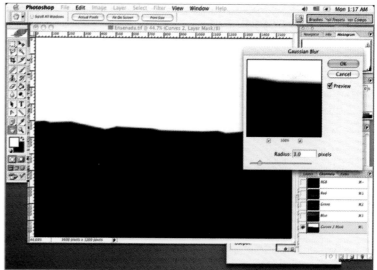

Figure 16.30 Adding the blur to the mask before painting out the flag gives a more natural integration.

Lens Flaring Up

You need a few lens flare lights up near the front. Yeah, you heard me right. You break the rule of "No lens flares and no spaceships," which is advice given to students fresh out of school on making their demo reels. Here you use the lens flare options for the streetlights closest to you. (There will be no spaceships, however.)

1. Create a new layer and use a yellow airbrush in Color Dodge mode to dab on some lights.

    This creates some light locations.

2. Create a copy of the entire merged image:

    ▪ Press Command+A (Win: Ctrl+A) to Select All.

    ▪ Press Command+Shift+C (Win: Ctrl+Shift+C) to copy the image as it is.

    ▪ Press Command+V (Win: Ctrl+V) to paste into a new layer.

    Now use the Lens Flare filters.

3. Use the Marquee tool to select a light to augment.

4. Go to **Filter** > **Render** > **Lens Flare**, as shown in Figure 16.31.

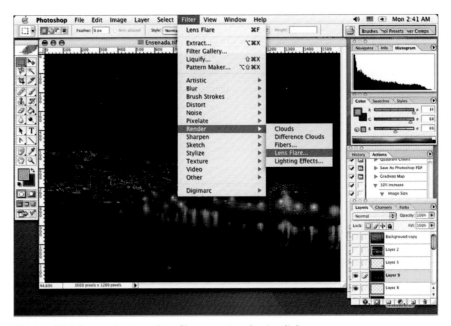

Figure 16.31 Use the Lens Flare filter to paint glowing lights.

5. Choose the type of lens flare you like and use the interactive preview to place it exactly where you want it.

    Figure 16.32 shows this being done.

Take a look at the original image (in Figure 16.33) and compare it to your finished image (in Figure 16.34).

Note

If this were for a movie, you would have to paint out the flag and put in a 3D flag or a 2D composited flag instead.

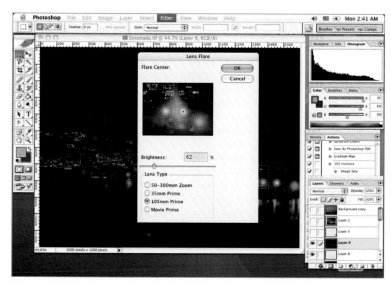

Figure 16.32 You need to do this individually to each light. If you don't give a selection, one huge flare is created—the kind that spaceships fly out of.

Figure 16.33 Your before image.

Figure 16.34 Your after image. Not too shabby!

INDEX

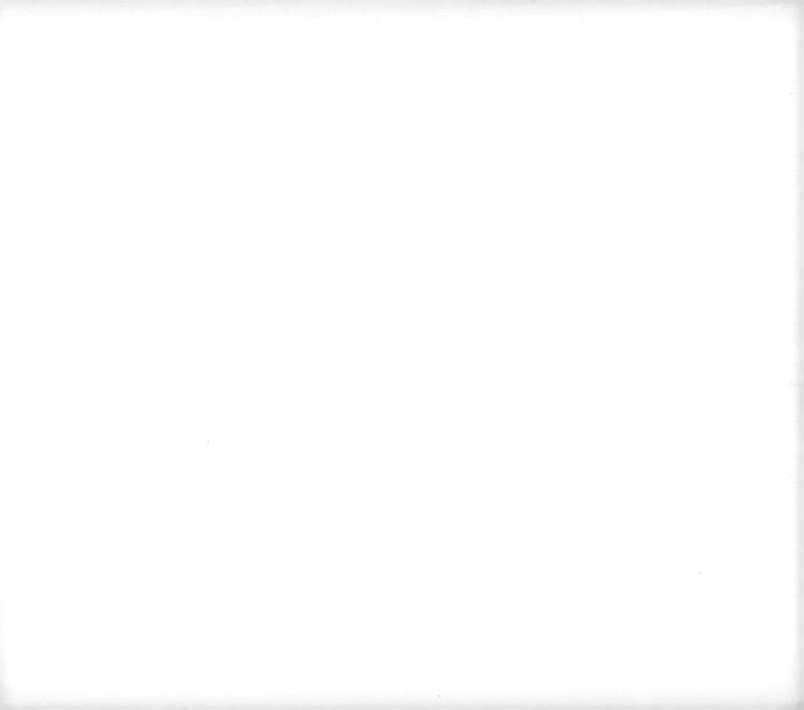

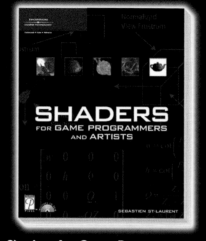
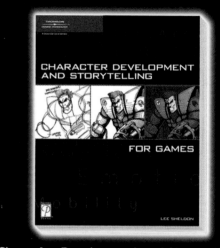

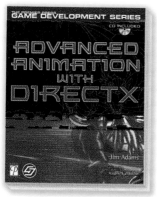